Sponsored by
# THE MONTEREY VINEYARD®

Proceeds to support efforts of
**LAKEFRONT PARTNERSHIP**
to preserve and enhance
Chicago's lakefront.

# CHICAGO Celebrity C·H·E·F·S

Compiled by
**LAKEFRONT PARTNERSHIP**

Foreword by
**Mike Ditka**

Introduction by
**Cary Gott**

Preface by
**Perry Duis**

Cover illustration by
**Chapman Kelley**

Design by
**Adele Kingan** and **Camy Fischer**

**PEANUT BUTTER PUBLISHING**
SEATTLE, WASHINGTON

Second Printing—July 1989
10  9  8  7  6  5  4  3

Copyright © 1989 by Peanut Butter Publishing.
All rights reserved. No portion of this book
may be reproduced without written permis-
sion from the publisher

Peanut Butter Publishing
200 - 2nd Avenue W.
Seattle, WA 98119
(206) 281-5965

ISBN 0-89716-306-0

Art Direction: Josh Moyer

# CHICAGO Celebrity C·H·E·F·S

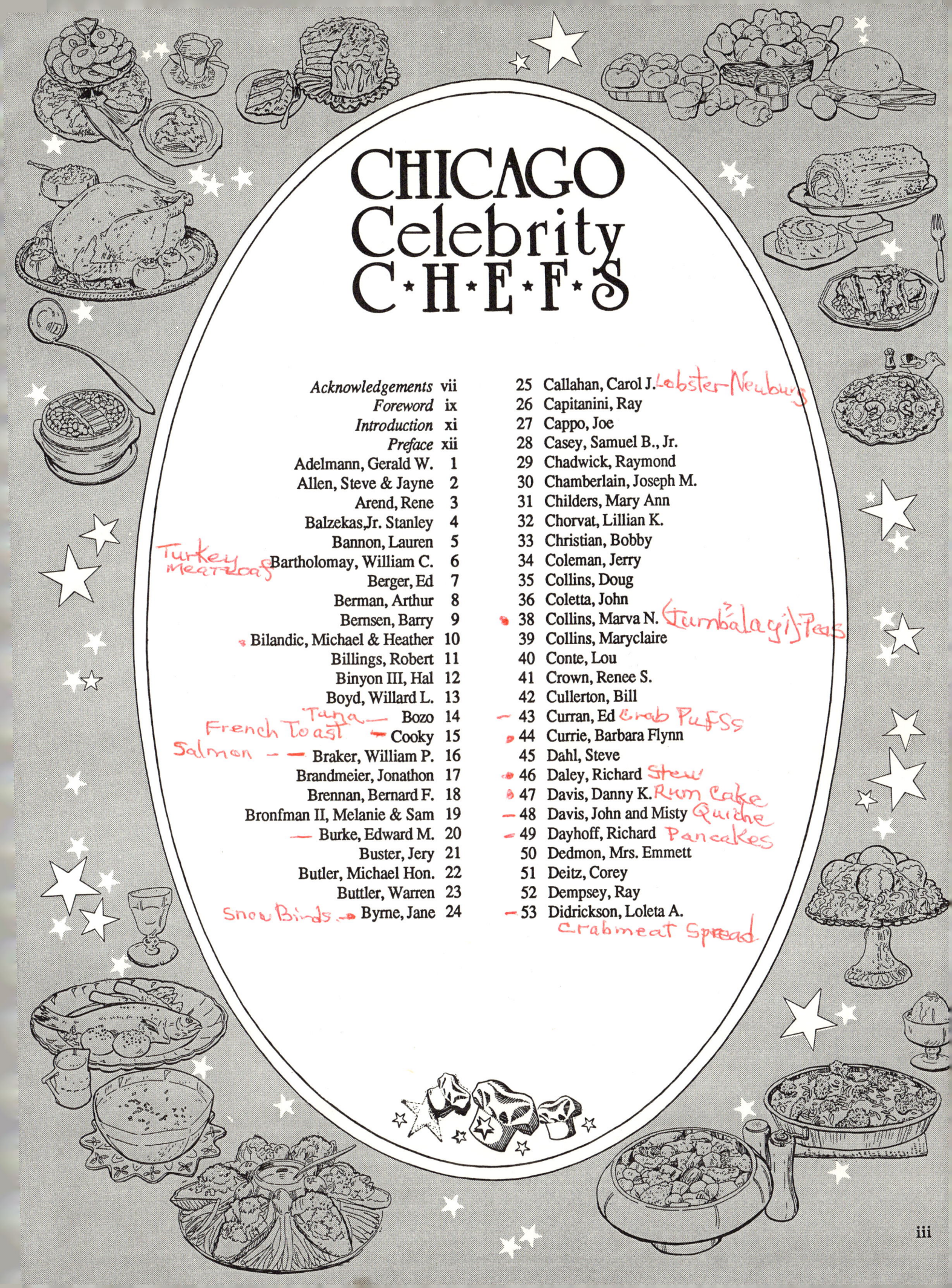

| | |
|---|---|
| *Acknowledgements* | vii |
| *Foreword* | ix |
| *Introduction* | xi |
| *Preface* | xii |
| Adelmann, Gerald W. | 1 |
| Allen, Steve & Jayne | 2 |
| Arend, Rene | 3 |
| Balzekas, Jr. Stanley | 4 |
| Bannon, Lauren | 5 |
| Bartholomay, William C. | 6 — *Turkey Meatloaf* |
| Berger, Ed | 7 |
| Berman, Arthur | 8 |
| Bernsen, Barry | 9 |
| Bilandic, Michael & Heather | 10 |
| Billings, Robert | 11 |
| Binyon III, Hal | 12 |
| Boyd, Willard L. | 13 |
| Bozo | 14 — *Tuna* |
| Cooky | 15 — *French Toast* |
| Braker, William P. | 16 — *Salmon* |
| Brandmeier, Jonathon | 17 |
| Brennan, Bernard F. | 18 |
| Bronfman II, Melanie & Sam | 19 |
| Burke, Edward M. | 20 |
| Buster, Jery | 21 |
| Butler, Michael Hon. | 22 |
| Buttler, Warren | 23 |
| Byrne, Jane | 24 — *Snow Birds* |
| Callahan, Carol J. | 25 — *Lobster Newburg* |
| Capitanini, Ray | 26 |
| Cappo, Joe | 27 |
| Casey, Samuel B., Jr. | 28 |
| Chadwick, Raymond | 29 |
| Chamberlain, Joseph M. | 30 |
| Childers, Mary Ann | 31 |
| Chorvat, Lillian K. | 32 |
| Christian, Bobby | 33 |
| Coleman, Jerry | 34 |
| Collins, Doug | 35 |
| Coletta, John | 36 |
| Collins, Marva N. | 38 — *(Tumbalagi) Peas* |
| Collins, Maryclaire | 39 |
| Conte, Lou | 40 |
| Crown, Renee S. | 41 |
| Cullerton, Bill | 42 |
| Curran, Ed | 43 — *Crab Puffs* |
| Currie, Barbara Flynn | 44 |
| Dahl, Steve | 45 |
| Daley, Richard | 46 — *Stew* |
| Davis, Danny K. | 47 — *Rum Cake* |
| Davis, John and Misty | 48 — *Quiche* |
| Dayhoff, Richard | 49 — *Pancakes* |
| Dedmon, Mrs. Emmett | 50 |
| Deitz, Corey | 51 |
| Dempsey, Ray | 52 |
| Didrickson, Loleta A. | 53 — *Crabmeat Spread* |

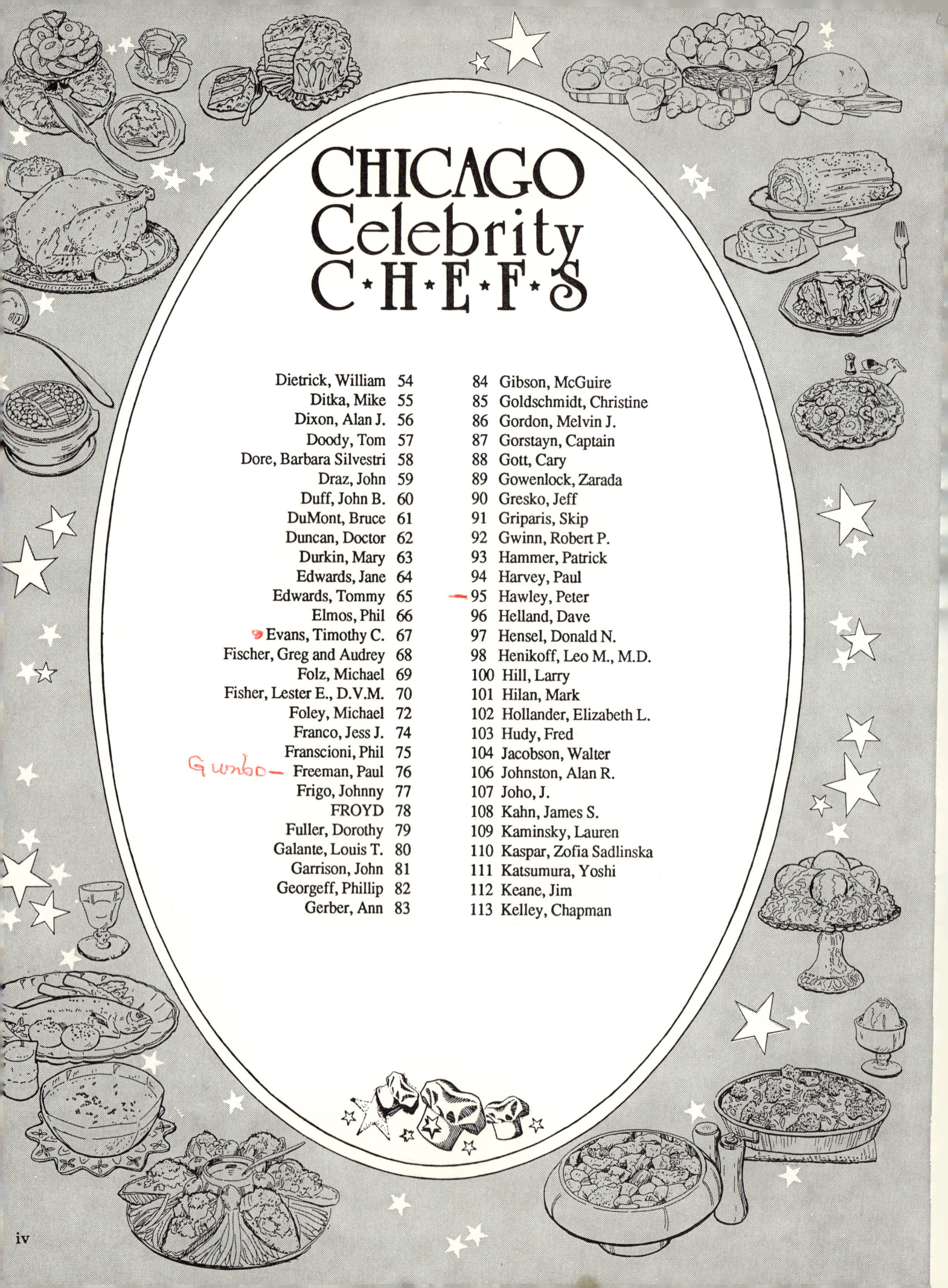

# CHICAGO Celebrity C·H·E·F·S

|  |  |
|---|---|
| Dietrick, William 54 | 84 Gibson, McGuire |
| Ditka, Mike 55 | 85 Goldschmidt, Christine |
| Dixon, Alan J. 56 | 86 Gordon, Melvin J. |
| Doody, Tom 57 | 87 Gorstayn, Captain |
| Dore, Barbara Silvestri 58 | 88 Gott, Cary |
| Draz, John 59 | 89 Gowenlock, Zarada |
| Duff, John B. 60 | 90 Gresko, Jeff |
| DuMont, Bruce 61 | 91 Griparis, Skip |
| Duncan, Doctor 62 | 92 Gwinn, Robert P. |
| Durkin, Mary 63 | 93 Hammer, Patrick |
| Edwards, Jane 64 | 94 Harvey, Paul |
| Edwards, Tommy 65 | 95 Hawley, Peter |
| Elmos, Phil 66 | 96 Helland, Dave |
| Evans, Timothy C. 67 | 97 Hensel, Donald N. |
| Fischer, Greg and Audrey 68 | 98 Henikoff, Leo M., M.D. |
| Folz, Michael 69 | 100 Hill, Larry |
| Fisher, Lester E., D.V.M. 70 | 101 Hilan, Mark |
| Foley, Michael 72 | 102 Hollander, Elizabeth L. |
| Franco, Jess J. 74 | 103 Hudy, Fred |
| Franscioni, Phil 75 | 104 Jacobson, Walter |
| Freeman, Paul 76 | 106 Johnston, Alan R. |
| Frigo, Johnny 77 | 107 Joho, J. |
| FROYD 78 | 108 Kahn, James S. |
| Fuller, Dorothy 79 | 109 Kaminsky, Lauren |
| Galante, Louis T. 80 | 110 Kaspar, Zofia Sadlinska |
| Garrison, John 81 | 111 Katsumura, Yoshi |
| Georgeff, Phillip 82 | 112 Keane, Jim |
| Gerber, Ann 83 | 113 Kelley, Chapman |

iv

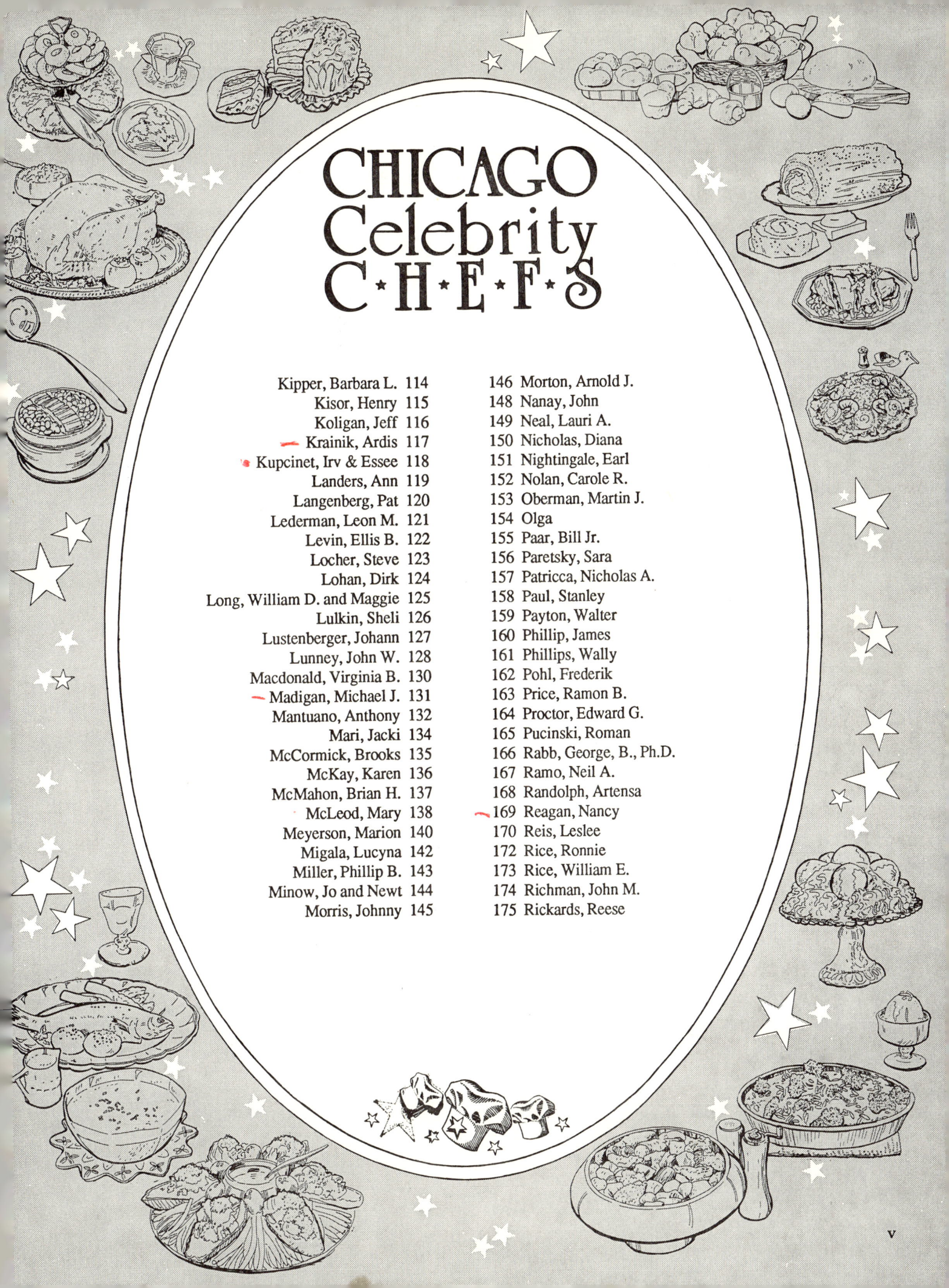

# CHICAGO Celebrity C·H·E·F·S

Kipper, Barbara L. 114
Kisor, Henry 115
Koligan, Jeff 116
Krainik, Ardis 117
Kupcinet, Irv & Essee 118
Landers, Ann 119
Langenberg, Pat 120
Lederman, Leon M. 121
Levin, Ellis B. 122
Locher, Steve 123
Lohan, Dirk 124
Long, William D. and Maggie 125
Lulkin, Sheli 126
Lustenberger, Johann 127
Lunney, John W. 128
Macdonald, Virginia B. 130
Madigan, Michael J. 131
Mantuano, Anthony 132
Mari, Jacki 134
McCormick, Brooks 135
McKay, Karen 136
McMahon, Brian H. 137
McLeod, Mary 138
Meyerson, Marion 140
Migala, Lucyna 142
Miller, Phillip B. 143
Minow, Jo and Newt 144
Morris, Johnny 145

146 Morton, Arnold J.
148 Nanay, John
149 Neal, Lauri A.
150 Nicholas, Diana
151 Nightingale, Earl
152 Nolan, Carole R.
153 Oberman, Martin J.
154 Olga
155 Paar, Bill Jr.
156 Paretsky, Sara
157 Patricca, Nicholas A.
158 Paul, Stanley
159 Payton, Walter
160 Phillip, James
161 Phillips, Wally
162 Pohl, Frederik
163 Price, Ramon B.
164 Proctor, Edward G.
165 Pucinski, Roman
166 Rabb, George, B., Ph.D.
167 Ramo, Neil A.
168 Randolph, Artensa
169 Reagan, Nancy
170 Reis, Leslee
172 Rice, Ronnie
173 Rice, William E.
174 Richman, John M.
175 Rickards, Reese

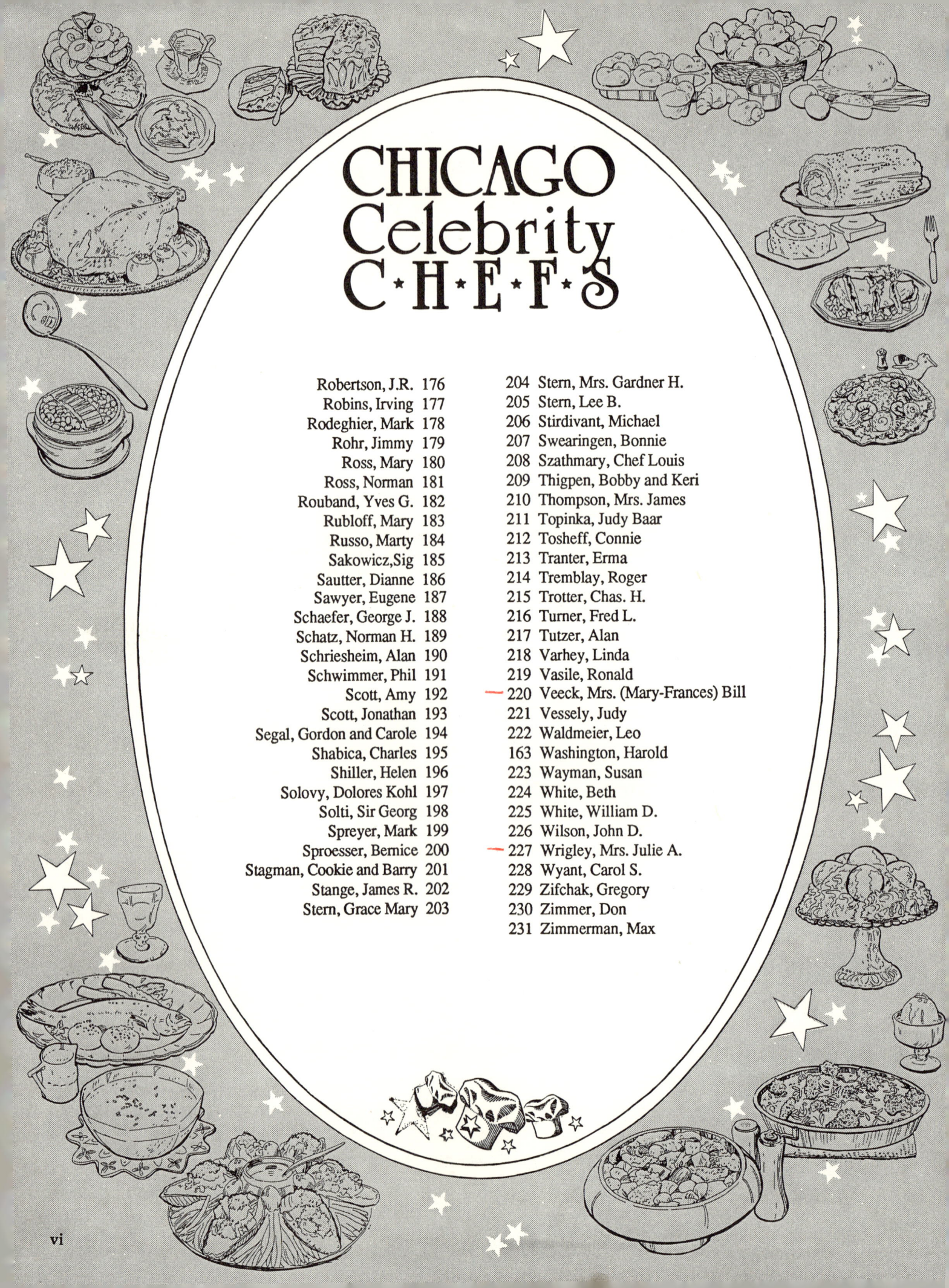

# CHICAGO Celebrity C·H·E·F·S

| | |
|---|---|
| Robertson, J.R. 176 | 204 Stern, Mrs. Gardner H. |
| Robins, Irving 177 | 205 Stern, Lee B. |
| Rodeghier, Mark 178 | 206 Stirdivant, Michael |
| Rohr, Jimmy 179 | 207 Swearingen, Bonnie |
| Ross, Mary 180 | 208 Szathmary, Chef Louis |
| Ross, Norman 181 | 209 Thigpen, Bobby and Keri |
| Rouband, Yves G. 182 | 210 Thompson, Mrs. James |
| Rubloff, Mary 183 | 211 Topinka, Judy Baar |
| Russo, Marty 184 | 212 Tosheff, Connie |
| Sakowicz, Sig 185 | 213 Tranter, Erma |
| Sautter, Dianne 186 | 214 Tremblay, Roger |
| Sawyer, Eugene 187 | 215 Trotter, Chas. H. |
| Schaefer, George J. 188 | 216 Turner, Fred L. |
| Schatz, Norman H. 189 | 217 Tutzer, Alan |
| Schriesheim, Alan 190 | 218 Varhey, Linda |
| Schwimmer, Phil 191 | 219 Vasile, Ronald |
| Scott, Amy 192 | — 220 Veeck, Mrs. (Mary-Frances) Bill |
| Scott, Jonathan 193 | 221 Vessely, Judy |
| Segal, Gordon and Carole 194 | 222 Waldmeier, Leo |
| Shabica, Charles 195 | 163 Washington, Harold |
| Shiller, Helen 196 | 223 Wayman, Susan |
| Solovy, Dolores Kohl 197 | 224 White, Beth |
| Solti, Sir Georg 198 | 225 White, William D. |
| Spreyer, Mark 199 | 226 Wilson, John D. |
| Sproesser, Bernice 200 | — 227 Wrigley, Mrs. Julie A. |
| Stagman, Cookie and Barry 201 | 228 Wyant, Carol S. |
| Stange, James R. 202 | 229 Zifchak, Gregory |
| Stern, Grace Mary 203 | 230 Zimmer, Don |
| | 231 Zimmerman, Max |

vi

# ACKNOWLEDGEMENTS

Our first thanks goes to all who treasure the lakefront and to those who have given their encouragement and support along the way: Cary Gott and The Monterey Vineyard for sponsoring this project and their concern for our cause; Sam Bronfman II, President, The Seagram Classics Wine Co.; Raymond Chadwick, Vice President, The Seagram Classics Wine Co.; Elliott Wolf and Susan Peder of Peanut Butter Publishing; Coach Mike Ditka; Chapman Kelley, artist; Perry Duis, historian; Adele Kingan of Creative Connection; Camy Fischer of Cameo Art Studio; Dave Sickinger of I.P.P. Lithocolor; Andrea Pawlisz of Typeset/Offset; Pat Manthei, Linda Ziemer and the Chicago Historical Society; Laurie Leigh, Photographer, Kee Chang of The Chicago Association of Commerce and Industry; Johnny Morris, Channel 2; Members of The Chicago Shoreline Protection Commission including: Ed Uhlir, Research and Planning, Chicago Park District; Neal de Snoo, Department of Planning, City Hall; Henry Henderson, Chief Council; Dr. Charles Shabica, Northeastern Illinois University; other friends and members of Lakefront Partnership including: Peggy Andrews, Marianne Andrews, Ed Proctor, James Harbert, Barry Rustin, Liz Cunningham, Mary Ann Ellefson, Marlene McIntosh, Darlene Chorney of Young Variety Club of Illinois, Patrick Hammer of Scuba Emporium, Al Benedict of the Chicago Air Show and The Chicago Hang Gliding Organization.

A special thank you to each of our celebrities who contributed their special recipe.
We wish to thank the Chicago media, associations and organizations for their cooperation and help.

About our cover painting:
Islands off Chicago's lakefront have been the dream of many visionary people dating back to Burnham's Plan of 1909. This conceptual work by Chapman Kelley reflects one of the possiblilties and opportunities we have for the protection and enhancement of our lakeshore environment.

**CHICAGO CELEBRITY CHEFS** was made possible only through the teamwork of many, a partnership, creating this cookbook we know you will enjoy. Everyone can do the same for the shoreline by working together in a partnership for its improvement. Through the purchase of this book you are contributing to the lakefront and our goal.

And now we would like to propose a toast:

- to The Monterey Vineyard for their generosity, **Chicago Celebrity Chefs** has become realized;

- to the people, places and things that help flavor Chicago;

- and finally to **Chicago,** *a beautiful city still learning, growing and living!*

**GREG R. FISCHER**    **AUDREY FISCHER**

**LAKEFRONT PARTNERSHIP**
10035 S. WESTERN AVENUE
CHICAGO, ILLINOIS 60643
PHONE 312: 239.LAKE

# CHICAGO BEARS

Pride is essential to the success of any individual, team, or group venture. We must set goals and then develop methods to reach them.

I love Chicago, its people, its sights, its sounds, but particularly the lakefront and the beaches that set it apart from other cities.

The beauty of the lakefront area of Chicago is something that not only has to be preserved and protected, but also developed for our future generations to appreciate.

It gives me great pleasure to write this forward for the Chicago Celebrity Chefs Cookbook because these people are working to raise capital and support to continue the development of our treasured lakefront.

We need to support this team because their cause is so worthwhile.

Thanks for your help.

## THE MONTEREY VINEYARD®

CARY GOTT
Executive Vice President
and Winemaster

Dear Chicago —

Let me confess that this is one Californian who can't wait to get to Chicago to put on running shoes and head for the shores of Lake Michigan!

There is no question that Chicago's lake front is one of America's natural wonders. I enjoy meandering and mingling there with the hot-dog-eaters and sun-worshippers and snow-trekkers. At the same time, I respect the history of the lake and its city setting, and know that maintaining its beauty depends on all of us.

At The Monterey Vineyard, we depend on natural wonders in our immediate neighborhood, from the Gabilan and Santa Lucia mountains to the boar roaming the edges of our vineyard, Paris Valley Ranch. We know that these "wonders" need careful looking-after and support.

In that spirit, we are proud to have made possible the publication of the Chicago Celebrity Chefs' Cookbook. We salute all of the contributors, and you, who are about to partake!

Purchasing—and enjoying—this Cookbook will add to the resources for restoring the lake front, and we thank you.

When you lift your next glass of The Monterey Vineyard Chardonnay, think of us toasting you "back" from our shores of the Monterey Bay.

*Cary Gott*

800 SOUTH ALTA STREET • POST OFFICE BOX 780-GONZALES, CALIFORNIA 93926 • (408) 675-2316

## CHICAGO'S GREATEST CIVIC ASSET

Lake Michigan is a utility to most Chicagoans. Like the gas or electric company, we take it for granted most of the time and direct grumbles its way only when we think that it is too expensive or realize how much it is a monopoly. On occasion, we also worry about it when we realize that, despite its might, it is also very fragile. But few of us realize that our treatment of the Lake Michigan shoreline has also been a mirror which has reflected what each passing generation of Chicagoans thought about themselves and the metropolis they created.

Initially, the lake was regarded as a purely utilitarian avenue of opportunity. In the city of O'Hare, the Dan Ryan and Union Station, it is often difficult to realize what early explorers and the first permanent settler, Jean Baptiste Point DuSable, knew well: that Lake Michigan was the very reason for Chicago's existence. What crude roads made land travel difficult, there was a great advantage in being at the southwestern end of a water highway that extended to the Atlantic coast. The dream of an all-water route to the Mississippi--finally realized with the completion of the Illinois and Michigan canal in 1848--made Chicago a major port before railways were little more than speculators' toys.

Gradually the fur trade gave way to the handling of grain, lumber and livestock, and by the middle of the 19th century, Chicagoans were beginning to discover what would become their endless dilemma. The burgeoning commerce and industry found new uses for lake water, which returned as untreated sewage. But the city's growing population also drew its drinking water from the same lake that the sewer system befouled. Almost

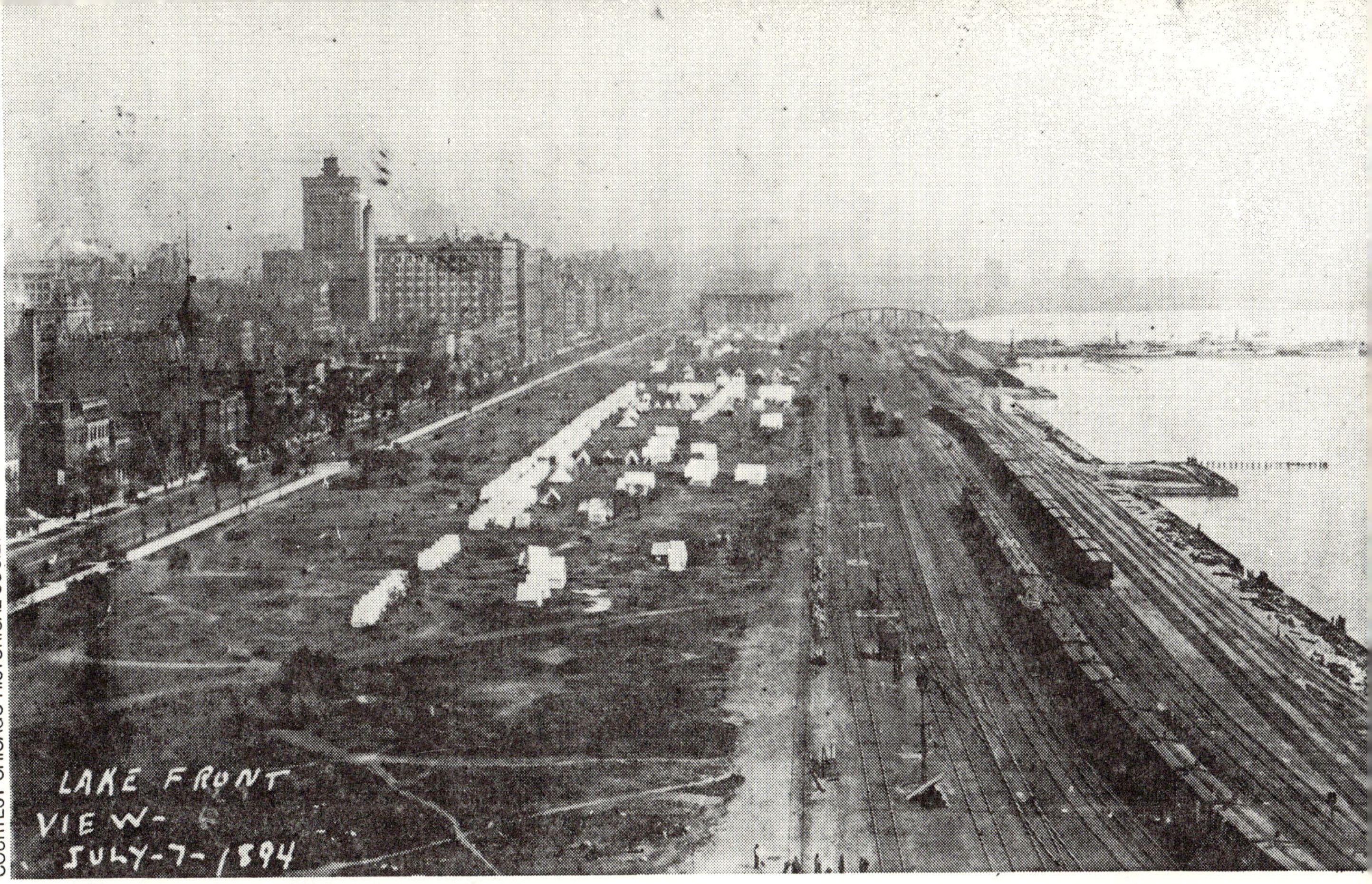


COURTESY CHICAGO HISTORICAL SOCIETY

*EARLY VIEW OF LAKE SHORE DRIVE 1894*

in desperation, city officials turned to technological solutions, none of which worked very well. One was an effort to pump the Chicago River backwards, carrying the pollution, which was obvious to the eye and nose, downstream instead of into the lake. Massive pumps at Bridgeport failed to work properly, and typhoid epidemics were a regular summertime occurrence. Not even a second technological wonder, the new water tower and pumping system of 1868 could extend far enough out from the shore to solve the problem.

Meanwhile, this utilitarian public attitude toward the lake also shaped the uses of the shoreline. Chicagoans claimed to be "too busy" for aesthetics and thought little of developing its recreational possibilities. As a consequence, when an 1850 storm blew record-high water all the way to State Street, city leaders were all too delighted to accept the offer of the Illinois Central Railroad to provide shoreline protection all the way from the river's mouth to presentday Hyde Park in exchange for exclusive rights to the shoreline. Few people complained about the smoke and noise because they were regarded as signs of economic progress.

Perhaps the low point in the neglect of the lakefront was reached with the arrival of George Wellington Streeter. A former showman and captain of a

LOCAL ODDITIES . . . In and About Chicago
By Bob Mills



THE building which is now the 999 Lake Shore Drive address was the first building to be erected on what was called Capt. Streeter's District of Lake Michigan.

—From Fred Rusch, 109 East Oak St.

COURTESY CHICAGO HISTORICAL SOCIETY

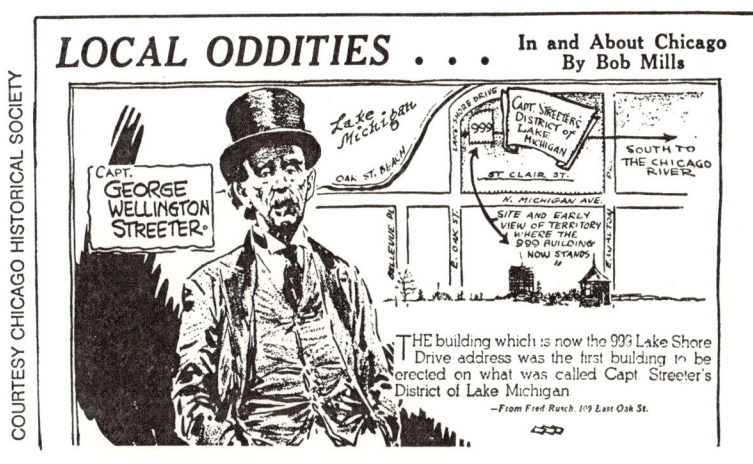

*GEORGE WELLINGTON STREETER*
*THE CHICAGO DAILY NEWS JANUARY 21, 1935*

leaky tub called the "Reutan," he had set out for South America on a stormy night in December 1886, but the wind blew his rig ashore near Chicago Avenue. When the sands began to accumulate around the hull, "Cap" and his wife decided to stay for the rest of the winter. As the months passed, the beach grew larger, leading Streeter to a brilliant scheme. Because the considerable "made land" was not on any map, he reasoned, it could not be part of Illinois or Chicago. He officially declared it the "District of Lake Michigan" and began what would be decades of physical and legal confrontation with the authorities. Wealthy owners of adjacent lands took offense at the scruffy interloper, and the police tried with little success to shut down the unlicensed saloon he opened. Although Cap died in 1921, for the next thirty years his second wife continued to claim the territory which ironically became known as "Streeterville."

The 1890s proved to be a turning point in the story of Chicago's attitude toward its lakefront, as utilitarianism began to give way to the realization of aesthetic potential. The creation of the Metropolitan Sanitary District in 1889 led quickly to plans for a new canal that would successfully reverse the flow of the river. When that massive project was completed on January 1, 1900, the shoreline lost most of its smell and the drinking water its bad taste. When typhoid rates fell, the average Chicagoan saw the lakefront as less of a disease threat and dreamed of large public beaches. Then, the World's Columbian Exposition of 1893 transformed Jackson Park in a well-ordered and pleasing environment that was in sharp contrast with the chaotic city outside its gates. Many Chicagoans looked north from the fairgrounds for the first time and saw the beauty of the shimmering reflection of the Loop at night. Soon after the fair closed Daniel Burnham and other architects began sending to newspapers their plans for the beautification of the

*World's Columbian Exposition of 1893*

*1909 PLAN OF CHICAGO*

central city, especially the open space opposite the downtown. Chicagoans became increasingly uneasy about what they had given the Illinois Central, especially when the line's allies in the City Council tried to take over Lake Front (now Grant) Park to become the site of a new depot. That space was saved, and in a related series of Supreme Court cases the city eventually won the riparian rights along the I.C. right-of-way. This allowed landfill and public use east of the tracks.

The 1893 fair, the fresher breezes, and victory in the "Battle of Grant Park" represented a new era in thinking about the lakefront that culminated in the historic 1909 Plan of Chicago. Working with the support of the business community, architect Daniel Burnham and his assistant, Edward H. Bennett, made the lakefront the focus of their complex regional blueprint. The downtown harbor was the "front door"; a widened Michigan Avenue was for casual strolling; and a linear shoreline park, lagoon, and a string of recreational islands south from downtown were a triumphal celebration of victory in the Illinois Central riparian rights cases.

Chicagoans generally celebrated the Burnham Plan and its preservation of over 16 miles of lakeshore for recreation, but one of its features touched off a debate that remains unresolved to this day: should parks be sylvan retreats, either wilderness or formally landscaped, or should they be intensively developed with public buildings that uplift and enrich the community. The Plan envisioned Grant Park as a cultural campus that was dotted with museums and libraries, an idea single-handedly challenged by the mail-order mogul Aaron Montgomery Ward. Through a series of court cases

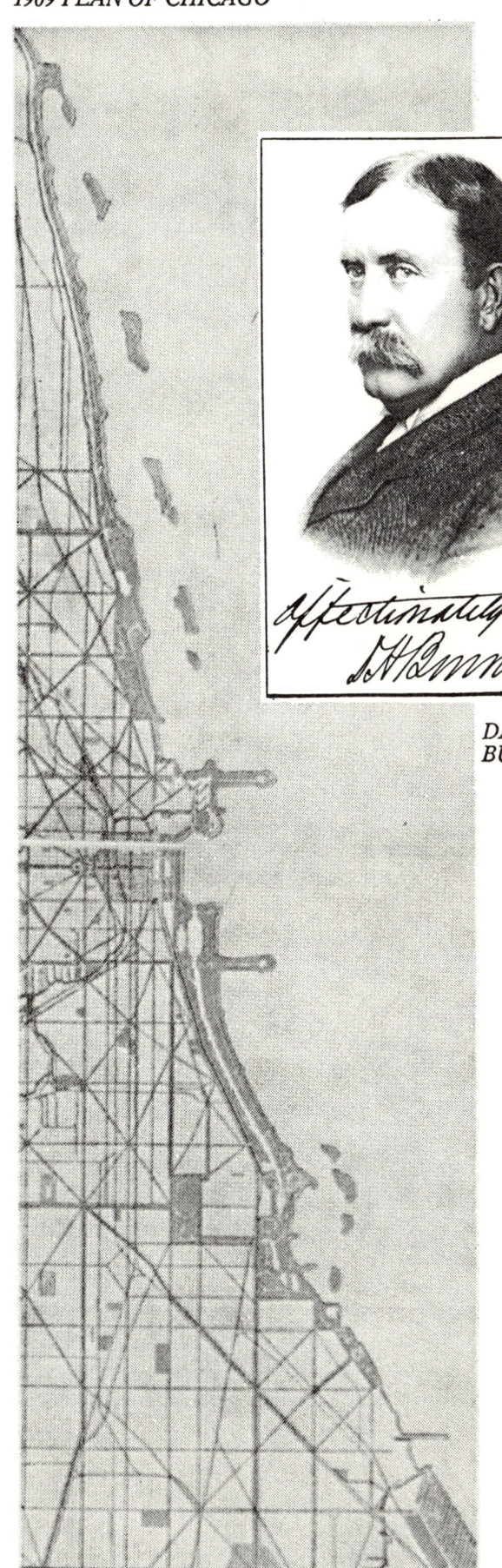

*DANIEL BURNHAM*

xv

ALL COURTESY CHICAGO HISTORICAL SOCIETY

*EARLY VIEW OF LAKE SHORE DRIVE*

*LAKE SHORE DRIVE FROM DRAKE HOTEL, 1926*

*VIEW SOUTH ON LAKE SHORE DRIVE, 1940*

Ward invoked a clause in an 1830s government land grant which gave property-owners along what became Michigan Avenue the right to veto anything built across the street in what became Grant Park. Ward did not challenge the Art Institute building, which had already been constructed, but he did force the Field Museum to settle for a site technically just outside Grant Park. The other target of Ward's litigation, the John Crerar Library, was later contructed as a skyscraper on the west side of Michigan Avenue. (To this day, Ward's legacy lives. The Art Institute's additions are exempted as additions to the original building, and all other above-ground structures are technically temporary.)

For the most part, however, the era of pure aesthetics quickly gave way to one of development. In 1914 the city completed Municipal (now Navy) Pier, in large part to appease the federal government, which thought that Chicago was frittering away the economic development potential of its lakefront by turning it to parklands. Then came the museums. Back in 1892 the Lincoln Park Commissioners had allowed the Chicago Academy of Sciences to build on park land, but the prosperity of the 1920s led to a new round of construction that included the new Shedd Aquarium, Museum of Science and Industry, and Adler Planetarium, as well as a new home for the Chicago Historical Society. The open space and free site costs also proved an irresistible lure to politicians who built Soldier Field. Completed in 1926, it cost five times as much as the larger Los Angeles Coliseum.

During the 1920s, another non-recreational use began to intrude on the lakefront. While there had been a Lake

Shore Drive since the 1870s, it had been a Lincoln Park pleasure road for carriages. A half century later, the name would refer to one of America's first expressways, a limited-access, multi-lane highway that pioneered in the use of the cloverleaf. Depression-era public works projects added reversible traffic fins in 1935 to aid rush hour traffic flow. Two years later the long-delayed Outer Drive Bridge with its famous "S-Curve" provided a link between north and south sides. In the minds of many Chicagoans, the word "lakeshore" would forever after automatically be followed by "drive" and images of traffic jams.

The era of development also included the use of the lakefront to promote the local economy. It took the planning for the 1933 Century of Progress Exposition to initiate construction of the Burnham Plan's string of park islands. Northerly Island, which constituted much of the fair site, would be the only one constructed, but it never would be used for picnics and baseball games. In 1948 federal funding created Meigs Field on the site. That same year saw 50 acres near the foot of 23rd street transformed in the Chicago Railroad Fair to commemorate the centennial of Chicago's first train. It was a huge success that was extended a second summer. Then, in 1950, there was a disastrous effort to hold what was to become an annual Chicago Fair at the same site. When that failed, city officials devised a plan to use a state racetrack tax to construct a new convention and exhibition hall there. In 1959 Mayor Richard J. Daley cut the ribbon on the new McCormick Place which was criticized as a stupefying concrete box.

It burned in January, 1967. Its replacement is widely regarded as more gracefully designed. Meanwhile, the privately-owned lakefront areas were intensely developed in the years following World War II. A wall of highrise apartments lined Sheridan Road north of Hollywood Avenue. Ironically, the last northward Outer Drive extension in the mid-1950s led to the bankruptcy and razing of the most successful private shoreline use, the grand Edgewater Beach Hotel, which found itself cut off from the water. Then, the Illinois Central began to reap a second benefit from their 1850 agreement with the city with the creation of Illinois Center, a dense concentration of office, hotel, and residential towers.

*CENTURY OF PROGRESS*

COURTESY CHICAGO HISTORICAL SOCIETY

LAKE SHORE DRIVE AT NORTH AVENUE, FEBRUARY 8, 1987

By the 1960s a reaction to the era of intense development began to surface, as the lakefront seemed to be the focus of events that symbolized that turbulent decade. The atmosphere of protest was evident among those who chained themselves to trees in a futile effort to block widening of South Lake Shore Drive and in the efforts to force a removal of the Nike missile installation on the 55th Street promontory. The central event in the 1968 Convention disorders was appropriately a lakefront event, another kind of Battle of Grant Park. When America finally became worried about the environment, Chicagoans had to look no further than the lake. There were concerns, once more, about the pollution of drinking water supplies. The stench from rotting alewife kills reminded us of the real possibility of a "dead" lake. New anti-pollution laws, especially a ban on phosphates in laundry detergents, were important first-steps toward improvement. The debate over the degree to which the shoreline parks should be developed also continues. As a counter to adverse headlines, Mayor Daley frequently announced plans for a domed stadium to replace Soldier Field. His administration also produced conflicting plans for the South Side shoreline, at one point suggesting that the linear islands that Daniel Burnham had suggested would soon be built.. But,

**Perry Duis,** *Chicago historian and author, teaches at the University of Illinois in Chicago.*

faced with the prospect of O'Hare reaching its flight traffic capacity, Daley also vigorously promoted the idea of a third major airport on landfill.

Chicago's lakefront has continued to mirror the changing nature of the city, including the ongoing transformation toward an economy based less on manufacturing and more on services. Just as world's fairs and other expositions drew in tourist dollars in the past, modern "fests," "tastes," and similar celebrations lure suburban and regional visitors whose dollars circulate and grow in the local community. Similarly, McCormick Place has functioned as its promoters promised: a magnet that attracts conventioneers by the hundreds of thousands each year. Sadly, the condition of the lakefront also parallels the deteriorating infrastructure of streets and sewers in the city at large. The high lake levels of 1987 forced the city at least to realize that years of neglect had left much of the shoreline walls and piers in dilapidated condition. Massive stones, once thought an eternal protection, have shifted, threatening an erosion of the landfill behind them. The repair bill could exceed $800 million.

Yet, despite crisis and controversy, the lakefront remains Chicago's greatest civic asset. At a time when glass-walled buildings and automobile sprawl threaten to homogenize the appearance of uniqueness. Few of the world's metropolises can boast of a shoreline half as long, and none have taken the care to preserve it for open public use. Instead of treating it like a utility, taken for granted and frequently ignored, we need to treat it like the true celebrity that it is.

**Open Lands Project**

*Preserving the
quality of life
through open
lands since 1963.*

53 West Jackson Boulevard
Chicago, Illinois
60604
312 427 4256

H. James Fox
*President*

George W. Davis
*Vice President
Program*

Frederick N. Bates
*Vice President
Development*

Gerald B. Frank
*Vice President
Administration*

Sarah N. Rossett
*Treasurer*

Patricia Rosenzweig
*Secretary*

Gerald W. Adelmann
*Executive Director*

*Directors*
John W. Andresen, Ph.D.
Donn F. Bailey, Ph.D.
Stephen Baird
William J. Beecher, Ph.D.
Shaun C. Block
George E. Bullwinkel
Anthony T. Dean
Richard L. Ettlinger
Leon D. Finney, Jr.
Kenneth V. Fiske
Thomas M. Flavin
Kay V. Ganser
Sylvia Gordon
Jacques A. Gourguechon
Aubrey J. Greenberg
Beverly A. Kimble
Samuel T. Lawton, Jr.
Jocelyn S. Nebenzahl
David Novick
George W. Overton
Albert E. Pyott
Charles Saltzman
Jeffrey R. Short, Jr.
Mrs. William L. Taylor, Jr.
Clarence S. Wilson, Jr.
Michael B. Witte

*Honorary Directors*
Gaylord Donnelley
Marshall Field V
Jack E. Guth
Brooks McCormick
Harry M. Weese
Louise B. Young

*Affiliates*
Corporation for Open Lands
(CorLands)

Wetlands Research, Inc.

*Printed on recycled paper.*

Since 1963 Open Lands Project, a non-profit agency, has worked throughut northeastern Illinois to preserve and protect natural open lands. Our efforts have helped to preserve over 12,000 acres of woodlands, parks and nature trails for everyone's enjoyment.

DILL CARROTS*

1 lb carrots cut julienne style
3 tbsp unsalted butter
1/2 tsp sugar
pinch of salt
pinch of white pepper
1/2 cup chicken stock
2/3 cup creme fraiche**
2 tbsp fresh dill, minced

Melt the butter. Add the carrots, sugar, salt and pepper. Saute over medium heat for 3 minutes stirring constantly. Add chicken stock, cover and reduce heat to low. Simmer for 5 minutes. Uncover and raise heat to medium high and cook until the stock is reduced. Add the creme fraiche* and bring to a boil till the mixture thickens. And, just before serving, add the dill.

Enjoy!

Gerald W. Adelmann
Executive Director

*Submission by Deborah Gillespie, Financial Manager
**If you are unable to find creme fraiche at your grocery store, try a specialty store (e.g., Treasure Island).

**STEVE ALLEN**
15201 BURBANK BOULEVARD
SUITE B
VAN NUYS, CALIFORNIA 91411
(818) 988-3830

Steve & Jayne Allen's
Chocolate Mousse

## Ingredients

- 4 egg yolks
- 3/4 cup finely granulated sugar
- 1/4 cup orange liqueur
- 6 ounces or squares semi-sweet baking chocolate
- 6 ounces or 1½ sticks soft unsalted butter or margarine
- ¼ cup diced (finely) glazed orange peel
- 4 egg whites
- pinch of salt
- 1 tablespoon granulated sugar
- 4 tablespoons strong coffee
- Sauce- lightly whipped, sweetened whip-cream.

## Utensils

- 3-quart porcelain mixing bowl
- wire or electric beater
- pan of not quite simmering water
- basin cold water
- small saucepan

## Directions

A. Beat egg yolks & sugar together until thick, pale yellow and forms a slowly dissolving ribbon off spoon. Beat in liqueuer.

B. Set mixing bowl over not quite simmering water and continue beating for 3 or 4 minutes until mixture is foamy & too hot for finger touch.

C. Beat over cold water for 3 or 4 minutes until mixture is cool and again forms a ribbon or the consistency of mayonnaise.

D. Melt chocolate with coffee over hot water; remove and beat in butter (slowly to make a smooth cream).

E. Beat chocolate mixture into egg yolks and sugar then, beat in orange peel.

F. Beat egg whites and salt until soft peaks form; sprinkle gran. sugar and beat until stiff peaks form. Stir 1/4 of egg whites into chocolate mixture and fold in other 3/4.

G. Turn into dessert petit pots or serving dish. Refrigerate minimum 2 hours and preferably overnight.

H. Add whip cream to choice.

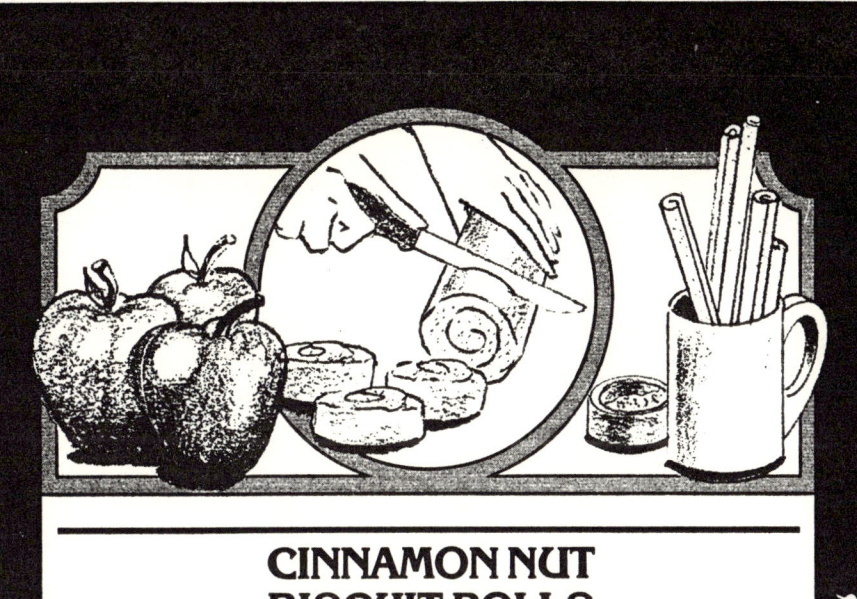

# CINNAMON NUT BISCUIT ROLLS

*(Yield 12 biscuit rolls/ preheat oven to 425°)*

2¼ c. sifted flour
2½ tsp. baking powder
½ tsp. baking soda
½ tsp. salt
2 tsp. sugar
4 T. solid vegetable shortening
1 c. buttermilk
2 T. melted butter
2 T. granulated sugar
1 tsp. cinnamon
2 T. chopped pecans
½ c. white (store-bought) cake frosting

Combine dry ingredients in mixing bowl. Cut in shortening, add buttermilk until soft dough forms. Place on floured surface and knead for 30 seconds. Roll out into a rectangle on floured board until dough is a very flat ¼". (Thinness allows for more even rolling and for the finished swirl design.) Brush entire surface with melted butter. Sprinkle mixture of cinnamon and sugar — using sifter — to dust over surface of dough. Then sprinkle with pecans. Roll from the longer side of the rectangle like a jelly roll and cut into 12 one-inch pieces. Place them side by side on baking sheet. Cover with wax paper and press gently to flatten with underside of a baking sheet. Remove wax paper and bake at 425° for 15 minutes. Remove from oven and frost with white cake icing while still hot (forms glaze-like topping). Sprinkle with additional pecans if desired.

## Variations:

### CINNAMON RAISIN BISCUIT ROLLS
— add ½ cup raisins instead of pecans.

### CINNAMON APPLE BISCUIT ROLLS
— add ½ cup diced and peeled tart apple pieces.

### CINNAMON COCONUT BISCUIT ROLLS
— add ½ cup shredded coconut.

Rene Arend, Executive Chef
McDonald's Corporation

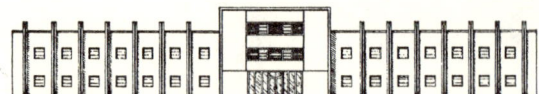

**Balzekas Museum of Lithuanian Culture**

6500 South Pulaski Road     Chicago, Illinois 60629     312 - 582 - 6500

FROM:

"KUGELIS"
Stanley Balzekas, Jr.
Lithuanian Potato Pudding

Pre-heat oven to 400 degrees:

10 Large White Potatoes
   (Use old ones)

1 Medium Onion

5 Thick Slices of Lean Bacon

4 Eggs (Separate egg yolks and beat egg whites in advance)

2 tsps. Salt

Chop bacon and begin frying. Add chopped onion. Fry until bacon bits are crisp.

Peel and grate potatoes. Pour fried bacon over the potatoes, add salt, egg yolks and mix well with a wooden spoon. Fold in beaten egg whites. Pour into a greased baking dish (depth of grated potato mixture should be at least 2½ inches).

Bake in the oven at 400 degress for 15 minutes, then reduce heat to 375 degrees and bake 45 minutes longer. Remove from oven and let cool 10-15 minutes before serving.

Cut into squares and serve with sour cream, cranberry sauce, or additional fried onions and bacon.

Enjoy a Lithuanian favorite!!!!

(Left-overs can be refrigerated and later re-heated or fried in a pan with a little butter.)

*Enjoy*
*Stanley Balzekas*

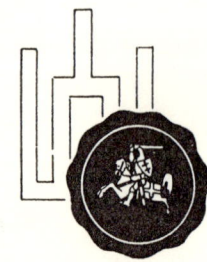

*Pasta is the traditional pre-race meal for runners. This is a favorite recipe from my files:*

## Tagliatelle with Zucchini and Walnut Sauce

2 cups toasted walnuts
1 cup olive oil
1/2 cup freshly grated parmesan cheese
1/4 cup chopped onion
1 clove garlic, peeled & chopped
2 tsp. chopped fresh basil ( or 1 tsp. leaf basil, crumbled)
2 tsp. chopped fresh oregano (or 1 tsp leaf oregano crumbled)
1/2 tsp. salt
1/4 tsp. pepper
2 medium zucchini, sliced
16 oz. tagliattele or other flat pasta

Combine walnuts, olive oil, parmesan cheese, parsley, onion, garlic, basil, oregano, salt and pepper in electric blender or food processor. Cover. Whirl until smooth.

Blanch zucchini in boiling salted water to cover for 3 minutes.
Drain. Add to blender/processor, cover, whirl until smooth.
Cook pasta in boiling, salted water until al dente. Drain.

Place sauce in medium saucepan. Cook over medium heat until heated thoroughly. Pour over pasta; toss to mix well.

Serves 4. Serve with additional grated Parmesan, Garlic Bread & Salad.

◇◇◇◇◇◇◇◇◇◇◇◇◇◇◇◇◇◇◇◇◇◇◇◇◇◇◇◇

While some athletes practice the rules of carbohydrate loading most of us are simply looking for an excuse to sit down to a delicious pasta dinner. Whether it's a 10K or a marathon. The night before the race, participating runners, race workers and fans seem to enjoy with equal enthusiasm pasta with zucchini and walnut sauce. Call the CARA office for information on upcoming races and schedule your next pasta dinner party!

*Best wishes on your fundraising efforts from Chicago Area Runners Association!!*
*Lauren Bannon*

**Chicago Area Runners Association**
708 N. Dearborn
Chicago, IL 60610
(312) 664-0823

**Board of Directors**
**Keith Holzmueller**
President
**Sue Nebel**
Vice-President
**Anne E. Simpson**
Treasurer
**Marjorie Doolan**
Secretary
**Rob Williams**
Past President
**Ernest Billups**
**Phil Blumenfield**
**Peg Cronin**
**Leah Hake**
**Edwin Hill**
**Sarah Linsley**
**Tom McCall**
**Matthew Mimlitz**
**Janine Minichello**
**John Nair**
**Noel Nequin, MD**
**Ray Vandersteen**
**Stephen Weinberg, DPM**
**Lauren B. Bannon**
Executive Director

# Chicago Park District

425 EAST McFETRIDGE DRIVE
CHICAGO, ILLINOIS 60605

WILLIAM C. BARTHOLOMAY
PRESIDENT

Turkey Meatloaf

1-2 lbs. ground turkey
2-3 egg whites
1/2 cup seasoned bread crumbs
Seasoned pepper
Fresh chopped parsley

Mix together and form loaf.
Slice onions on top.
Put in 9X13 pan and bake at 400 degrees for 15 minutes.
Pour off any grease.
Cut up several potatoes into quarters and place around loaf.
Add large can of tomato sauce and a little water, if needed, to cover and cook potatoes.
Reduce heat to 325 degrees. Bake 30 minutes.

Optional: You may add any other spices you prefer, such as basil and oregano to the tomato sauce, as well as sprinkle shredded cheese on top just before it's done.

*William C. Bartholomay*

**SOLA'S**
14420 South Indiana Avenue
Riverdale, Illinois 60627
(312) 841-1700

EDWARD F. BERGER
Wine Director

WINE MERCHANTS

## Pasta with "Clam Sauce - Eduardo"

While having dinner with my good friend, audio wizard, Bob Zickus, I was impressed with his Linguini & clam sauce. I developed this souped-up version, which became totally different than Bob's.

- 2 Large onions
- ¼ cup olive oil (virgin preferred)
- ½ stick melted butter
- 2 cloves garlic (crushed)
- 2 cans minced clams
- 2 teaspoons Dijon mustard
- dash Worcestershire (to taste)
- pinch - dill
- Homemade Linguini or "Kluski" style noodles

Saute onions in olive oil & melted butter mixture, add clams, garlic, mustard, worcestershire & dill. Simmer uncovered until sauce thickens slightly. Serve over hot noodles.

Best with Chardonnay & crusty French bread.

Enjoy,

Ed Berger

| | | |
|---|---|---|
| **SPRINGFIELD OFFICE**<br>ROOM 605E<br>STATE CAPITOL BUILDING<br>SPRINGFIELD, ILLINOIS 62706<br>PHONE: 217/782-8492<br><br>**LEGISLATIVE SERVICE OFFICE**<br>2705 W. HOWARD STREET<br>CHICAGO, ILLINOIS 60645<br>PHONE: 312/764-2200<br><br>**CHICAGO OFFICE**<br>111 W. WASHINGTON<br>SUITE 1505<br>CHICAGO, ILLINOIS 60602<br>PHONE: 312/346-8620 | **ILLINOIS STATE SENATE**<br><br>**ARTHUR L. BERMAN**<br>SENATOR<br>2ND LEGISLATIVE DISTRICT | CHAIRMAN • ELEMENTARY AND<br>SECONDARY EDUCATION COMMITTEE<br>CHAIRMAN • JOINT COMMITTEE ON THE<br>OVERSIGHT OF EDUCATION REFORM<br>VICE-CHAIRMAN • INSURANCE AND<br>LICENSED ACTIVITIES COMMITTEE<br>CO-CHAIRMAN • CITIZENS COUNCIL<br>ON SCHOOL PROBLEMS<br>MEMBER<br>  FINANCE AND CREDIT<br>    REGULATIONS COMMITTEE<br>  JUDICIARY COMMITTEE<br>  ADVISORY COUNCIL ON AGING<br>  SENATE SPECIAL COMMITTEE<br>    ON CONSUMER BANKS<br>  SENATE SELECT COMMITTEE<br>    ON INSURANCE AVAILABILITY |

## ART BERMAN'S FAVORITE CHOCOLATE CHIP COOKIES

1 C. Butter or margarine, softened
3/4 C. white sugar
3/4 C. brown sugar
1 T. vanilla
2 eggs

2 1/4 C. unsifted all-purpose flour
1 t. baking soda
1 t. salt
2 C. semi-sweet chocolate chips
  (12 oz. package)

1 C. chopped walnuts or pecans

Cream butter and sugars with vanilla until light and fluffy. Add 2 eggs and beat well. Combine flour, baking soda and salt in small bowl--mix lightly. Gradually beat into creamed mixture. Stir in chips and nuts. Drop by spoonfuls onto an ungreased cookie sheet. Cook at 375° for 8-10 minutes. Cool before removing from cookie sheet. Makes 3-6 dozen.

***********************

This is the recipe my mother used. She would make chocolate chip cookies when I was sick. They seemed to work even better than chicken soup!

*Arthur Berman*

5759 N. Broadway • Chicago, Illinois 60660 • 769-2900
2714 W. Peterson • Chicago, Illinois 60659 • 465-2900

Barry's Secret Receipe
Lake Michigan Smelt

When the smelt are running on the shores of Lake Michigan, that's when I head for Navy Pier to make a deal with a pizza loving fisherman.

Five pounds of fresh smelt will get him a Barry's Spot Pizza covered with sausage, pepperoni, mushrooms, onions, green peppers and lots of cheese.

While the fisherman is enjoying his pizza, I head home to make fresh fried smelt.

> 5 pounds fresh smelt
> (remove heads and slit bellies)
> 3½ cups flour
> ½ cup fine grain corn meal
> 1 teaspoon salt
> 1 teaspoon paprika
> ¼ teaspoon white pepper
> 1 cup peanut oil
> ¼ pound margarine

Wash, clean and pat dry smelts. Cover with mixture of flour, corn meal, salt, paprika and white pepper. Let the smelts stand for ten minutes then cover with flour mixture again.

Put the oil and margarine in a large frying pan and heat until the oil starts popping.

Add the smelts and fry golden brown on each side, turning them once only.

For a tangy special mix sauce:

> 1 cup ketchup
> 1 tablespoon horseradish (hot)
> 1 tablespoon Worcestershire sauce

Enjoy!

*Barry Berhsen*
Barry Berhsen
Barry's Spot Pizza

## Michael A. Bilandic

### GRANDMA BILANDIC'S FRIED CHICKEN

1 frying chicken, cut-up
1 cup flour
1 cup fresh bread crumbs
2 large eggs, beaten
½ teaspoon salt
¼ teaspoon pepper
¼ teaspoon paprika
6 tablespoons butter
6 tablespoons Crisco

Mix flour, bread crumbs and seasonings in one bowl. Place beaten eggs in another bowl. Dip chicken pieces first in egg and then in flour mixture. Store in refrigerator for about one hour.

Fry chicken pieces in a mixture of butter and Crisco until golden in color. Place chicken in a buttered pan, covered with foil, and bake in a 325 degree oven for 1-1½ hours. Remove foil after ½ hour.

Serve hot or cold.

*Heather and Mike Bilandic*

# MUSEUM OF HOLOGRAPHY / CHICAGO

1134 W WASHINGTON BOULEVARD / CHICAGO, ILLINOIS 60607

FETTUCCINE ROBERT

Fettuccine from scratch

    3 cups semolina flour (Beware of putting semolina in a plastic pasta maker)

    4 eggs, salt, tablespoon of olive oil or water.

    Form well with flour, break in eggs and blend in salt and oil or water. Mix with flour and knead until a firm but moist ball is formed.

    Cover dough and let sit for 10 to 15 minuts, then roll by hand with rolling pin or run through a stainless steel pasta machine. (An absolute bargain at about $30)

Sauce Robert

    Halve about 30 or 40 large stuffed spanish olives and soak for 2 to 12 hours in a sauce pan containing a cup or more of top quality olive oil. (The amount of olive oil depends on your tolerance for oil.)

    After marinating, place pan over low heat and add 1½ pints heavy cream. Bring to simmer, stirring occassionaly, until oil and cream have blended.

    When pasta is cooked (only a couple of minutes for fresh made) drain quickly, put in large bowl and pour sauce over pasta. Toss and top with fresh ground black pepper, ½ cup of pine nuts, and fresh ground parmesan or romano cheese.

    Serves 4

Pasta mangia,

Robert Billings
Trustee

# Binyon's Restaurant
### 327 SOUTH PLYMOUTH COURT - CHICAGO, ILLINOIS 60604
### TELEPHONE: 341-1155

SHRIMP BINYON

Yield:   6 appetizers

Ingredients:

| | |
|---|---|
| Bread | ¾ lb. |
| Butter | ½ lb. |
| Cloves garlic, minced | 2 |
| MONTEREY CHARDONNAY | 1 oz. |
| Monosodium glutamate | ½ tsp. |
| Shrimp, jumbo, cooked and cleaned | 30 |
| Paprika | ½ tsp. |
| MONTEREY DRY SHERRY | 1 oz. |

Method:

Trim all the crust from the bread and chop bread into fine crumbs. Cream butter and combine with bread crumbs, garlic, MONTEREY CHARDONNAY and monosodium glutamate. Knead the mixture thoroughly the way you would bread dough, then roll into a cylinder about three inches in diameter and refrigerate for an hour or until hardened. Divide the cooked shrimp into six coquille shells and pour the MONTEREY DRY SHERRY over them. Slice the butter mixture into quarter inch slices and lay evenly on top of shrimp. Sprinkle with paprika and bake in oven at 450 degrees for eight to ten minutes or until the shrimp are a bubbling golden brown.

*Hal Binyon III*

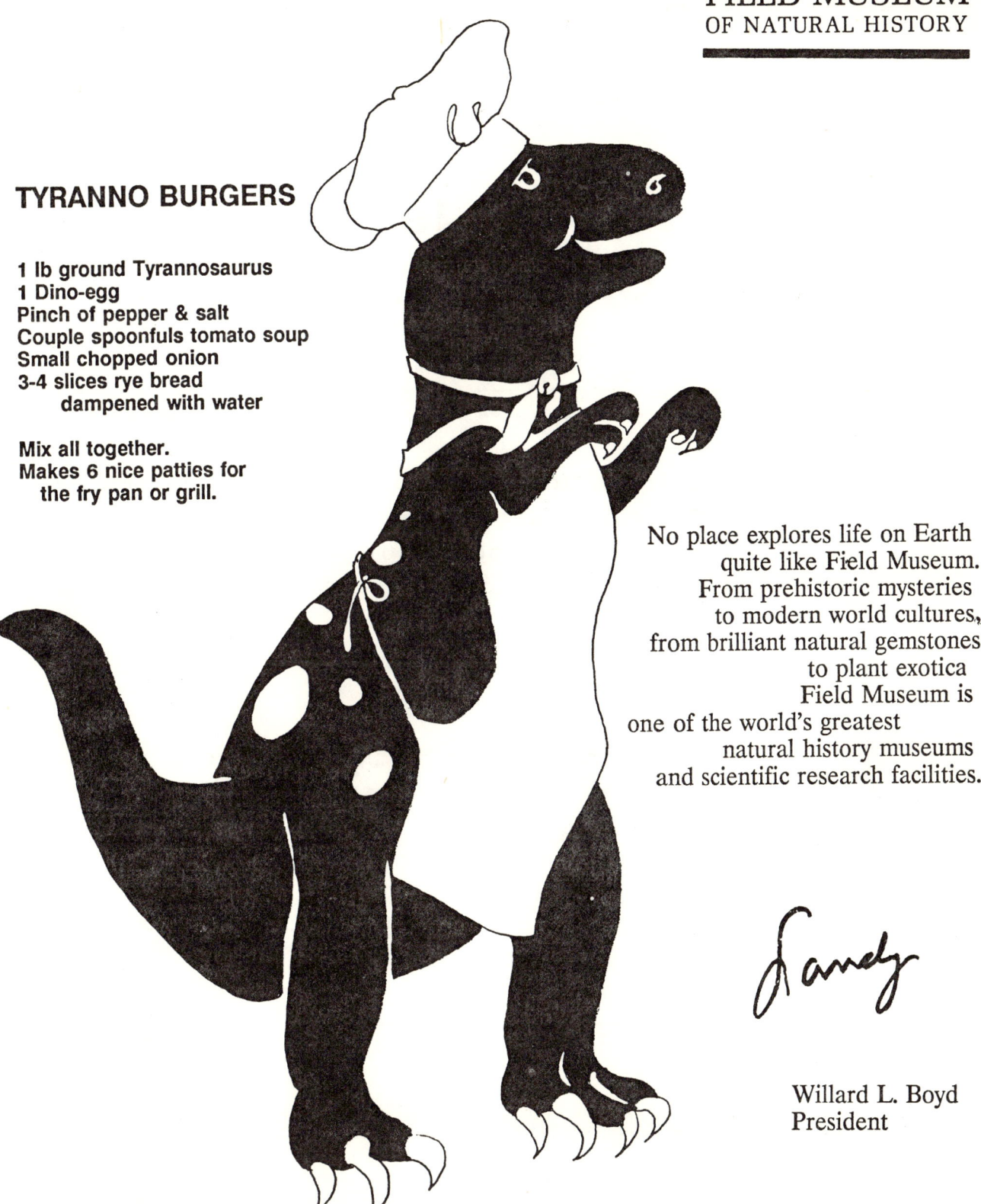

# FIELD MUSEUM
## OF NATURAL HISTORY

## TYRANNO BURGERS

1 lb ground Tyrannosaurus
1 Dino-egg
Pinch of pepper & salt
Couple spoonfuls tomato soup
Small chopped onion
3-4 slices rye bread
    dampened with water

Mix all together.
Makes 6 nice patties for
    the fry pan or grill.

No place explores life on Earth quite like Field Museum. From prehistoric mysteries to modern world cultures, from brilliant natural gemstones to plant exotica Field Museum is one of the world's greatest natural history museums and scientific research facilities.

*Sandy*

Willard L. Boyd
President

Hours: Monday - Sunday, 9am - 5 pm . EVENTS HOTLINE (312) 322-8854

13

ROOSEVELT ROAD AT LAKE SHORE DRIVE • CHICAGO, ILLINOIS 60605-2496 • TELEPHONE 922-9410, AREA CODE 312

2501 Bradley Place
Chicago, Illinois 60618
312-528-2311

**WGN-TV CHICAGO**

♫♪♫♪♫♪♫♪♫♪♫♪♫♪♫♪♫♪♫♪♫♪♫♪♫♪♫♪♫♪♫♪

# BOZO'S MUSICAL CASSEROLE

♫♪♫♪♫♪♫♪♫♪♫♪♫♪♫♪♫♪♫♪♫♪♫♪♫♪♫♪♫♪♫♪

YOU NEED:
- 1 can of chunk tuna packed in water (BEST IF IT'S A PIANO TUNA)
- 1 can of mushroom soup
- 1 small bag of potato chips or nacho chips
- 1/3 cup of milk
- 1 cup of noodles

FIRST:
Cook the noodles until they're done
Drain the tuna and empty into baking dish (break up the chunks a bit)
Add noodles (DRAIN OFF FIRST OR THE TUNA WILL SWIM AWAY)
Add soup, milk and some of the potato (nacho) chips--about a handful
Mix up well
Add remaining chips on top

Bake for about 30 minutes in 350 degree oven

THEN:     ENJOY!

*BOZO*

♪♫♪♫♪♫♪♫♪♫♪♫♪♫♪♫♪♫♪♫♪♫♪♫♪♫♪♫♪♫♪♫♪

14

Tribune Broadcasting Company

2501 Bradley Place
Chicago, Illinois 60618
312-528-2311

**WGN-TV CHICAGO**

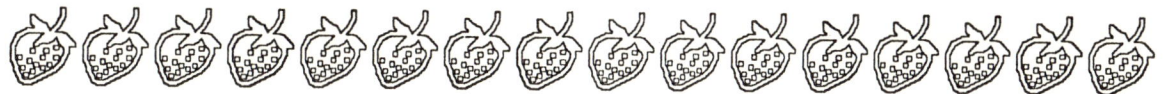

# COOKY'S BERRY BUTTER & FRENCH TOAST

YOU NEED:
- 1/4 CUP POWDERED SUGAR
- 3/4 CUP FROZEN STRAWBERRIES
- 1 CUBE SOFTENED BUTTER
- 2 EGGS
- 1/2 CUP MILK
- A TEASPOON CINNAMON
- 4 SLICES BREAD

FIRST: BLEND THE BUTTER, FROZEN STRAWBERRIES AND POWDERED SUGAR (IN A BLENDER OR FOOD PROCESSOR). SET ASIDE.

THEN: MIX EGGS, MILK AND CINNAMON AS BATTER

AND DIP BREAD SLICES IN BATTER AND FRY TO GOLDEN BROWN ON BOTH SIDES.

SERVE TO YOUR FAMILY. COOKY ALWAYS ADDS CHOCOLATE SAUCE BUT MAYBE YOU WOULDN'T LIKE IT.

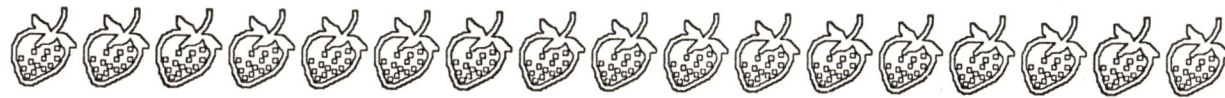

Tribune Broadcasting Company

**JOHN G. SHEDD AQUARIUM**

1200 SOUTH LAKESHORE DRIVE  CHICAGO  ILLINOIS 60605
312-939-2426

WILLIAM P. BRAKER DIRECTOR

## Salmon a la Shedd

| | |
|---|---|
| 4 lb. salmon filets | 1/4 tsp. dill seed |
| 2 sticks butter or margarine | 1/4 tsp. caraway seed |
| 1 cup freshly squeezed lemon juice | Pinch onion salt |
| 1/2 cup dry white wine | 2 bay leaves, finely crushed |
| 2 tsp. celery salt | |
| 1 tsp. celery seed | 1/4 cup capers |

Melt butter or margarine over low heat, add lemon juice, wine and rest of ingredients. Mix thoroughly.

Filet salmon and remove skin. Cut into pieces approx. 4" square. Arrange in pyrex baking dishes. Divide sauce between dishes and make sure sauce runs under filets to prevent sticking. Sprinkle fish with additional celery seed, celery salt, dill, caraway. Place 1/2 bay leaf on each piece of fish. Place approx. 6 capers on each piece.

Bake in oven at 350 degrees or Weber charcoal grill, covered. Baste at regular intervals to keep fish moist. Fish is done as soon as it loses glistening pearly appearance and becomes opaque. Filet must be separated with knife to determine this. DO NOT OVERCOOK.

William P. Braker
Director

/mld

# THE LOOP. AM 1000 / FM 98

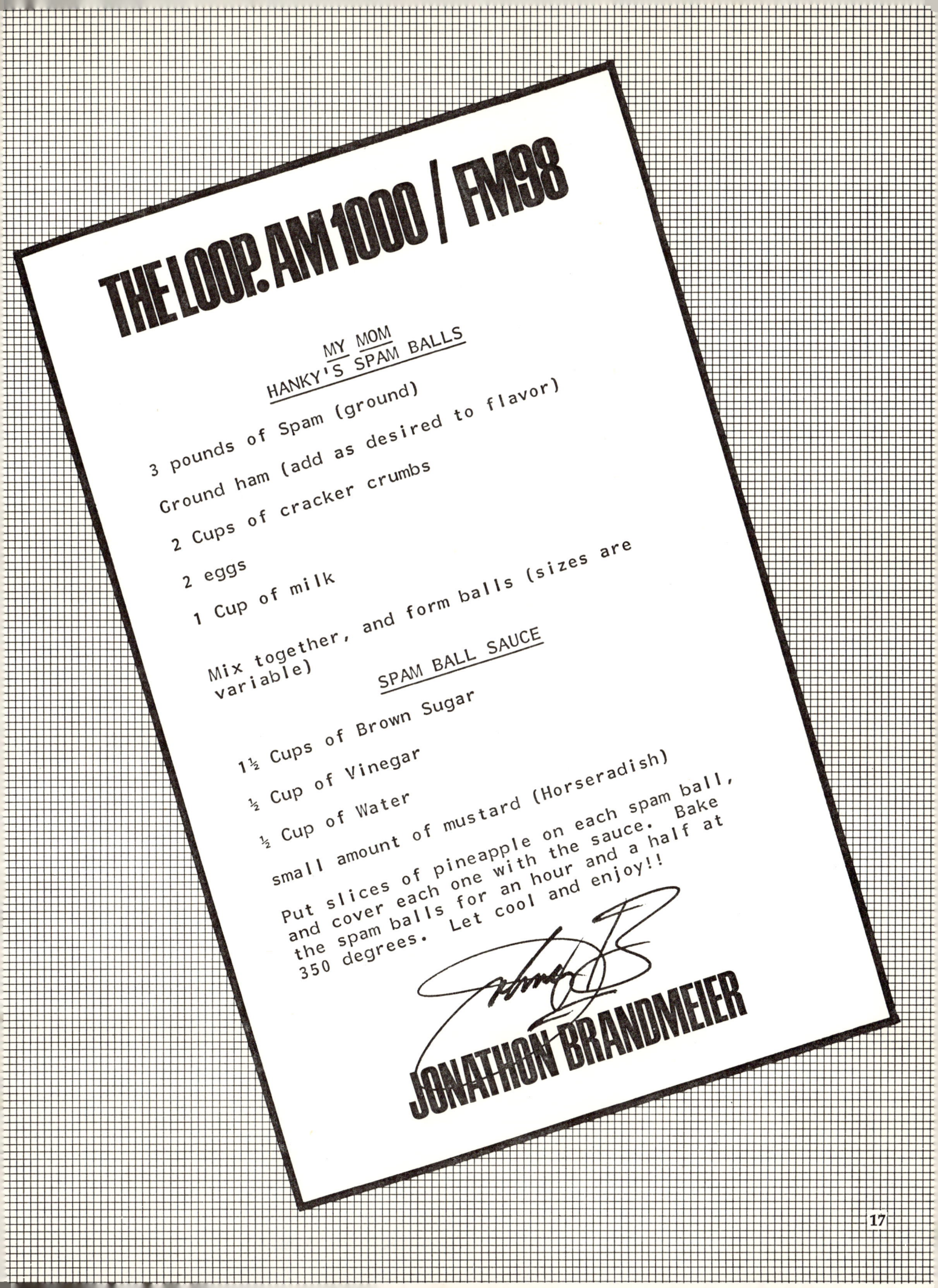

## MY MOM
## HANKY'S SPAM BALLS

3 pounds of Spam (ground)

Ground ham (add as desired to flavor)

2 Cups of cracker crumbs

2 eggs

1 Cup of milk

Mix together, and form balls (sizes are variable)

## SPAM BALL SAUCE

1½ Cups of Brown Sugar

½ Cup of Vinegar

½ Cup of Water

small amount of mustard (Horseradish)

Put slices of pineapple on each spam ball, and cover each one with the sauce. Bake the spam balls for an hour and a half at 350 degrees. Let cool and enjoy!!

*Jonathon Brandmeier*

## JONATHON BRANDMEIER

Montgomery Ward
Corporate Offices
Montgomery Ward Plaza
Chicago, Illinois 60671

**Bernard F. Brennan**  President and Chief Executive Officer

312-467-2849

## FISH SOUP

1 large onion - chopped
1/2 cup celery - chopped
1 large clove of garlic - chopped
2 tblsp. butter
2 cans (16 oz.) crushed tomatoes
1/2 cup white wine
1 tsp. salt
1/4th tsp. pepper
1/4th tsp. thyme
1 pkg. or (1 lb.) fish fillets (can substitute shrimp, tuna or crab)

Saute' onions, celery, garlic and butter until tender. Stir in tomatoes, wine, salt, pepper and thyme. If you are preparing this ahead of time, refrigerate at this point.

When ready to serve, add fish cut in chunks and simmer 10 to 15 minutes.

*Bernard F. Brennan*
Bernard F. Brennan

**Montgomery Ward**

# The Seagram Classics Wine Company

2600 CAMPUS DRIVE • SAN MATEO, CA 94403

(415) 378-3939

SAM BRONFMAN II
PRESIDENT

## Marinated Grilled Chicken

```
3       tablespoons Dijon mustard
   3/4  cup olive oil
2       cloves garlic, crushed
1-1/2   teaspoons ground pepper
1-1/2   teaspoons dried thyme
1       large bayleaf, crumbled
pinch   of cayenne pepper
2-1/2   tablespoons The Monterey Vineyard Chardonnay
2-1/2   tablespoons wine vinegar
salt    to taste
6       chicken breasts
```

1) In a small bowl, whisk together mustard and oil.

2) Add all other ingredients except chicken.

3) In large rectangular baking dish, arrange chicken and pour marinade over.

4) Leave to marinate overnight, turning occasionally.

5) Grill 10 to 15 minutes on each side on the bar-b-que, using marinade for basting.

Delicious!

*Melanie & Sam Bronfman*

## OFFICE OF THE ALDERMAN, FOURTEENTH WARD

**EDWARD M. BURKE**
ALDERMAN
2650 W. 51ST STREET
CHICAGO, ILLINOIS 60632
471-1414

COUNCIL CHAMBERS
CITY HALL—ROOM 207
121 N. LA SALLE ST.
CHICAGO, ILLINOIS 60602

Plum Pie

Filling:

2 to 2-1/2 Cups of Dark Italian Seeded Plums, Sliced in Half
1/4 Cup Brown Sugar
1/4 Cup Granulated Sugar
1 Tablespoon of Cinnamon
1 Teaspoon Small Pearl Tapioca
1 Wedge of Lemon--Squeezed

---

Crust: (Makes 2 bottom and 2 top crusts)

2 Cups Flour
2/3 Cup Lard
Sprinkle of Salt

Mix all of the above until it forms grainy texture (like oatmeal).

Add: 1/4 Cup Water, 1 Egg Yolk, 1 Tablespoon Lemon and mix. Sprinkle on top of dough gently.

Work dough with fork until all is combined. Don't make it too moist. Set in refrigerator one-half hour, then roll out. (Makes two bottoms and two tops, thin crusts, not thick.)

# The Cottage restaurant

525 TORRENCE AVENUE
CALUMET CITY, ILLINOIS 60409

312/891-3900

When my dear friend invited me over and I first laid eyes on the dish that he prepared, I thought to myself "What is that?". Being a Chicagoan, "chili" always meant to me a sort of soup, not too spicey and not too complex. Needless to say I was hooked after the three bowls I had that night.

The following recipe is an approximation of what he serves, but it's never as good as when I have it every year, when the weather gets nippy, at his home, in the warm glow of our friendship.

## Five-Way Chili

2 lbs. ground sirloin
1 lb. Spanish onions, finely chopped
4-5 cloves garlic, crushed thru press
1/2 c. corn oil (plus 3 T. additional)
8 c. crushed tomatoes
1 quart tomato juice
2 c. grated light cheddar cheese
2 c. additional diced Spanish onions
4 c. red beans, cooked
2 lbs. cooked, thin spaghetti

Spices & Seasonings:
6 oz. hot or mild chili powder
2 T. salt
1 crushed red jalepeno pepper
1 T. crushed black peppercorns
2 T. ground cinnamon
1 T. dried oregano
1/2 T. ground cumin
2-3 bay leaves
1 T. good quality cocoa
few dashes Tabasco sauce, opt.

Combine spices, then mix half into ground meat. Heat oil until smoking, add seasoned meat in batches, and brown. Separately saute onion in additional oil being careful not to brown. Add onions to meat, then add tomatoes, juice, and remaining spice mixture. If mixture seems too thick, add about 1 quart water (this will depend on amount of juice in tomato product). Cook, stirring occasionally for about 2 hours. If desired, beans can be added towards end of cooking time, or they can be offered separate.

To serve: Ladle hot chili over warm pasta in large bowls. Allow guests to add their own amount of cheese and onions.

GOVERNORS

HON. MICHAEL BUTLER
CHAIRMAN
VISCOUNT COWDRAY
MAJOR RONALD FERGUSON
GEOFFREY J.W. KENT
JORIE BUTLER KENT
STUART MACKENZIE
CECIL SMITH

## BLACK CHERRY PUDDING

1 pound can black Bing cherries
1 cup sugar
1 cup flour
1 teaspoon soda
1 egg beaten
1 tablespoon melted butter
1 cup chopped nuts

Sauce

1 cup sugar
½ cup butter or margarine
½ cup cream
1 teaspoon vanilla

If you like the big black Bing cherries you will find this an outstanding desert.
1. Mix the sugar, flour, soda, and the egg beaten with the melted butter. Stir in the cherries, well drained (but save the juice).
2. Add enough juice to the mixture to make a rather thick batter.
3. Add the nuts and pour into a shallow casserole or large pie plate, or, best of all, a Pyrex dish about 7½"x12" and shallow.
4. Bake in a 350° oven about 30 minutes, or until it is firm to the touch.
   Serve warm with hot sauce or ice cream, Serves 7-8.

Sauce: Mix the sauce ingredients in the top of a double boiler and cook over boiling water until it thickens somewhat. Keep warm until serving. Or make early in the day and reheat in a double boiler at serving time.

Michael Butler

HEADQUARTERS • OAK BROOK HILLS • 3500 MIDWEST ROAD • OAK BROOK, IL 60522 • (312) 325-5566 • FAX (312) 325-5573

# WOODFIELD HILTON AND Towers

## PEPPERLOIN

One whole Tenderloin cleaned. Four to seven pounds marinated in Olive Oil and 6 Bay Leaves, sliced onions, white pepper for about 36 hours.

Pepper Corn Mix:
- 16 oz. ½ cracked black pepper
- 1 cup rock salt
- Handful of bay leaves crushed
- 6 garlic cloves chopped

Mix all the above together. Roll the whole tenderloin in the mix and grill

## MUSTARD SAUCE

- 1 chopped onion
- 4 chopped garlic cloves
- 1 cup chopped celery
- 1 bunch chopped parsley
- Few pinches of oregano

- 8 oz. White wine
- 8 oz. Dry wine
- ½ gallon Cider Vinegar or Apple Cider
- 2 oz. Lee & Perrin
- ½ gallon prepared Mustard
- 1 gallon brown sauce

Saute vegetables with herbs. Add wine, Lee & Perrin, Cider vinegar, dry mustard, prepared mustard and brown suace and let simmer for about an hour or so.

3400 West Euclid Avenue   Arlington Heights, Illinois 60005   312/394-2000
Reservations 1-800/HILTONS

# JANE BYRNE

Snow Birds ---- Jane Byrne

Starting with a whole pineapple -- leaving leaves on, cut in half through leaves.

One banana - cut in half (do not peel).

Cube out pineapple with sharp knife.

Fill scooped out pineapple with chicken salad or shrimp salad (whatever you prefer).
Place cubed pineapple on side with toothpicks creating a nest.

Take one half of banana attaching it with toothpick to top of "bird" (bottom of pineapple) with toothpicks. Use two raisins for eyes.

Sprinkle entire "bird" with coconut.

This is a very pretty arrangement, but also a healthy natural food to serve your guests.

*Jane Byrne*

# CHICAGO ARCHITECTURE FOUNDATION

1800 South Prairie Avenue
Chicago, Illinois 60616

(312) 326-1393

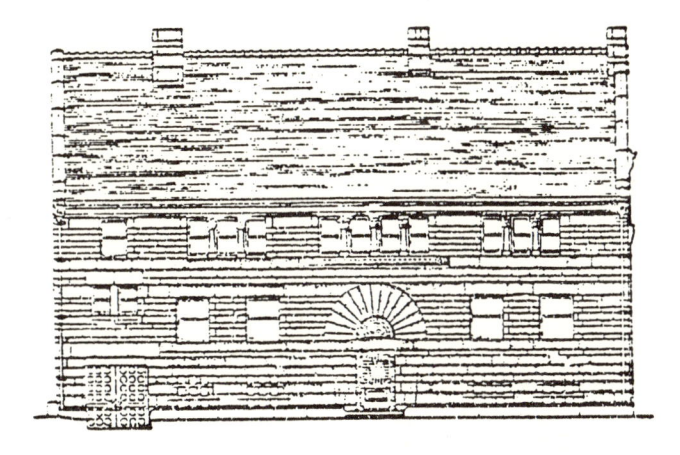

John J. and Frances Glessner loved to entertain in their new home at 1800 South Prairie Avenue, Chicago's most elegant neighborhood in the 1880's. At one event, a reading of Faust held for friends and members of the Chicago Symphony Orchestra, guests Robert Lincoln and Allison Armour prepared the following Lobster Newburgh recipe.

### LOBSTER NEWBURGH

- 4 TBSP Butter
- 2 C Lobster Meat, Cooked and Diced
- 3 Eggs
- 1 C Cream
- 1/3 C Sherry
- Dash of:
    - Salt
    - Nutmeg
    - Paprika

To 4 tablespoons of butter add 2 cups cooked diced lobster meat. Stir for 3 or 4 minutes and season with a dash of paprika and nutmeg. Add yolks of 3 eggs and 1 cup cream beaten together. Stir continuously for several minutes. Add 1/3 cup sherry and salt to taste. Serve at once. (Serves four)

*Carol J. Callahan*

Submitted by: Carol J. Callahan
Glessner House Curator*

*Glessner House Museum in the Prairie Avenue Historic District is open to the public. For information call 326-1393.

# Italian Village INCORPORATED

TELEPHONE DEarborn 2-7005 ✶ Chicago, Illinois 60603

Sauteed Sea Scallops with Capers and Roasted Red Peppers

yield: 4 servings

1½ pound fresh sea scallops
    flour
1 teaspoon garlic (chopped fine)
1 tablespoon parsley (chopped fine)
2 ounces white wine
8 tablespoons chopped roasted red peppers, preferably freshly home-roasted (see below) or from a water packed jar
1 tablespoon chopped nonpareilles capers
4 bay leaves (crumbled)
2 tablespoons red wine vinegar
4 tablespoons parmesan cheese
    salt
    freshly ground black pepper
    olive oil

Roasted Red Peppers

Place 2 large red peppers under broiler until skin blackens and blisters. Transfer to saucepan and keep under cover for 15 minutes. Remove and hold each pepper under cold running water peeling off skin and removing seeds.

1. Wash the sea scallops thoroughly in cold water, drain and pat dry with cloth kitchen towling.

2. Dredge sea scallops in flour and shake off excess.

3. Saute' sea scallops in olive oil on both sides.

4. Drain excess oil. Add garlic and parsley and cook for 1 minute.

5. Deglaze pan with white wine. Add roasted peppers, capers, bay leaf, red wine vinegar and parmesan cheese. Season to taste with salt and pepper. Cook for 1 minute and serve.

*Buon Appetito,*
*Ray Capitanini*

# Crain's Chicago Business

740 Rush Street, Chicago, Illinois 60611

**Joe Cappo**
Vice President/Publisher
312/649-5358

PASTA ALLEGRA

1/4 pound butter
1/4 cup olive oil
3/4 cup chopped onions
1 large can of tomatoes, pureed
1 1/2 teaspoons salt
1/2 teaspoon black pepper

1 teaspoon oregano
1 pound egg noodles, cooked al dente
1/4 cup grated parmesan cheese
1/2 pound mozzarella, in dice-sized cubes
1/2 cup sliced ripe black olives

Heat half the butter and the oil in a saucepan. Saute the onions 5 minutes. Add the tomatoes, salt and pepper; bring to a boil and cook over high heat for 10 minutes. Mix in the oregano.

Melt the remaining butter in a casserole. Add the noodles, 2 tablespoons parmesan cheese and the mozzarella. Toss well. Pour the sauce over the mixture; sprinkle with the remaining parmesan cheese and arrange the olives on top. Bake in a 350 degree oven 10 minutes or until the mozzarella cheese begins to melt.

Enjoy!
Joe Cappo

**CRAIN COMMUNICATIONS INC.**

Advertising Age • Business Marketing • Modern Healthcare • Business Insurance • Pensions & Investment Age • Crain's Chicago Business • Crain's Cleveland Business • Autoweek • Automotive News • Rubber & Plastics News • Crain's New York Business • Crain's Detroit Business • Monthly Detroit • Electronic Media • City and State

## DIXON
DIXON TICONDEROGA COMPANY

756 Beachland Boulevard
P.O. Box 3504
Vero Beach,
Florida 32964

Telephone:
305 +
231-3190

Samuel B. Casey, Jr.
CHAIRMAN OF THE BOARD

300 S. Riverside Plaza
Suite 1100 N
Chicago, Illinois 60606

Telephone
312 +
648-0555

POPOVER POWER

Basic Recipe

Makes 12 popovers if a standard
Roshco Co. anodized aluminum pan
is used, 24 if a muffin tin is used

- 2 cups sifted all-purpose flour
- 1 tsp. salt
- 6 jumbo eggs, lightly beaten
- 2 cups milk
- 6 T. unsalted butter, melted and cooled, or meat drippings or vegetable oil

1. Heat oven to 375°. Generously butter popover cups.
2. Combine flour and salt in the bowl of an electric mixer. Add eggs, milk and butter and beat until smooth, scraping sides frequently with a spatula. Do not overbeat.
3. Fill popover cups ½ full with the batter. Bake in the center of the oven for 40-45 minutes. Do not peek or the popovers will collapse.

For drier interiors prick the popovers in several places with a bamboo skewer during the last 5 minutes of baking time. Loosen popovers from pan and serve at once with my favorite strawberry preserves, or your personal favorite.

*Samuel B. Casey Jr.*

**THE SEAGRAM CLASSICS WINE COMPANY**

95 EAST ALGONQUIN ROAD

DES PLAINES, IL 60016

(312) 699-5270

RAYMOND S. CHADWICK
VICE PRESIDENT
CENTRAL DIVISION MANAGER

## IRISH SODA BREAD

```
4 cups sifted flour          1 1/2 cup raisins
1/4 cup sugar                1 1/3 cup milk
1 tbsp. white vinegar        1 tsp. salt
1 tbsp. baking powder        1 egg
1/4 cup butter               1 tsp. baking soda
          1 tbsp. carroway seeds
```

Sift together flour, sugar, salt and baking powder. Stir in carroway seeds. Cut in butter. Stir in raisins.

In another dish combine milk, egg, baking soda and vinegar. Stir into other mixture.

Knead until smooth. Form into ball - Grease round (approx. 9") Pyrex bowl with shortening. Place batter in bowl. Make cross with knife in top. (Separate slightly)

Bake 1 hour-1 hour 10 min. in 375 degree oven. Let cool. Serve with butter and/or favorite preserves.

This recipe for Irish Soda Bread originates from Slea Head, County Kerry, Ireland.

My wife's paternal grandmother, Johanna Long Hoar, brought this tradition to America in the early 1900's. Irish Soda Bread graces our table on special holidays, especially St. Patrick's Day!

ENJOY!

Ray Chadwick

**The Adler Planetarium**

1300 South Lake Shore Drive
Chicago, Illinois 60605
312-322-0304

☆ ☆ ☆ ☆ ☆ ☆

## HEAVENLY BROWNIES

From an old and (until now) top-secret family recipe. Also known as "Port-Tack Brownies" - a label any sailboat sailor will understand.

MIX:     1 stick melted butter
         1 cup granulated sugar
         1/4 cup unsweetened cocoa powder

BEAT IN: 2 eggs
         1 teaspoon vanilla
         3/4 cup flour
         1/4 teaspoon salt
         3/4 cup chopped nuts

Spread in 8" x 8" buttered pan.
Bake at 350° for 20 minutes.

Submitted by:
Dr. Joseph M. Chamberlain*
President and Director
The Adler Planetarium
Chicago

*AKA: Chief cook and Navigator

*Joseph M. Chamberlain*

☆ ☆ ☆ ☆ ☆ ☆

WLS-TV   190 North State   Chicago, Illinois 60601   Telephone 312 750-7777

THIS IS EASY....AND SO GOOD!!!

BLUEBERRY SCONES

3 cups buttermilk baking mix
2 tablespoons sugar
1 cup fresh or frozen blueberries (I use fresh)
¼ cup milk
2 eggs

FOR GLAZE:

1 egg, well beaten
2 tablespoons sugar

Preheat oven to 400°. In medium bowl, combine the baking mix, 2 T. sugar and blueberries. Pour milk in measuring cup. Add the eggs to the milk and beat with a fork until well mixed. Stir liquid into baking mix until moistened. (Dough will be crumbly.)

Turn the dough onto a lightly floured work surface, and pat into a 9" round, about ½" thick. Brush the dough with the beaten egg, then sprinkle with 2 T. sugar. Cut the round into twelve wedges. Place on ungreased cookie sheet and bake for 10-12 minutes until golden.

Serve immediately with butter or cream and jam. Makes 12 scones, 165 calories each.

TIP: For the lightest scones, handle the dough as little as possible. Overmixing and overshaping can toughen it. If the dough seems a bit sticky when cutting, dip the knife in flour, then cut.

Baked scones freeze and re-heat beautifully!

*Enjoy!*
*Mary Ann Childers*

# CSA Fraternal Life
*Formerly Czechoslovak Society of America*

Museum, Library and Archives
**LILLIAN K. CHORVAT**
(Museum Curator and Librarian)

<u>MAMA'S CHICAGO BEACH SALAD</u>  (Jackson Park, Montrose, Oak St., 12th St.,)

Weekly outings to Chicago's beaches in the mid 1930's thru 1940's were anticipated with much happiness. A hearty lunch included Mama's famous summer vegetable salad. It is delicious and did not spoil before picnic time!

    2 large potatoes, cooked in their jackets
    1 or 2 green peppers
    3 stalks celery
    1 medium onion
    2 large tomatoes
(Dice all vegetables fine.  Dice potatoes, combine with diced vegetables.)

    <u>Dressing</u>

    1 tsp salt
    3 tsp sugar
    1/4 tsp pepper
    2 T vegetable oil
    About 3 oz vinegar
    About 3-4 oz water
(Mix well, and pour over diced vegetable.  Delicious.)

*Lillian K. Chorvat*
Lillian K. Chorvat

2701 So. Harlem Ave., (P.O. Box 249) Berwyn, IL 60402-0249  Phones: (312) 242-2224 or 795-5800

# bobby christian

**COMPOSER - CONDUCTER - ARRANGER**

531 NORTH EAST AVENUE • OAK PARK, ILLINOIS 60302 • VILLAGE 8-3250

BOBBY CHRISTIAN'S HOTDOG SCALOPPINE  (ORIGINAL RECIPE)

For six to eight servings

    12 Hotdogs
     6 tablespoons of GOOD Italian Olive Oil
     2 cloves of garlic (at least)
     ¼ teaspoon of oregano
     ¼ teaspoon of parsley (dried leaves)
     1 large cup (12 ounces) bell tomatoes (canned - Italian brand)
     1 PINCH of salt
     1 PINCH of mint leaf (if desired)
     ½ cup of Chianti wine (or similar Italian wine)

In a large frying pan (skillet) heat olive oil on a low flame and then add diced garlic. Slice hotdogs about ¼ inch thick and fry adding salt, oregano, parsley, and mint (if desired). Fry medium well (until slightly browned). Put stove on high for a couple of minutes and add all of the wine and cook on high for two minutes. Pour tomatoes over this and cook for 20 minutes on low flame. Let cool - cover - let stand.

About twelve minutes before serving put on high flame for two minutes (leaving cover on)...turn stove off and let stand for ten minutes. Serve with rice, spaghetti, linguine, mashed potatoes, etc.

Serve with salad tossed with wine vinegar Italian dressing.

This recipe was first introduced to the public on the "JIM CONWAY RADIO SHOW" in 1941 on radio station WBBM. Bobby Christian is the inventor of this great concoction.

P.S.: For better health use turkey dogs!!!

*Bobby Christian*

## Jerry Coleman's Paella   Serves 12

This is a festive party dish that can be made in advance so that you have time to spend with your guests.

### Ingredients

Chicken stock ( about 4 cups for every cup of rice )

Black pepper/ saffron/ bay leaf / thyme/ fresh parsley (a hand full)

4 cloves garlic

Yello onions (2 large)

White rice (1/2 cup for each man 1/4 cup for each woman to be served)

Olive oil (1 cup)

Italian plum tomatoes (large can)

Dry white wine (1/2 cup)

* Spanish chorizo (4 or 5)
* Camarones secos (sun dried shrimp 3 oz.)

  Boned chicken brest (1 1/2 lb)

  Medium fresh shrimp (1 1/2 lb)

  scallops (3/4/lb.)

  Mussels (4 Doz.)

  Clams (1 Doz.)

  Red pimientos (small jar)

  Peas (1pk. frozen)

  Green beans (1 pk. French)

-----------------

Heat a large iron skillet (15in.) and add 3/4 cp. oil. Fry chicken (cut in bite size pc.) remove. Chorizo (sliced) remove. Now saute the shrimp & scallops and remove. Put all of the meats in a bowl and hold.
Now add chopped onion'chopped garlic' camarones secos' & rice to the skillet & saute in the oil that was used for the meats.
Scrub Mussels & clams & steam until cooked. Combine liquor of clams & mussels with chicken stock & juice of tomatoes.Combine saffron & wine and bring to simmer. Add to other liquid. Add tomatoes to rice/onions/ dried shrimp/&garlic.Add liquid to pan and cook rice until almost done. Put meats/clam & mussel meats back in skillet and continue to cook. Add frozen peas and mix in. When done 'spread green beans on top and then pimientos. Decorate top with empty clam & mussel shells.

* Without the Spanish chorizo and Camarones secos this dish is a poor imatation.

They can be purchased at "La Unica" 1515 W. Devon"Chicago

This dish is a traditional NewYears Day dinner at our house. The many different tastes make for exciting eating. ENJOY

# CHICAGO BULLS

Sour Cream Chocolate Chip Cake.

1/4 lb. margarine  ⎫
1 1/2 c. sugar       ⎬ Cream together
1 1/2 tsp. vanilla   ⎭

*Doug Collins*

Add 3 eggs, one at a time
3 cups flour          ⎫
1 T. baking powder    ⎬ Blend

16 oz. sour cream     ⎫ Blend in
1 1/2 tsp. baking soda ⎬ sour cream
                       ⎭ container

Combine all ingredients —

Topping — 1/2 c. sugar
          1 t. cinnamon
          6 oz. choc. chips

Grease & flour 9x13 pan.
Spread — 1/2 of batter
         1/2 of chocolate chips
         1/2 of topping — press
                      down & repeat.
Bake at 350° for 30 mins.

980 N. Michigan Ave. • Suite 1600 • Chicago, IL 60611-4501 • (312) 943-5800

HOTEL · AT ILLINOIS CENTER, 200 NORTH COLUMBUS DRIVE, CHICAGO, ILLINOIS 60601 · (312) 565-8000

# The Fairmont Hotel's
# Baked Alaska
### served at the Moulin Rouge

10 Eggs          1 oz Salad Oil
10 oz Sugar      1 oz Vanilla
10 oz Flour      1 oz Salt

Heat the eggs and sugar together over a double broiler. When about 120°, remove from heat and mix at medium speed until eggs are thick and fluffy. While eggs are mixing, sift flour and salt together. Fold by hand into the whipped eggs, then fold in salad oil and vanilla. Spread onto a greased or paper-lined baking sheet, approx. ¼" thick and bake at 450° until light brown for about 3-5 minutes. Let cool.

Cut out rectangular piece of cake, 10" x 4". Layer vanilla, strawberry, and chocolate ice cream on cake, about 1" of each. Cover the ice cream with strips of remaining cake and freeze.

*Continue:*

**HOTEL** · AT ILLINOIS CENTER, 200 NORTH COLUMBUS DRIVE, CHICAGO, ILLINOIS 60601 · (312) 565-8000

## Meringue

1 cup Egg Whites
2 cups Sugar

Beat egg whites on high speed until stiff peaks are formed. Add 2/3 of sugar slowly. Fold remaining sugar in by hand.

Spread immediately onto ice cream cake and brown in a very hot oven or with a torch. Serve with a thickened Bing Cherry Sauce.

Yield – 10 servings.

## Bing Cherry Sauce

1 #5 can of Bing Cherries with juice
3 oz Kirshwasser
1 oz Cornstarch
3 oz Sugar

Strain cherries and put into a sauce pan. Add sugar and bring to a boil. Dissolve cornstarch in Kirshwasser and add to boiling cherry juice. Cook until thick and clear. Add strained cherries. Serve warm.

Yield – 1 quart sauce

Bon Appetit!

John Coletta
Executive Chef – Fairmont Hotel

# Memo

**From** MARVA N. COLLINS

**To** ALL PEA LOVERS

### BLACKEYED PEAS JUMBALAYI

ONE PACKAGE BLACKEYED PEAS

THREE CANS OF STEWED TOMATOES

THREE LARGE RED PEPPERS

THREE LARGE GREEN PEPPERS

FIVE LARGE ONIONS

DIRECTIONS:

SOAK THE PEAS IN WATER OVERNIGHT. PUT PRESOAKED PEAS IN A POT OF WATER AND BOIL UNTIL PEAS ARE TENDER TO TOUCH. CUT THE RED, GREEN PEPPERS, AND ONIONS INTO THE BOILING POT OF PEAS. POUR CANS OF STEWED TOMATOES INTO POT. SIMMER FOR ONE HOUR UNTIL PEAS ARE COMPLETELY TENDER TO TOUCH.

*Marva N. Collins*
9/88

WESTSIDE PREP. SCHOOL
4146 W. Chicago Avenue
Chicago, Il 60651
(312) 227-5995

**WINDY CITY SPORTS**

P.O. Box 817, Wilmette, IL 60091  312-492-1080

Recipe submitted by
Maryclaire Collins
Editor, **Windy City Sports** magazine

Szechuan steak shish kebabs

1-1/2 lb. lean flank steak
1/3 to 1/2 cup low-sodium soy sauce
2 Tbls. sesame seed oil
2 Tbls. molasses
2 Tbls. sherry
1 Tbls. vinegar
1-2 Tbls. hot chili oil
2 tsp. dry mustard
1-2 tsp. ground fresh ginger
5 garlic cloves, chopped
Zest from 1 lemon
Juice from half lemon

Keep steak well-chilled, almost frozen, for easier slicing.  Then thinly slice it into strips, across the grain.
   Mix together the marinade ingredients:  soy sauce, sesame oil, molasses, sherry, vinegar, chili oil, mustard, ginger, garlic, lemon zest and lemon juice.  Mix well.  Add the meat to marinade and let stand 15 to 30 minutes at room temperature.  Then string the strips loosely onto shish kebab skewers.  Save the marinade for basting if desired.  Barbecue the shish kebabs over a hot fire for about 4-6 minutes. Turn once.
   Serve piping hot over couscous or thin pasta.  Great with a caesar salad and a full-bodied Cabernet Sauvignon.  Serves 5-6.

I call this a healthy beef recipe with some pizzazz.  If you really want to turn up the olfactory flames, just add more hot chili oil.

*Maryclaire Collins*

PUBLISHED BY CHICAGO SPORTS RESOURCES, INC.

Lou Conte, Artistic Director of the Hubbard Street Dance Company, has created a popular but serious style that combines the strength, technique and grace of ballet, the explosive energy and style of jazz, and the neat rhythmic footwork of tap, often incorporating American themes and music -- a style with roots in musical theatre. The year 1988 celebrates the Company's Tenth Anniversary of entertaining audiences with its highly acclaimed, unique and polished style of dance.

## CREVETTES ARMORICAINE

6 large prawns, shelled and deveined
4 tbs. butter
1 tsp. chopped shallots
1 tsp. chopped garlic
2 tbs. brandy
2 tbs. dry sherry
2 tbs. finely chopped parsley
1 large tomato, peeled, seeded and diced
1 pinch salt

Split prawns partially up back. Saute in butter.
Add shallots and garlic and saute briefly.
Flambe with brandy and dry sherry.
Add tomato and simmer briefly.
Remove prawns and reduce sauce to desired consistency.
Swirl in 3 tbs. butter and add chopped parsley.
Remove from heat immediately and pour sauce over prawns.

*Lou Conte*

*Memorandum from . . .*
RENEE S. CROWN

## CORN SOUFFLE

4 cups canned corn (drained)
8 T. flour
2 T. margarine
4 t. sugar (level)
2 t. salt
4 whole eggs - well beaten
4 cups milk

Mix corn, flour, sugar, salt. Melt butter. Combine with eggs. Put everything together. Mix well. Pour into greased baking dish.

Bake at 350° for 1 hour.
Stir in the beginning.

*Easy and delicious*

## MILE-HI STRAWBERRY PIE

1 baked pie shell
2 eggs (whites only)
1 c. sugar
1 t. cream of tartar
1 -8 oz. pkg frozen strawberries
1 c. whipping cream

In large electric mixer bowl, beat 2 egg whites until firm, gradually beating in sugar and cream of tartar.

Beat in package of partially thawed strawberries. Continue beating for 20 minutes, or until the meringue is a "mile-hi".

Fold in whipped cream. Fill pie shell with mixture. Put in freezer for at least 6 hours. Better still, make it the day before..
but always freeze.

*Always a winner -
Enjoy
Renee Crown*

41

**WGN CONTINENTAL BROADCASTING COMPANY**
**WGN RADIO 720**
A TRIBUNE BROADCASTING STATION
435 NORTH MICHIGAN AVENUE • CHICAGO, ILLINOIS 60611
312/222-4700

One of my favorites (Hush Puppies Bass N' Beer Batter)

1 pkg. Lake Of The Woods Batter Mix.

1 can/bottle Beer (not light)

½ cup chopped onions

½ cup chopped green peppers

Mix with 1 cup cubed Bass (or Chicago Lakefront Perch) ½" cubes

Batter should be thick enough to "dollop" into HOT oil - NOT paste but THICK.

The Hush Puppies will sink slowly then rise to the top - as soon as they are brown take out, don't try too many at one time. Serve hot - you'll never keep up with guests.

REPLY: BILL CULLERTON • OUTDOOR EDITOR • WGN RADIO
3 EAST PARK BLVD. • VILLA PARK, ILLNOIS 60181
312/530-2191

You lucky WGN listener! You certainly know a good thing when you hear it ( I guess that's why you listen to Al and/or Ed) so here are <u>two</u> of my favorite recipes. Don't get all excited, I'm sure they originally came from some very reputable cooking source and were not created by any relative of mine.

## Aunt Lana's Curran(t) Cookies

This recipe makes 2 and a half dozen

1 cup flour
1/4 cup brown sugar
1/2 cup softened butter
1/2 teaspoon vanilla
1/4 teaspoon salt
1 separated egg
3/4 cup chopped walnuts
and a jar of Smuckers Currant Jelly

Mix the flour, brown sugar, butter, vanilla, salt and yolk. Mix at low speed. Mold into one inch balls. Egg white to foam. On waxed paper, dip the balls into the egg white and roll in the nuts. Indent center of ball with thumb. It'll now look flattened with an indentation in the center. Bake 15 minutes at 350 degrees or until golden. When cool scoop jelly into the center and enjoy. Delicious!

## Aunt Barb of Bloomingdale's Crab Puff Appetizer

Aunt Barb makes these on every special occasion. On Christmas they always show up on her special Santa Claus plate. If you wait more than a few minutes you'll get a good look at Mr. Claus ...because these babies disappear fast!

Step one:   Buy, or make, creampuff pastry shells. Smaller size is best.

Step two:   Drain a 6oz package of Wakefield Crabmeat
Add two 8oz packages of warm cream cheese
1/2 cup of mayo
3 tablespoons of onion
1 teaspoon of Worcesterchire
1 teaspoon lemon juice

Mix it all together and fill the pastry shells with the mixture. Keep refrigerated but allow them to warm up a bit before serving.

We really do enjoy these two recipes at holiday time. Hope you'll give them a try and that they'll become part of the tradition at your home as well.

Ed Curran

**DISTRICT OFFICE**
5650 S. HARPER AVENUE
CHICAGO, ILLINOIS 60637
312/643-5237
312/667-0550

**CAPITOL OFFICE**
2107 STRATTON BUILDING
SPRINGFIELD, ILLINOIS 62706
217/782-8121

**ILLINOIS HOUSE OF REPRESENTATIVES**
**BARBARA FLYNN CURRIE**
STATE REPRESENTATIVE ● 26TH DISTRICT

**CHAIR**
SELECT COMMITTEE ON THE 1992 WORLD'S FAIR

**VICE CHAIR**
APPROPRIATIONS II
REVENUE

**MEMBER**
ENERGY, ENVIRONMENT AND NATURAL RESOURCES

SESAME CHICKEN WITH CUMBERLAND SAUCE

The Chicken:
    Mix 1/2 cup grated parmesan cheese
        2 cups seasoned bread crumbs
        3 tablespoons sesame seeds

    Dip six to eight chicken pieces in melted
        butter, then in crumb mixture

Bake one hour at 350-degree oven

The Cumberland Sauce:
    Combine and simmer until smooth
        1 cup red currant jelly
        1 6-ounce can frozen orange juice, defrosted
        4 tablespoons dry sherry
        1 teaspoon dry mustard
        1/8 teaspoon ground ginger
        1/4 teaspoon Tabasco sauce

Serve the sauce with the chicken--and enjoy!

*Barbara Flynn Currie*

## STEVE DAHL'S TACOS

1 HEAD ICEBERG LETTUCE
(2/14 OZ) CANS CHOPPED OR SLICED BLACK OLIVES
2 RIPE TOMATOES, CUT IN THIN WEDGES
1 RIPE AVOCADO, CUT IN CHUNKS
1/2 BUNCH SCALLIONS, SLICED
LAWRY'S SEASONED SALT
3 TABLESPOONS BUTTER
1 MEDIUM ONION, CHOPPED
4 POUNDS GROUND ROUND OR CHUCK
1 (1 LB) CAN SOLID VEGETABLE SHORTENING
2 DOZEN CORN TORTILLAS
1 POUND CHIHUAHUA, FARMER'S, MONTEREY JACK
OR BRICK CHEESE, GRATED
2 CUPS SOUR CREAM
HOT SAUCE
SALT

Prepare salad: Cut lettuce into thin slices, then chop if desired. Toss with olives, tomatoes, avocado and scallions. Season with seasoned salt to taste. Refrigerate for 1 hour, tossing occasionally.

In large skillet or saute pan, heat butter. Saute onion for 5 minutes until soft. Add beef and cook for 10 minutes until browned. Season with salt to taste. Drain juices from meat; reserve.

In 2-quart dutch oven or heavy saucepan, heat shortening until almost smoking. Place 1 tortilla in pan, fry for 5 seconds.

Flip and fold with tongs and fork. Quickly fry each side of fold until crisp. Pat dry. Serve right away or fill with meat and place in pan in oven under low heat. Fry remaining tortillas.

To assemble tacos: Fill each taco with meat, cheese, salad, sour cream and hot sauce. Serves 6 to 8.

I really get into making tacos, I don't just go to Dominick's, I go to Del Rey on 18th Street for hot corn tortillas. I buy the real buttery Chihuahua cheese at a place across the street. If you can't get Chihuahua, farmer's cheese is a good substitute.
I prefer to mix the lettuce, olives, scallions, tomatoes and avocado as a salad. I set up the taco ingredients assembly-line style, letting everyone make their own. My preferred technique: Meat first, then the cheese, so it melts on the meat a little bit. Salad, sour cream and hot sauce top the taco.

211 EAST OHIO STREET • PH 16 • CHICAGO, ILLINOIS 60611 • 312-822-9740

# DALEY
## FOR MAYOR

## Rich's Favorite Stew

3 lbs cubed stewing beef
1 large can tomatoes
1 bag frozen peas or green beans
1 bag whole carrots or bag frozen carrots
4 potatoes, cubed
4 onions, cubed
3 Tbsp minute tapioca
1 Tbsp sugar
1 Tbsp salt
Season by grinding black pepper
Pinch of thyme, marjoram & rosemary
2 oz. red wine

Put all ingredients in deep casserole, cover and bake 5 hours at 225 degrees.

*Serves 8*

*Enjoy!*
*Margaret and Rich Daley*

RICHARD M. DALEY FOR MAYOR • 108 N. STATE STREET, CHICAGO, IL 60602 • 269-1989

## CITY COUNCIL
### CITY OF CHICAGO

**COUNCIL CHAMBER**
CITY HALL, ROOM 209-7
121 N. LaSalle Street
CHICAGO, ILLINOIS 60602
TELEPHONE: 744-3070

**DANNY K. DAVIS**
ALDERMAN, 29TH WARD
5730 W. DIVISION
CHICAGO, ILLINOIS 60651
TELEPHONE: 626-2700

**COMMITTEE MEMBERSHIPS**
- Budget and Government Operations
- Claims and Liabilities
- Finance
- Health
- Human Rights and Consumer Protection
- License
- Local Transportation
- Police, Fire and Municipal Institutions
- Streets and Alleys

---

FROM THE KITCHEN OF

ALDERMAN DANNY K. DAVIS

### RUM CAKE

WALNUTS OR PECANS BROKEN
2 BOXES YELLOW CAKE MIX-WITH PUDDING
1 CUP DARK RUM
2/3 CUP OIL
6 WHOLE EGGS
1/2 CUP COLD WATER

### GLAZE

1/2 CUP SUGAR
1/2 STICK BUTTER
1/8 CUP WATER
1/2 CUP RUM

### DIRECTIONS

GREASE AND FLOUR A BUNDT PAN. LAYER BOTTOM OF THE PAN WITH BROKEN NUTS. MIX REMAINING INGREDIENTS AND POUR INTO PAN. BAKE AT 325 DEGREES FOR 1 HOUR.

COMBINE ALL GLAZE INGREDIENTS IN A SMALL PAN AND BRING TO A BOIL FOR 5 MINUTES. ALLOW CAKE TO COOK COMPLETELY. BRUSH GLAZE OVER CAKE AFTER PIERCING CAKE WITH FORK SO GLAZE WILL DRIP INTO INSIDE OF CAKE.

*Danny K. Davis*
DANNY K. DAVIS
ALDERMAN, 29th WARD

**CHICAGO WHITE SOX**
324 W. 35th STREET
CHICAGO, ILLINOIS 60616
(312) 924-1000

**CHOLESTEROL FREE QUICHE ***

(MAKES 2 QUICHES)

INGREDIENTS:
- 2 readi-crust made with pure vegetable oil
- 12 egg whites
- 1-2 egg yolks
- 1/4 c. non-fat milk
- 2 T flour
- 1 c. part-skim mozzarella cheese
- 10 mushrooms, diced
- 1/2 lb. smoked turkey sausage (in bacon section of store)
- 1 c. broccoli florets
- 1/2 c. diced onions
- Any other vegetables (bell peppers, snow peas, zuccini, etc.)

DIRECTIONS: Thaw readi crusts and preheat oven to 425 degrees. Blend the egg whites and 1-2 yolks with 2 T. flour, milk, pepper (curry optional). Mix cheese (grated) with egg mixture. Slowly sautee onion and mushrooms to get excess water out. Mix all of the vegetables and egg mixture together. Pour into crusts. Sprinkle 2 T. parmesan on top of both. Bake until golden brown and firm.

*My minor degree from San Diego State University is in nutrition and my major is in exercise physiology. I know what cholesterol does to the body--eggs are the leading cholesterol-rich food. This quiche has almost no cholesterol. It is extremely high in the most complete protein and also very low in calories.

MISTY DEAN-DAVIS

JOHN K. DAVIS

## STRAWBERRY/BANANA WHEAT PANCAKES

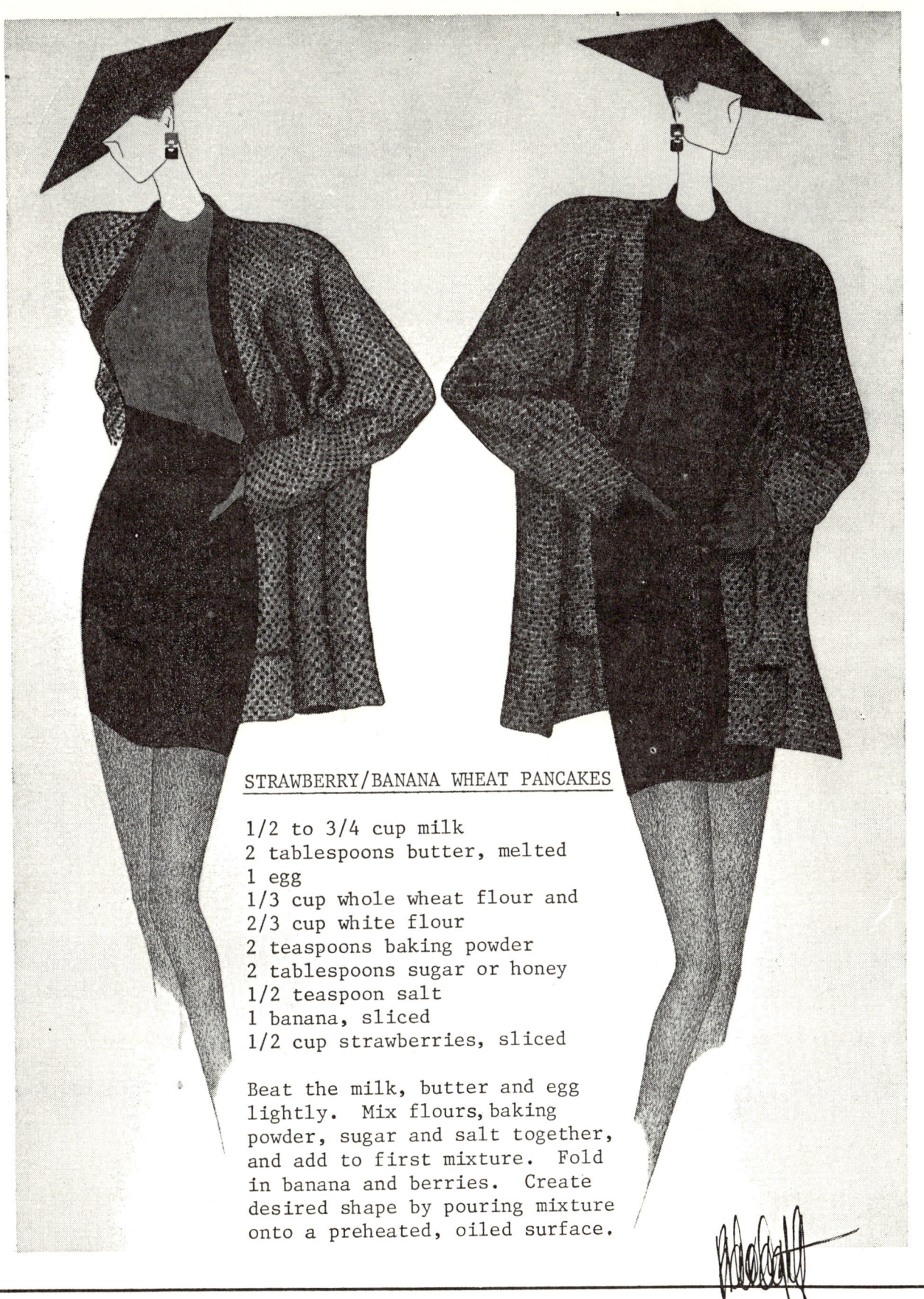

1/2 to 3/4 cup milk
2 tablespoons butter, melted
1 egg
1/3 cup whole wheat flour and
2/3 cup white flour
2 teaspoons baking powder
2 tablespoons sugar or honey
1/2 teaspoon salt
1 banana, sliced
1/2 cup strawberries, sliced

Beat the milk, butter and egg lightly. Mix flours, baking powder, sugar and salt together, and add to first mixture. Fold in banana and berries. Create desired shape by pouring mixture onto a preheated, oiled surface.

# RICHARD DAYHOFF

CHICAGO HISTORICAL SOCIETY • *Clark Street at North Avenue, Chicago, Illinois 60614*

## Mrs. Emmett Dedmon's
## "Fabulous Cookies"

1/2 cup butter
1 teaspoon vanilla
1 cup of graham cracker crumbs
1 cup coconut
1 (6 oz.) package of chocolate chips
1 (6 oz.) package of butterscotch chips
1 cup of chopped nuts
a can of sweetened condensed milk

Melt butter in 9 x 13 inch pan. Add vanilla. Sprinkle crumbs over butter and vanilla. Over this spread coconut, then add a layer of chocolate chips and one of butterscotch chips. Next spread on the nuts. Finally drizzle on condensed milk. Bake for 30 minutes at 350 degrees.

*Claire Dedmon*

Editor's note: "Fabulous Cookies" is surely a fitting title given her husband's famous book entitled <u>Fabulous Chicago</u>. Mrs. Dedmond played an active role in the research of this wonderfully informative book.

# WFYR V 103.5 FM

PRUDENTIAL PLAZA
130 E. RANDOLPH
SUITE #2303
CHICAGO, ILLINOIS 60601
(312) 861-8100

COREY DEITZ'S "CROCK-A-SMILE DONEWELL CHILI"

(MY APOLOGIES TO "CROCODILE DUNDEE"!)

WE'RE CRAZY IN CHICAGO. IN THE DEAD OF WINTER, NOTHING MAKES US HAPPIER THAN GETTING MORE CHILI. BUT, WHAT BETTER FOOD TO SUPPLEMENT OUR RAW HUNGER DURING A BEARS GAME THAN MY SECRET RECIPE FOR "CROCK-A-SMILE DONEWELL CHILI"? IT'S EASY:

2 POUNDS OF GROUND BEEF (YOU MAY SUBSTITUTE SAUSAGE)
2 CANS OF RED KIDNEY BEANS
2 FRESH TOMATOES OR 1 CAN OF TOMATOES (SLICED UP)
ENOUGH FRESH ONIONS TO EQUAL 1 CUP (CHOPPED UP)
GREEN PEPPERS CHOPPED UP TO EQUAL 1 1/4 CUPS
(OPTIONAL) 1 SMALL CAN OF TOMATOE PASTE
GARLIC
SALT
CHILI POWDER

DIRECTION: COOK UP THAT FINE-LOOKIN' GROUND BEEF AND BROWN TO TASTE. POUR OFF THE EXTRA FAT AND THROW IT IN A CROCK-POT. (THE GROUND BEEF, NOT THE FAT!) 2 POINTS FOR TOSSING IT ACROSS THE KITCHEN WITH EXACT AIM. ADD BEANS, TOMATOES, ONION, GREEN PEPPERS. IF A MORE TOMATOEY (IS THAT A WORD) CONSISTENCY IS DESIRED, GO FOR ANOTHER 2 POINTS WITH THE CAN OF TOMATOE PASTE. ADD ABOUT 2 TEASPOONS OF SALT, CHILI POWDER AND GARLIC. MORE LATER TO SUIT YOUR OWN TASTE. COOK IN THE CROCK POT ON LOW FOR ABOUT 9 HOURS...WHICH MEANS IF YOU WANT IT DONE IN TIME FOR A BEARS GAME, START IT SUNDAY MORNING AT 4AM. WHEN READY, YOU CAN INCREASE THE FLAVOR BY EATING IT OUT OF A FOOTBALL HELMET. PUT LEFTOVERS IN THE REFRIGERATOR. I'M SURE HE'LL COME OVER TO HELP YOU OUT.

ENJOY!

*Corey Deitz*

COREY DEITZ
3-7PM   103.5 FIRE

# Chicago Lions Rugby Football Club
### Established 1964

PLEASE REPLY TO:

RUGBY (MEAT-)BALLS

SAUCE:  1 JAR CHILI SAUCE

1 CAN CRANBERRY SAUCE

2 TB BROWN SUGAR

1 TB LEMON JUICE

COOK IN PAN ON STOVE, LONG ENOUGH TO MELT CRANBERRY, THEN POUR OVER MEATBALLS MADE AS FOLLOWS:

2 LBS. HAMBURGER

1/3 CUP BREAD CRUMBS

2 EGGS

1 LARGE CHOPPED ONION

3 TB ketchup

2 TB soy sauce

GARLIC, PEPPER, PARSLEY - q.s.

BAKE 30 MINUTES AT 350°.

*Ray Dempsey*
RAY DEMPSEY, PRESIDENT

MEMBER, THE MIDWEST RUGBY FOOTBALL UNION; MEMBER, THE CHICAGO AREA RUGBY FOOTBALL UNION

# STATE OF ILLINOIS
## GENERAL ASSEMBLY

**LOLETA A. DIDRICKSON**
HOUSE OF REPRESENTATIVES
SPRINGFIELD, ILLINOIS
217/782-8017

POST OFFICE BOX 98
FLOSSMOOR, ILLINOIS
312/957-3710

## CRABMEAT REMOULADE

1 7-ounce can crab meat
1 cup mayonnaise
1/4 cup olive oil
2 tablespoons lemon juice
2 cloves garlic, crushed
1 teaspoon celery seed
2 stalks celery, finely chopped
1/4 teaspoon salt
1/8 teaspoon pepper

Pick over and shred crab meat. Blend all ingredients by hand. Refrigerate. Serve with crackers, chips and raw vegetables. Yield: 3 cups.

*Loleta Didrickson*

Loleta A. Didrickson
State Representative
37th District

A Didrickson family tradition on Thanksgiving Day!

# Chicago Mountaineering Club

*Here are three recipes used by the club.* **ONA'S POTATOES** *are cooked over an open fire in the morning.* **THE GLOGG** *is the party drink for an end-of-the-season party.* **HELENA'S BBQ SAUCE** *is applied to a lamb roasted over an open fire:*

---

## HELENA'S BBQ SAUCE AND LAMB

2 Bottles dry red wine  
1 quart olive oil  
1 c real lemon juice  
3 c tomato sauce  

2-3 t allspice  
1 1/2 T salt  
1 T pepper  
1 t ginger  

3 finely chopped onions  
3 cloves finely chopped garlic  
1/2 t cloves (powdered)  

Mix ingredients; bring to boiling point (do not boil). Cool. Ready to use.
Fasten Lamb to a rod or pipe extending through the body and support lamb 3-4' above an open fire. Cook for several hours, brushing on BBQ sauce while rotating. Remove from fire and carve when cooked.

---

## GLOGG RECIPE

1/2 c sugar  
1/2 c raisins  
5 figs  
6 almonds  
1 tsp. cloves  

2-3 pcs. cinnamon  
1/4 tsp. cardamom  
1 orange peel, dried  
(1/4 orange per recipe)  

5 c wine (dry red)  
1 c brandy  
1 c grain alcohol  
1 btl. beer  
1 btl. stout (Ginnes 6-7 oz.)  

Simmer spices 5-10 minutes in beer and stout. Add wine and bring to boiling point. (DO NOT BOIL.) Add brandy and alcohol; flame. Ready to serve.

---

## ONA'S POTATOES (2 servings)

4 strips bacon  
1/2 onion, chopped  

1-2 potatoes, cooked & chopped  
3-4 eggs  

Cut bacon and cook to desired crispness. Remove from pan. Drain excess fat and add onion. Fry until almost done. Add potatoes and fry until crisp. Add eggs and bacon. When eggs are cooked, serve.
Note: Amounts may vary depending on your preference. It is easy to make larger quantities.

\* \* \* \* \* \* \* \* \* \* \* \* \* \* \* \* \* \* \*

*Members of the Chicago Mountaineering Club have enjoyed climbs all over the world including Alaska's Mt. McKinley, the U.S. and Canadian Rockies, Devil's Tower in Wyoming, the European Alps, and Cord. Blanda in Peru. Excellent fun and weekend training can be found in the relatively nearby Devil's Lake area.*

*William F. Dietrich*, president

*Secretary: Rich Ranney, 22 S. Thurlow St, Hinsdale 60521*

# DITKA'S

PAGLIA E FIENO

Ingredients:

½ lb Spinach Linguini
½ lb Egg Linguini
1 C  Baby Green Peas
1 C  Sliced Mushrooms
½ C  Diced Ham
Sauce Alfredo (recipe follows)

Cook pasta until soft, approximately 7-8 minutes, DO NOT OVERCOOK! After cooking shock in cold water. Put aside.

Sauce Alfredo:
1 qt Chicken Stock
½ C  Romano Cheese
½ C  Parmesan Cheese
½ C  Gorganzola Cheese
2 T  Sweet Basil
1 C  Heavy Cream
Salt and Pepper to taste

Bring chicken stock to a boil. Add roux of butter and flour with a wire whip. When sauce is medium thickness add all cheeses and basil. Cook out for 5 minutes. Add cream. Salt and pepper to taste.

Add 8 ounces of Alfredo sauce to a 9" saute pan. Take equal amounts of Spinach and Egg Linguini to pan. Add equal amounts of Ham, Peas, Mushrooms. Saute for 3 minutes. Serve in a casserole dish.

Serves 8.

BON APPETIT!!! GO FOR IT!!!

Chef Mike Ditka

ALAN J. DIXON
ILLINOIS

# United States Senate
WASHINGTON, DC 20510-1301

COMMITTEES:
ARMED SERVICES
BANKING, HOUSING, AND URBAN AFFAIRS
SMALL BUSINESS

## Al's Favorite Chili

### Ingredients

2 lb. ground chuck
1 large onion
1 large stalk celery & top
1/2 green pepper
2 tomatoes (fresh or canned)
1/2 lb. mushrooms
3 cans kidney beans
1 small can tomato paste
1-3 tsp. chili powder
1-2 tsp. garlic powder
salt & pepper
1 tsp. sugar or black strap molasses
1 large can tomato sauce
1 large can water
1 tsp. celery salt

### Directions

Brown ground chuck and chopped onion and drain, leaving some for moisture.
Add chopped celery and green pepper.
Add remaining ingredients and let simmer very slowly -- about 1/2 hour.
Add kidney beans and simmer another 30 minutes slowly.

Makes 8-10 servings

*Alan J. Dixon*

# LIMELIGHT

## NEW YORK · LONDON · CHICAGO

"Party Stew ala Limelight"

PREPARE:
: Dry cleaning and party shopping needs, make hair stylist appointments, light work schedule for following day.

REMOVE:
: The gristle and fat from your already so lengthy guest list.

SIMMER:
: The remaining "meat" at 98.6 for approximately 3 to 4 weeks. Occasionally adding an aura of intrigue and mystique.

ADD:
: A liberal pinch of interesting pre-publicity to the appropriate media.

: Spicy bite-size morsels of slightly marinated entertainers.

: Tropical beverages containing finely distilled spirits. (all moisture will eventually be absorbed by the main ingredients.)

: Several bolts Silk, 12 dozen black ties and the imported hides of 20 unfortunate steer.

Bring to a full boil for approximately 6-8 hours, (constantly stirring, shaking and churning), until a rich stew develops.

Turn on the lights, turn off the music and serve steaming hot to a safe means of transportation home!

LEFTOVERS OF THIS DISH LEND THEMSELVES PARTICULARY WELL TO BEING SERVED THE NEXT DAY AFTER BEING ALLOWED TO COOL.

(They are often best served with aspirin, bed rest and an understanding spouse.)

Prepared, tested and endorsed,

*Tom Doody*

TOM DOODY

DIRECTOR OF EVENTS (MENU ITEMS), LIMELIGHT CHICAGO

632 North Dearborn Street, Chicago, Illinois 60610 312 · 337 · 2985

**The Christmas Seal People**®            ✝ **Chicago Lung Association**

1440 West Washington Blvd.
Chicago, Illinois 60607.1878

312.243.2000

*President*
Willard A. Fry, M.D.
*Executive Director*
John L. Kirkwood

---

BROCCOLI-STUFFED SHELLS
8 servings

---

3 c broccoli florets
1 15-oz container part-
   skim ricotta cheese
2 eggs, beaten
1/4 c grated parmesan
   cheese

1/4 t black pepper
1/2 t nutmeg
1/2 t oregano
24 jumbo shells, cooked
3 c spaghetti sauce

Steam or boil broccoli florets until crunchy tender. Allow to cool. Mince florets, either with a sharp knife or in the base of a food processor fitted with a steel blade. Combine minced broccoli with ricotta, eggs, parmesan, pepper, nutmeg, and oregano and stir until well combined. Stuff each cooked shell with approximately 1 tablespoon of the ricotta-broccoli mixture. Place shells in baking dish, cover with sauce and bake 40 minutes at 350°F.

Nutrition information per serving: Calories: 235. Calories from fat: 28%. Protein: 15 g. Sodium: 490 mg. Cholesterol: 129 mg.

Serve with a green salad and a dish of steamed zucchini with onions.


*Barbara Silvestri-Dore*

Barbara Dore
Director of Smoking or Health

**LAKE TROUT BRAISED WITH RIESLING AND SAVOY CABBAGE**
(8 main course servings)

| | |
|---|---|
| 8 | 6 oz. portions of fileted lake trout |
| 2 oz. | unmelted butter |
| 1/4 cup | minced shallots |
| 1 pint | Dry Riesling wine |
| 1 pint | fish stock |
| 1 1/2 qt. | shredded savoy cabbage |
| 1 quart | cream |

lemon juice, salt, and white pepper, to taste.

1. Preheat oven to 400°.

2. Coat bottom of pan with butter.

3. Add shallots and place filets on top.

4. Add Riesling and fish stock. Place on medium flame and bring to a simmmer.

5. Cover fish with buttered parchment or foil.

6. Place in 400° oven approximately 7 minutes, or until done.

7. Remove filets from pan and keep warm.

8. Add cabbage and cream to the poaching liquid and simmer to reduce until the liquid reaches the consistency that it coats the back of a spoon.

9. Adjust the seasoning of the sauce to taste with salt, pepper, and lemon juice.

10. Serve fish filets on top of cabbage and sauce, accompanied by boiled potatoes and chilled dry Riesling.


Submitted by: Chef John Draz
Coordinator of Culinary Instruction
The Culinary School of Kendall College
2408 Orrington Ave.
Evanston, IL 60201

**City of Chicago**
Eugene Sawyer,
Mayor

**The Chicago Public Library**

John B. Duff
Commissioner

Samuel F. Morrison
First Deputy Commissioner/
Chief Librarian

**Board of Directors**

James W. Compton
President

Edwin Claudio

J.S. Fuerst

James H. Lowry

Cindy Pritzker

Dr. Cannutte N. Russell

Jerome Stone

John L. Waner

Bernarda Wong

Administrative Center
1224 West Van Buren Street
Chicago, Illinois 60607
(312) 738-7600

---

Oscar Wilde once remarked that the "simple pleasures are the last refuge of the complex," and I am reminded of this every time I enjoy the following desert, for although simple, it triggers lingering memories of the delicate tarts served in Vienna and throughout France.

This pear tart makes a wonderful finale to a fine dinner. It is a beautiful open tart displaying layers of thinly sliced pears, and I like it with New Orleans coffee which is strong and laced with chickory, followed by a sniffer of warmed cognac.

PEAR TART
Line a 9 inch tart pan with pastry, trim and prick the bottom of dough with a fork. Freeze until ready for the filling.

FILLING
Peel, half and core five medium pears. Carefully cut each half in thin slices, working slowly to keep the pear half intact. Fan four of the pear halfs in the tart shell, and fill in the gaps with the last pear half. If accomplished with care, the pears will resemble a blossom.

Sprinkle pears with 5 tablespoons sugar, and dot with half a stick of butter, cut into small pieces.

Sprinkle with 1 tablespoon pear liquor.

Bake in a preheated 400 degree oven until the pears are carmelized, approximately one hour. Cool.

When cool spoon a glaze mixture over the baked tart. The glaze of 1/3 cup of apricot jam and 2 tablespoons of pear liquor should be heated in a small saucepan until the jam is melted.

PASTRY
1 cup all purpose flour
1 stick unsalted butter, cut into small pieces
1 1/2 tablespoons sugar
pinch of salt
2 to 3 tablespoons ice water

To make pastry, process the flour, butter, sugar and salt in a food processor until the mixture resembles coarse meal. With machine running add enough water until dough gathers into a ball. Refrigerate one hour before rolling out to fit tart pan.

This tart will serve eight. A nice addition is to serve a dollop of whipped cream on each piece. Flavor the cream with pear liquor. The tart is best served at room temperature.

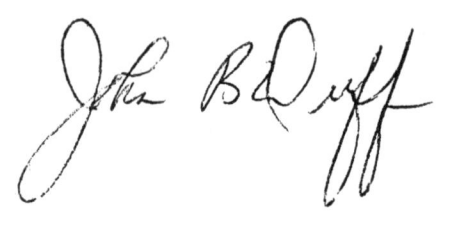

*John B Duff*

# MUSEUM OF BROADCAST COMMUNICATIONS
AT RIVER CITY / 800 SOUTH WELLS STREET / CHICAGO, IL 60607-4529 / (312) 987-1500

**BOARD OF DIRECTORS**

**Chairman**
Arthur C. Nielsen, Jr.
*A.C. Nielsen Company*

**President**
Bruce DuMont
*WTTW Television*

**Vice Presidents**
Richard C. Christian
*Kellogg Graduate School of Management Northwestern University*

Norman Goldring
*CPM, Inc.*

Red Quinlan
*IDC Services*

**Secretary**
Wally Gair
*Illinois Broadcasters Ass'n.*

**Treasurer**
Gerald W. Agema
*Tribune Broadcasting Co.*

Steve Allen
*Meadowlane Enterprises*

Tom Bauer
*Mediatech*

Patricia A. Cafferata
*Young & Rubicam Chicago*

Joe Cappo
*Crain's Chicago Business*

Gertrude Crain
*Crain Communications*

Rance Crain
*Crain Communications*

Anne Potter DeLong
*Rock Island Communication Co.*

Andrew B. Derrow
*Goldman, Sachs & Co.*

James Dowdle
*Tribune Broadcasting Co.*

Stephen P. Durchslag
*Sidley & Austin*

Barrett H. Geoghegan
*WAND Television*

Angel Harvey
*Capital Cities/ABC Inc.*

Joel Hochberg
*DDB Needham Worldwide*

Jeffrey D. Jacobs
*Jacobs & Assoc., Ltd.*

Ronald B. Kaatz
*The Medill School of Journalism Northwestern University*

Essee Kupcinet
*Academy School of the Performing Arts*

Lucy Salenger
*Consultant, Illinois Film Office*

Chuck Schaden
*Hall Closet Productions*

Frank Sullivan
*Frank Sullivan & Assoc.*

Dempsey Travis
*Travis Realty Company*

Joel Weiner
*Kraft, Inc.*

Michael L. Weiser
*Weiser Group*

Derk Zimmerman
*Group W Productions*

Joseph H. Zoller
*The Zoller Organization*

**Curator**
J. Fred MacDonald, Ph.D.

---

### BRUCE DUMONT'S BURGER BOATS

#### INGREDIENTS

1 pound lean ground beef
1 loaf of Italian bread
1 bottle K. C. Masterpiece Barbecue Sauce
1 stick butter
1/2 package favorite packaged cheese
1 green pepper
garlic powder

#### DIRECTIONS

1. Using grapefruit knife, carefully cut the top off bread loaf, avoiding cutting through, to create a boat-like bread loaf. Carefully take top off and scoop out excess bread and discard. Keep top for later.

2. After spraying skillet, begin to cook beef a bit at a time over slow flame. After chopping green pepper (and/or onion) add to simmering beef a bit at a time. Periodically drain off fat so beef remains as dry as possible. Slowly add 1/4 cup of barbecue sauce and stir so all beef is covered. For heartier taste, add additional sauce.

3. Slowly melt stick of butter in sauce pan.

4. Using butter brush, spread melted butter all over your boat-like bread loaf (including the top).

5. Sprinkle garlic powder all over melted butter. Natural garlic clove adds an even zippier taste.

6. When beef is cooked to your satisfaction, and you've added the right amount of barbecue sauce for your taste, drain excess fat from beef one last time and spoon meat into the boat-like bread loaf.

7. When boat is filled with beef (you'll probably have some left over) add strips of your favorite sliced cheese so that all beef is covered. Place under broiler along with buttered and garliced loaf top until cheese melts and bread turns a bit crusty.
WATCH IT CLOSELY SO IT DOES NOT BURN.

8. After a few minutes under the broiler, the cheese will form a blanket over your beef boat. For cheese lovers, add an additional layer... and let it melt.

9. When cheese melts, remove from broiler and serve on large platter. Surround your beef-boat with remaining beef, forming a sea of meat. Slice loaf top and serve separately.

SERVES: 2

#### A WORD ABOUT THE CHEF

Bruce DuMont is a Political Analyst for WTTW's "Chicago Tonight", host of WBEZ Radio's "Inside Politics" and President of the Museum of Broadcast Communications at River City in Chicago.

# WCLR 102 FM

8833 GROSS POINT ROAD/SKOKIE, IL 60077/(312) 677-5900

## PUMPKIN BISQUE SOUP

2 tbs. butter or margarine
1 cup of diced onions
1 cup of diced celery
9 cups of pumpkin (pealed, seeded and cut into dice-size cubes)
3 13-oz. cans of chicken broth (College Inn brand is very good)
3/4 cup of milk
1/8 to 1/4 tsp. of hot sauce
some chopped parsley to sprinkle on top later

Melt the butter in a four quart sauce pan, add the onions and celery and cook over medium heat for five minutes until the vegetables are soft. Add the pumpkin and broth. Bring to a boil then reduce the heat, cover and simmer 15 minutes or until the pumpkin is tender. Uncover and cool slightly, then place in a blender and puree. Return puree to sauce pan, add milk, hot pepper sauce and salt. Heat and stir. If it's too thick, add additional chicken broth. Canned pumpkin can also be substituted for the real thing. It's all ready to go and is a lot easier than preparing the real pumpkin.

Makes 10 cups

Put some chopped parsley on before serving.


Thanks for listening to WCLR.

Best regards,

*Dr. Duncan*

Doctor Duncan

a *Bonneville* station

# LAKE MICHIGAN FEDERATION

**BOARD**
Henry T. Chandler
 President
Courtney Van Lopik
 First Vice President
Jame Schaefer
 Second Vice President
John J. McInerney
 Treasurer
Linda L. Long
 Secretary

John D. Banaszak
Kevin Bosman
Lee Botts
Paul Culhane, Ph.D.
Kai Enenbach
John V. Farwell IV
James D. Griffith
Dennis M. Grzezinski
David Haywood
Ralph L. Johnson
Alan R. Johnston
Christine Kostel
Michael Kraft, Ph.D.
Robert Kueny
Frank Lahr
George F. McKiernan
Dean S. McNeil
Thomas J. Murphy, Ph.D.
Frank Nesbitt
Jone Noyes
Ellen Partridge
Charles D. Porter
C. Frank Shaw III, Ph.D.
Janice Stowell
Sally Van Vleck
E. Michael Walsh
Florence Walsh
James H. Zimmerman

**STAFF**
Glenda L. Daniel
 Executive Director
Mary Durkin
 Administrative Associate
Cameron Davis
 Program Associate
Rebecca Leighton
 Green Bay Office Director
Kathy Bero
 Milwaukee Office Director

*Citizen Action
to Save a
Great Lake*

## SEDIMENT SOUP

2 cups Oil & Grease

1 pound Lead

3 ounces Arsenic

2 dashes Cyanide

1 bit Cadmium

1 smidgeon PCBs

1 gram Phenols

1 pinch Zinc

Add a little Maganese

*(Spice it up with any of hundreds of other available chemicals, pesticides or herbicides.) Let settle to bottom of Lake Michigan and wait for a storm to dredge it up.*
*OR--You can wait until you catch and eat a large salmon or trout who frequents toxic hotspots at harbor mouths and enjoy virtually the same dish, but once removed.*

Mary Durkin
Administrative Associate

# Mitchell Indian Museum

Kendall College     2408 Orrington Avenue     Evanston, Illinois 60201     (312) 866-1395

Wild rice was a staple food of many of the Indian tribes in the western Great Lakes area.

WILD RICE CASSEROLE

1 cup wild rice, washed
1 cup cheddar cheese, chopped
½ cup onion chopped
1 large can tomatoes (include juice)
1 can ripe olives, sliced
½ cup olive oil
salt and pepper to taste

Stir together in casserole. Add 1½ cups boiling water. Bake 1½ hours at 325°

This is excellent with fish, fowl, or beef. Check for moisture after one hour baking time. Boiling water can be added (¼ cup) if it appears too dry. It can be made a day ahead, the flavors blend together even better.

Bouillon cubes, either chicken or beef can be added to the boiling water.

Enjoy this favorite food of our native American brothers and sisters.

*Jane T. Edwards*
Jane Edwards
Curator

## LIL' TOMMY'S MUSHROOM SALAD
### (Tommy Edwards)

1 pound medium mushrooms
¼ cup salad oil
2 tablespoons lemon juice
¼ cup sliced green onions
1 tablespoon basil leaves, crumbled
1 teaspoon salt
¼ teaspoon ground cumin seed
a few dashes of pepper
2 tomatoes cut into wedges
1 green pepper, seeded, cut into chunks

Rinse, pat dry and halve mushrooms; set aside. In a large bowl combine oil, lemon juice, green onions and seasonings. Pour over mushrooms, toss well. Add tomatoes and green pepper and toss well. Cover and let stand at room temp for 15 minutes. Serve in lettuce lined bowls. Serves 8 to 10.

## REAL BOSTON TO CHICAGO FISH CHOWDER

Salt pork is crucial to the authentic flavor of this chowder. Don't bother making it if you don't have it. Salt pork is sold in grocery stores in the bacon or lard sections.

Dice a piece of salt pork the size of a large finger and place in your chowder pot over medium heat. Meanwhile, chop a very large yellow onion finely and cook in the rendered salt pork fat until onion turns clear. Then add 3 or 4 nice white potatoes, unpeeled but scrubbed and diced. Stir potato around in the pot and cook for 5 minutes being careful potato doesn't stick too much to bottom of pot. Add 2 cups of cold lake water or enough to cover potatoes; season with salt and black pepper.

As the potatoes are cooking, prepare the fish filets. Cod is traditional, but any white-meat Atlantic fish combination can be used such as haddock, flounder, or sole. A piece of lake whitefish is o.k. to use in this case. About 1 1/2 to 2 pounds are adequate, depending on the quantity of potatoes in the chowder and the sailors it's going to feed.

When the potatoes are nearly tender, reduce the heat and add large soup-spoon size chunks of fish, cover pot and simmer chowder gently, slowly for 5 or 10 minutes, until fish is done. Reduce heat again and add 1 or 2 cups whole milk or half-and-half. Stir chowder gently and cook until milk is hot, never boil. Adjust seasonings. Serve immediately with a pat of butter in each bowl and hot cornbread on the side. Chowder, however, is better as it ripens; let it sit peacefully on the stove top for a few hours or overnight in the refrigerator. Reheat without boiling, adding butter before serving.

Serves 6 or more.

*A "down east" recipe for FISH CHOWDER from our Boston-bred program director Lisa Johnson—*
*Phil Elmes, President*

**TIMOTHY C. EVANS FOR MAYOR**
30 West Washington, Suite 615
Chicago, IL 60602
(312) 701-1989

### CABBAGE TAMALES

1 medium white cabbage
1 small green cabbage

Fillings:

   1 large onion
   1 large bell pepper
   2 eggs
   1/3 cup of rice uncooked
   2 medium cans of tomatoes
   1 large can of tomato sauce
   1½ lbs. of ground beef
   ¼ lb. of pork sausage
   2 buttons of garlic

Seasonings: Accent, salt & pepper, chili powder, and a few cracker crumbs.

Cut bottom of white cabbage and remove all cabbage leaves. Do the same with green cabbage. Wash cabbage leaves of both cabbages and place them in a separate pot.

Cover each with water and heat until leaves are soft enough to fold. (DO NOT OVERCOOK)

Set aside a large mixing bowl and mix together ground beef and sausage, chopped onions, bell pepper, garlic and 1 can of tomatoes. Add rice, 2 eggs, and above seasonings to your taste. (Mix together like a meat loaf).

Stuff filling into white cabbage leaves and wrap small green leaves around white leaves with filling. Pin together with toothpicks. Pour 1 can of tomatoes along with large can of tomato sauce over cabbages and simmer on top of stove (in large pan) for 45-60 minutes.

Serves 4-6 people.

# C·H·G·O
## CHICAGO HANG GLIDING ORGANIZATION

10035 S. Western Avenue   Chicago, Illinois 60643
Telephone 312 - 233-5037 / 281-3338

**CHGO** is proud of all their pilots. Special congratulations goes to our celebrities ***Larry Bunner** for his 175-mile flight (*which broke the world distance record for cross-country flights launched from a tow vehicle and all launch types east of the Rockies.*) ***John Heiney**, World Aerobatic Champion and Guiness record holder for performing 52 consecutive loops (*from a balloon drop*) * **Marty Bunner**, our regional director, and ***Brad Kushner**, our founder.

And to answer the question "Why do we want to fly so high going cloud to cloud?" the answer is. . .

To Get to This Cake-- It's **SKY HIGH!!**

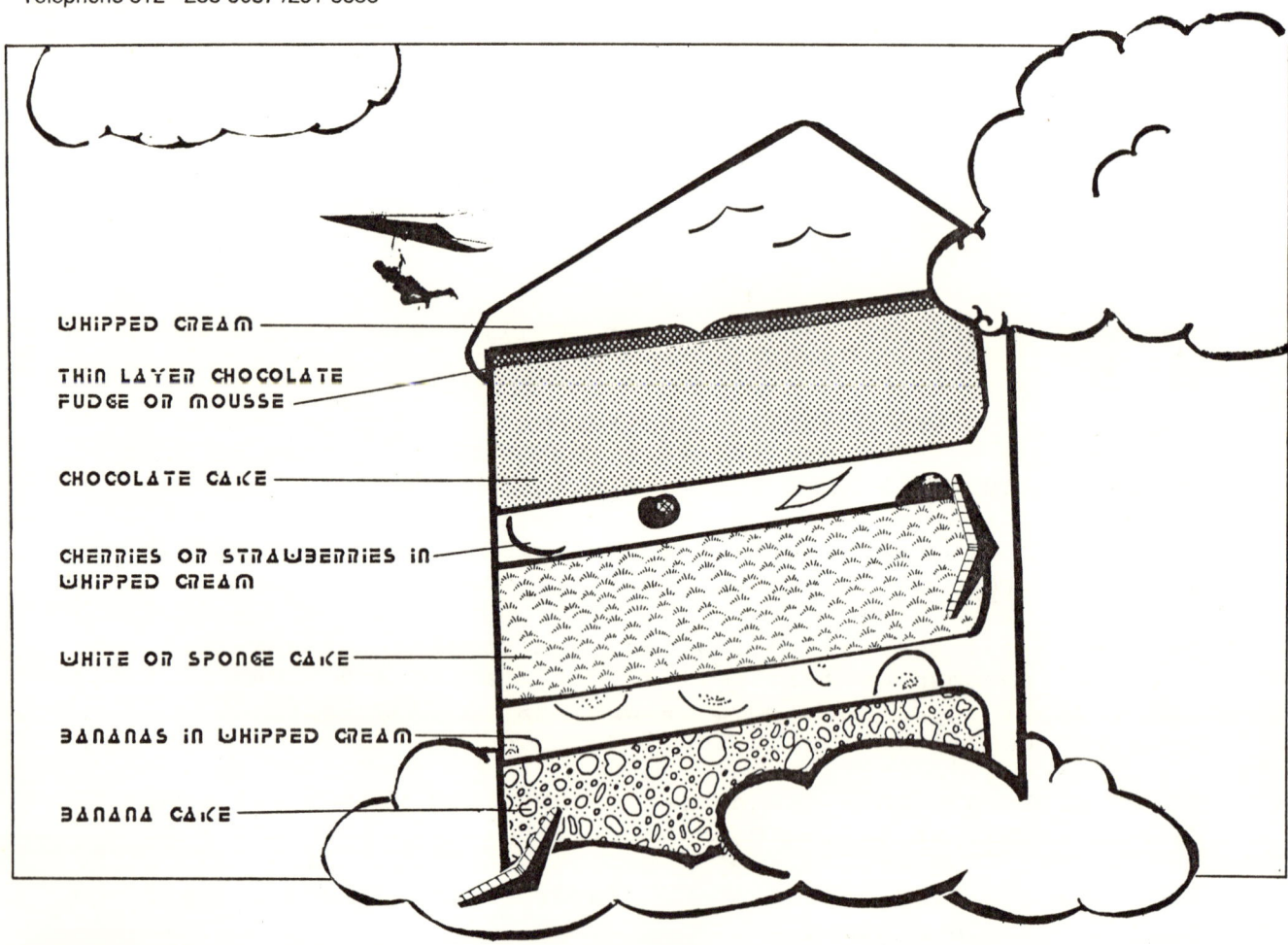

Cake diagram labels:
- WHIPPED CREAM
- THIN LAYER CHOCOLATE FUDGE OR MOUSSE
- CHOCOLATE CAKE
- CHERRIES OR STRAWBERRIES IN WHIPPED CREAM
- WHITE OR SPONGE CAKE
- BANANAS IN WHIPPED CREAM
- BANANA CAKE

**SKY HIGH** in calories

You'll Need:
* 1 non-flyable day
* 1 friend (It's a 2-person job--after all this recipe is for 2 great cakes!)
* Your favorite recipes for chocolate, sponge or white, & banana cake; chocolate fudge or mousse; also fresh cherries or strawberries, bananas & whipped cream

Then:
* Bake each cake in 2 round pans for a total of 6 layers. Let cool.
* Make the fudge or mousse. Sample often-- but save a little for each cake.
* Assemble 2 SKY HIGH cakes like the diagram above.
* ENJOY!

Gregory Fischer   Audrey Fischer
Pres.            V. Pres.

## Avalon

*The Stouffer Hamilton Hotel*
*400 Park Boulevard, Itasca, Illinois 60143*
*312-773-4000*

### Escargots With Herbed Brie In Phyllo Dough With A Lemon Caper Butter Sauce

12 Snails, diced fine
1/2 oz. ea. fresh basil, chives, garlic and shallots, chopped fine
12 oz. Brie cheese, rind removed and allowed to soften
9 sheets Phyllo dough

Cream Brie cheese in mixing bowl until smooth in texture. Add snails and herbs and blend until well mixed. Brush three sheets of phyllo with butter. Layer on top of each other. Repeat twice. Cut dough into 2" squares. Place a spoonful of cheese mixture in the center of each square. Fold dough into triangles. Bake in 350°F oven until golden brown, approximately 8-10 minutes.

Lemon Caper Butter Sauce

1 pound butter - softened
3 oz. capers, chopped
1 bottle dry white wine
1 shallot, chopped fine
3 oz. heavy cream

Reduce capers, shallots, and wine in saucepan until reduction covers only the bottom of the pan. Add cream and heat through. Slowly add butter keeping sauce warm; do not boil. Add salt and pepper to taste.

# chicago park district

## THE CUISINE OF THE CHILDREN'S ZOO
*Gourmet Goodies for Animals on the Go*

Listed here are many of the actual recipes used to create delicious and nutricionally-balanced meals for the animal residents of the Children's Zoo. Animal diets are prepared by zookeepers under the direction of Lincoln Park Zoo Veterinarian, Dr. Thomas Meehan, and consulting nutritional specialists. The tempting animal fare is prepared in the Children's Zoo Kitchen in full view of visitors.

### ARMADILLO'S SUPRISE

Appetizer:
Meal Worms

Main Couse Mush:
1 piece sweet potato
1 piece apple
1 slice banana
1/2 grated hard-boiled egg
1 cup meat mixture
Sprinkle with vitamin powder

*Feeds a three-banded armadillo or two hedgehogs*

### RABBIT'S SALAD BAR

Several leaves spinach and escarole, tossed lightly
2 carrots
1 sweet potato
1 apple
6 pieces rodent chow
2 biscuits monkey chow

### RACCOON'S DELIGHT

4 cups meat mixture
1 slice sweet potato
1/4 apple
1/4 orange
1/4 banana

Single serving

### FERRET'S FARE

1/2 cup meat mixture
1/4 hard-boiled egg
1 slice apple
Sprinkle with vitamin powder

### GUINEA PIG'S SALAD SUPREME

Begin with tossed green salad
Add slices: sweet potato
            carrot
            apple
Garnish with 1/2 cup guinea pig chow

### PORCUPINE'S PLEASURE

1 apple
1 sweet potato
5-6 pieces rodent chow
2 pieces monkey chow
1 carrot
10-15 peanuts

LESTER E. FISHER, D.V.M., Director
LINCOLN PARK ZOOLOGICAL GARDENS
2200 N. CANNON DRIVE, CHICAGO, ILLINOIS 60614-3895
PHONE: 294-4660

### TARANTULA'S TREATS

Crickets, sprinkled liberally with calcium powder.

### TURTLE'S HASH

Begin with diced and sliced smelt
Combine with bits of meat mixture
Blend in canned reptile diet
Arrange with tossed greens
1/2 sweet potato
2 apple slices
Carrot curls
Served with reptile fare, pre-mixed pellets

### CROW'S CUISINE

1/2 cup bird mix (equal parts dry dog food and fruit)
2 peanuts
2 grapes
1/2 hard-boiled egg, with shell
1 slice apple

### JUNIOR 'POSSUM'S PLATE

2 - 3 T. meat mixture
1/4 hard-boiled egg
1 slice apple
1/4 orange '2 slices banana
1 slice sweet potato
Garnish with shredded carrot or bits of celery

Increase portions as animals grow.

### PRAIRIE DOG'S PIE

6 pellets rodent chow (compressed alfalfa)
2 peanuts
3 pieces monkey chow
1 piece sweet potato
1 slice banana

### BOBCAT'S BURGERS

Meat mixture patties, 1 pound per day per animal
1 large rawhide bone, twice weekly

*AN ACCREDITED INSTITUTION OF THE AMERICAN ASSOCIATION OF ZOOLOGICAL PARKS AND AQUARIUMS*

*The gift of a pair of swans in 1868 began Lincoln Park Zoo and its commitment to the world's wildlife heritage.*

## Foley's

## Breast of Duck Grilled with Sesame Seed Oil, Sweet Potato Frites

Six 12 oz. Duck Breasts
2 oz. Sesame Seed Oil
1 Garlic Clove
Pinch of Fresh Lemongrass (optional)

### Method:

Heat coals to glowing ember stage. Trim the fat from the breast where the fat overhangs.* Remove the duck breast filet. Trim any silverskin from the meat side of the breast. Divide into halves.

Rub the breast with a clove of garlic. Brush lightly with the oil. Grill slowly to render the duck fat. Turn breast after skin side is rendered cook only two or three minutes more for medium rare. Sprinkle lightly with lemongrass. Continue to grill. Let duck rest. After five minutes slice each half into thin pieces. Arrange on plate. Sprinkle with a little additional oil. Garnish with frites and a vegetable if you choose. The dish can also be made in a cold salad form if you choose.

### Sweet Potato Frites

Using a knife or mandolin, cut peeled sweet potato into slicers the size of shoestring potatoes but a little shorter. Heat vegetable oil to 340 degrees. Drop fries into oil and cook until crisp. Season if you desire.

* If the cook leaves on too much of the fat, the breast will dry out before the fat is rendered. In addition to adding cooking time, the rendering fat will continuously drop on the coals and cause blackening of the breast with flair-up.

211 EAST OHIO STREET • CHICAGO, IL 60611 • 312-645-1261

## Calamari Risotto

1 lb of fresh peas or 3/4 cup of frozen
1/3 cup of olive oil
3/4 cup of finely chopped onion
3 tbls minced shallot
1 lb of fresh squid cut into 1/2 inch thick slices
1/2 cup of white wine
1/2 teas of saffron filaments
6 cups of chicken or fish stock
one tbl of fresh chopped tomato
a lb arborio rice
2 tbl of brandy
2 tbl of freshly chopped Italian parsley
1 clove of garlic worked into paste

### Method

Heat a one quart thick bottom saute pan. Add the olive oil. Warm lightly and add the onion and shallot. Add the garlic. Toss until opaque. Add the rice and cook for two minutes. Add the squid. Cook one minute. Add the wine, saffron and a pinch of salt and grind of white pepper. Previously heat the stock to boil. Pour over the rice. Bring to boil stirring so as to avoid burning. Cook on range top or in oven until the rice is creamy. Add more stock if necessary as liquid will vary depending on the absorption of the rice. When the rice is cooked but still has some bite, stir in the brandy, tomato and parsley. Add the peas. Adjust seasonings and serve immediately.

## Fresh Tuna Salad with Avocado and Pesto

One ounce of pesto
One ripe tomato cut into slices and then quarters
Four ounces of sushi quality tuna cut into 34 inch slice
Four ounces of assorted seasonal salad greens such as radicchio, butter lettuce, watercress, arugula and red leaf
Light Olive Oil for saute
One ripe avocado, cut into cubes

### Method

Heat oil in thick bottomed saute pan. Season tuna fish and brown on both sides until tuna is cooked to your desired degree of doneness. (With tuna this quality we prefer to cook it rare.) Remove the tuna to a plate and keep covered.

Plate three nice leaves from the radicchio in a bowl or on a plate. Toss the salad green with a little olive oil, the pesto and a squeeze of a lemon wedge. Add the tuna, tearing it into bite size pieces. Toss in the tomato pieces and avocado.

Arrange the salad in the middle of the radicchio. Serve with a fine rose.

**US Army Corps of Engineers**
Chicago District

COMMANDER'S 5-STAR PLATE

(Crab Alfranco)

1-3/4 Cups Water
2 Tbsp. Butter or Margarine
2 Tbsp. Sliced Green Onions
1/2 Tsp. grated Romano Cheese

1-1/4 Lb. Crab Pieces
  (Drained, in chunks)
1 Pkg. Uncle Ben's Country
  Inn brand Rice Alfredo
Dash of Pepper

SERVES FOUR

* Mix water, rice, seasoning packet, and butter in medium sauce pan. Bring to boil, reduce heat, cover and simmer for 20 minutes. Stir occasionally!!!

* Remove from heat, keep covered. Let stand for 5 minutes (or whenever). Pepper as will!!!

* Place crabmeat pieces in an 8-inch Corningware casserole dish. Top crabmeat w/cooked rice mixture. Sprinkle surface w/Romano and green onions.

* Cover and heat in Microwave for 2 minutes on high (or warm in conventional oven for 5 minutes or until ready to serve).

* Enjoy

# THE MONTEREY VINEYARD

Chicken Dijon
(Serves eight)

This is a fast easy dish we use for last minute entertaining. All of the ingredients are generally in the house.

In a medium bowl mix 2 cups bread crumbs, 1/4 cup parsley, 1 clove garlic mashed, salt & pepper to taste. In a second bowl mix 2 cubes melted butter, 1 tablespoon Dijon Mustard and 1 teaspoon Worcestershire sauce.

Dip eight boned chicken breast halves into the butter mixture and then roll in the bread crumb mixture. Arrange them in a foil lined baking dish and pour the balance of the sauce over them. Bake uncovered 1 hr in a 350° oven or until a fork pierce produces clear juice.

Serve with rice, your favorite vegetable and of course 2 bottles of Classic Sauvignon Blanc.

CHEERS!

Phil Franscioni
Winemaker

# Chicago Sinfonietta

**Board of Directors**
President
  *Dr. Paul Freeman*
Executive Vice President
  *James Paglia*
Vice President
  *Bettiann Gardner*
Vice President
  *Weldon Rougeau*
Secretary
  *Roger Wilson*
Treasurer
  *Howard Shapiro*
  *Bernard G. Allen*
  *George E. Ayers*
  *Anne Barlow*
  *Lenora Cartright*
  *M. Patricia Chapin*
  *Sr. Michelle Germanson, O.P.*
  *Dr. Robert C. Hsu*
  *Maureen Rita Kaucher*
  *John Lehman*
  *Tod Miles*
  *Maria Ojeda*
  *Clifford T. Osborn*
  *Quintin Primo III*
  *Alex Terras*
  *Elizabeth Wilkins*

**Honorary Board**
  *Lerone Bennett, Jr.*
  *Maestro Leonard Bernstein*
  *Martin Bookspan*
  *Wesley Buford*
  *Dr. George Butler*
  *Dr. J. Michael Channick*
  *Arnold Edinbrough*
  *Henry Fogel*
  *Clive Gillinson*
  *Richard Hunt*
  *Dr. Michael Jenne*
  *Sr. Jean Murray, O.P.*
  *Steven Ovitsky*
  *Professor Karl P. Pietsch*
  *Lorraine Pritzker*
  *Julian Rice*
  *Linda Johnson Rice*
  *Dr. Lucida Rita*
  *Joyce Rumsfeld*
  *Thomas Shepherd*
  *Honorable James Thompson*
  *Dr. W. Hazaiah Williams*
  *Francis G. Winspear*

## SEAFOOD GUMBO

Roux:
    1/3 cup oil
    1/2 cup flour
Place oil in large sauce pan and add flour stirring constantly until deep brown in color. Set aside.

    2 onions (chopped)
    1 bell pepper (chopped)
    3 cups okra (chopped)
    1 cup celery (chopped)
Add to roux and cook until onions are transparent.

Add the following spices:
    1 teaspoon thyme
    2 bay leaves
    1 teaspoon basil
    dash of red pepper
    dash of Lea & Perrins sauce
    salt, pepper, parsley to taste
Combine with vegetable mixture and 3 cups of water. Let simmer for 45 minutes.

Add:
    1/2 lb. crab meat
    1 lb. shrimp
    oysters (optional)
Serve over rice.

Rosary College • 7900 West Division Street • River Forest, Illinois 60305 • 312/366-1062
Paul Freeman, *music director* • Maureen F. Kaucher, *general manager*

## Johnny Frigo

Orchestras & Production

Twelve Twelve Lake Shore Drive

Chicago, Illinois 60610

Phone: (312) 943-5553

---

THE LOWLY BOWL OF OATMEAL COMES OF AGE!

I'M TOO BUSY PLAYING MUSIC
AND HAVE LITTLE TIME TO COOK
SO I'VE IMPROVISED A SIMPLE, HEALTHY DISH,
ONE WITH LOW CHOLESTEROL FOR THAT
COZY BREAKFAST NOOK.
IT'S DELIGHFUL AND DELECTABLY DELISH.

---

BOIL 12 OUNCES WATER — ADD 1/4 TEASPOON SALT —
ADD 12 OUNCES OATMEAL — STIR CONSTANTLY.
AS OATMEAL ABSORBS WATER, CONTINUALLY ADD
SMALL PORTIONS OF MILK FOR CORRECT CONSISTENCY.
REMOVE AFTER 2 1/2 MINUTES OR SO.
ADD LEVEL TABLESPOON LOW CAL MARGARINE —
ONE TEASPOON SYRUP — DASH OF CINNAMON —
ADD DESIRED LOW CAL SWEETENER — LASTLY,
ADD 3 LEVEL TABLESPOONS OF GRAPE NUTS — STIR.
WHEN PUT IN SEPARATE BOWLS, HAVE GLASSES OF
MILK AND PACKETS OF NUTRASWEET AT HAND
POUR ON PORTIONS OF MILK AS YOU EAT,
SPRINKLING ON SMALL PORTIONS OF NUTRASWEET
TO SUSTAIN IT'S SWEETNESS. MMM GOOD!

*Johnny Frigo*

### FROYD™ (For Reality Of Your Dreams)™
©1988 Carolyn Kidd

FROYD™ is a cheerful little yellow guy who helps us to believe in our dreams. Once you have found your dream FROYD is with you to help you never give up till you make that dream reality. Every one who has ever made their dream come true knows what FROYD knows, to make your dream possible you have to first believe you can make it happen.

A few people in Chicago came to FROYD and told him their dream was to save the Chicago lakefront. They want to make it a beautiful place for the people of Chicago to enjoy. FROYD pondered this dream and after careful calculations told them this dream was indeed possible. As a matter of fact he thought it was such a good dream he promised to share with them his secret recipe for making dreams come true.

### The FROYD secret recipe for making dreams come true.

Mix one part believing in dreams with two parts imagination. Stir in equal amounts of hard work, determination, patience, perseverance and practice and mix till well blended. Add lots of help from others who believe in you. And then bake for however long it takes (dreams can never overcook or become too well done). Follow The FROYD recipe and you can make just about any dream come true.

"If you believe in you like I believe in you there is nothing at all that we won't be able to do." FROYD

©1988 Carolyn Kidd

# CHICAGO APPAREL CENTER

**DOROTHY FULLER**
DIRECTOR

## CHIPPED BEEF IN WINE-MUSHROOM SAUCE

2 tablespoons butter
¼ pound sliced dried beef, shredded
2 tablespoons flour
1 can condensed cream of mushroom soup
½ cup California white wine
1 cup grated sharp cheddar cheese
2 ounces canned or fresh mushroom stems & pieces
2 tablespoons chopped parsley
1 tablespoon sherry wine

Shred beef and plunge into boiling water. Allow to stand 5 minutes. Drain. Combine wine with mushroom soup. Melt butter in skillet. Add shredded beef and saute for 3 minutes. Blend in flour. Add soup-wine mixture. Cook and stir until mixture boils and is rich and creamy. Add the cheese. Stir until cheese is melted. Add drained canned mushrooms (or fresh), parsley and sherry. Season to taste with freshly ground black pepper and salt, if necessary. Serve over steaming hot potatoes or scrambled eggs. Serves 4.

"Chipped beef not very trendy, you say? Well, in fashion we do make-overs to become more glamorous. And that's what this recipe does for plain-Jane chipped beef. I think this dressed-up version is almost gourmet fare and has been a favorite brunch or supper dish in our family for years. It is wonderful with scrambled eggs or baked potatoes."

*Dorothy Fuller*

OFFICE OF THE FIRE COMMISSIONER
CITY OF CHICAGO

LOUIS T. GALANTE
FIRE COMMISSIONER

## ITALIAN STYLE SALMON STEAKS ON A GRILL

2 lbs. salmon steak or other fish steaks, fresh or frozen
2 cups Italian salad dressing
2 tablespoons lemon juice
2 teaspoons salt
1/4 teaspoon pepper

Thaw fish, if frozen. Cut into serving size portions and place in a single layer in a shallow dish.

Combine salad dressing, lemon juice, salt and pepper, pour over fish and let stand 30 minutes, turning once.

Remove fish, reserving marinade for basting; place fish on a greased grill or well greased fish rack. Sprinkle fish with paprika. Cook about 4 inches from moderately hot coals about 8 minutes. Baste with sauce and sprinkle with paprika. Turn and cook about 10 minutes or until fish flakes easily when tested with a fork.

SMOKE DETECTORS SAVE LIVES

Louis T. Galante
Fire Commissioner

*The Power To Overcome*

## JOHN GARRISON'S SOUTH JERSEY BAKED LIMAS

Serves eight

Wash and soak 2 cups dried lima beans in 1 quart water overnight.

Simmer in same water for about half an hour.

Drain the beans, reserving liquor.

Layer into a baking dish:
- lima beans
- 1/4 pound of bacon, cut in pieces
- 1 medium onion, sliced

Combine:
- 1/4 cup light molasses
- 2 tablespoons chili sauce
- 1 1/2 to 2 1/2 tablespoons light brown sugar
- 2 teaspoons salt
- 1 cup tomato juice
- 1 teaspoon dry mustard (optional)

Pour mixture over beans, adding enough bean liquor to cover.

Cover casserole and bake until tender, 4 to 6 hours at 250.

Uncover casserole for the last half hour to brown, if necessary.

Don't let beans dry out -- use reserved liquor and add water to keep beans moist.

Serve with roasts or steak.

*John Garrison*

President and Chief Executive Officer

The National Easter Seal Society is a nonprofit, community-based health agency dedicated to increasing the independence of people with disabilities.  Easter Seals makes a difference in the lives of disabled adults, children and their families through a wide range of quality services, research and programs.  Easter Seals is in the forefront of advocacy efforts on behalf of people with disabilities.  Through 200 affiliates nationwide, more than a million people receive Easter Seal services each year.

**National Easter Seal Society**

*70 East Lake Street*
*Chicago, Illinois 60601*
*312 726.6200 (phone)*
*312 726.4258 (TDD)*

# NEWS FROM HAWTHORNE

Racing Season — Hawthorne Race Course
**STICKNEY, ILLINOIS 60650 — 780-3675, 780-3671**

Included in the
GUINESS BOOK OF WORLD RECORDS

**PHIL GEORGEFF**
**Director of Publicity**

QUICK BAKED MOSTACCIOLI CASSEROLE

Ingredients:

1# ground beef

32 oz. jar spaghetti sauce

1 - 12 oz. package of shredded Mozzarella Cheese

1 - 16 oz. package of thin Mostaccioli

2/3 cup of milk

Brown beef, add spaghetti sauce, simmer while cooking mostaccioli noodles.

Cook noodles as per instructions, drain & add milk.

Cover bottom of casserole dish with meat sauce then layer noodles, meat sauce & mozzarella cheese, noodles, meat sauce & cheese, etc.

Cover, bake in oven 350 degrees for 25-30 Min.

Serves 5 to 6

PHILLIP GEORGEFF

## Ann Gerber

### CHICAGO FUDGE PIE

1 unbaked 9-inch pie shell

1/2 cup butter (1 stick)

3 squares (3 ounce) unsweetened chocolate

1 1/2 cups sugar

4 eggs

3 tablespoons light corn syrup

1/4 teaspoon salt

1 teaspoon vanilla

1 quart vanilla ice cream (optional) or

whipped cream

Melt butter and chocolate together in a saucepan over very low heat. Beat in sugar, eggs, syrup, salt and vanilla with a rotary beater just until blended.

Pour into unbaked pie shell. Bake in a 350 degree oven for 40-45 minutes or until a knife inserted between center and edge comes out clean.

Do not overbake. Pie should shake a little. It will firm up in 15 minutes after being taken out of oven. Cool and serve with ice cream (or whipping cream) on top.

ANN GERBER
Society Columnist
Chicago Sun-Times

*I won Culinary Institute of America Award for this pie in 1985.*

# THE UNIVERSITY OF CHICAGO
## THE ORIENTAL INSTITUTE
### CHICAGO · ILLINOIS 60637

*Cables:* ORINST CHICAGO

1155 EAST FIFTY-EIGHTH STREET

## GREAT WALL CANNED CHINESE LAMB SPAGHETTI

*In February 1967, at Umm al-Jir in southern Iraq, I was at the end of a dig and all money, so I laid off the cook. For the last four days in the mud of the site, I did the cooking for the unfortunate government representative and myself. Wanting to keep things as simple and quick as possible, we ate mostly from cans. One of the last cans, lamb of the* **Great Wall** *brand from China, although not spoiled, had a strong odor. I decided to make spaghetti, since anything can be hidden under a tomato sauce as Europe found out after 1492. In great distress, try the following recipe:*

1 can **Great Wall** canned lamb
   (if you have no choice)
1 or 2 onions
1 teaspoon ground anise seeds
   (preferred over oregano)
a couple of tablespoons or so
   of olive or vegetable oil (whatever is available)

1 can tomato paste
3 or 4 fresh garlic
1/2 teaspoon oregano if available
salt to taste
1/2 teaspoon black pepper
half a pound of spaghetti

Heat oil in pan, add pepper, garlic, onions, salt and brown. Add lamb and stir occasionally. Add tomato paste and tomatoes, adding water if needed to make a fairly soupy mixture that should boil as you continue to cook. Add oregano or anise. Cook, covered, for about 20 minutes while preparing the spaghetti. Drain spaghetti when cooked to desired consistency (al dente, of course). This recipe serves at least 2 and can serve more depending on the success of the sauce in disguising the lamb. (Canned lamb was not a success in Iraq. It disappeared from the market very soon after its appearance.)

McGuire Gibson, Professor

Director, Nippur Expedition

**CHRISTINE GOLDSCHMIDT FOR**

# Christine

DESIGNER WOMEN'S APPAREL
FOR CAREER & SOCIAL LIFESTYLES

CHLOE' AND JOCKO COLNON

- MY HUSBAND JOCKO DOES MOST OF THE COOKING AT OUR HOME. IT GIVES ME TIME AFTER WORK WITH MY TWO BEAUTIFUL DAUGHTERS CHLOE' 3 YEARS AND CAROLINE 7 MOS.

- JOCKO HAS A "GREEN THUMB" IN THE COOKING DEPARTMENT AND DAUGHTER CHLOE' IS RIGHT IN THERE HELPING HER DAD. HER SPECIALTY IS GARLIC PEELING!

- THIS SIMPLE RECIPE MAKES BOTH COOKING AND EATING A JOY FOR ANYBODY WHO CAN BOIL WATER.

- EXCELLENT WITH LOAF OF ITALIAN PEPPER AND CHEESE BREAD AND A NICE RED OR WHITE ITALIAN TABLE WINE. ENJOY!

*Christine + Jocko*

## JOCKO'S NO COOK TOMATOE SAUCE
### FOR PASTA

1 CAN PLUM TOMATOES
1/2 CUP EXTRA VIRGIN OLIVE OIL
1/8 TSP. SALT
1/2 TSP. RED PEPPER FLAKES
2 TBS. BASIL (FRESH IS BEST)
6 ANCHOVY FILLETS (OPTIONAL)
3 CLOVES CRUSHED GARLIC
6 SHAKES BLACK PEPPER
1 LB BOX LINGUINI

**QUICK/EASY!! JOCKO'S NO COOK TOMATOE SAUCE**

BOIL WATER. COOK PASTA AL DENTE. SELECT LARGE SERVING BOWL TO PLACE SAUCE INGREDIENTS IN. DRAIN FLUID FROM CANNED TOMATOES. PUT IN BOWL. CHOP COARSELY WITH WOODEN SPOON. ADD OIL, SALT RED AND BLACK PEPPER, BASIL, GARLIC, (CHOPPED ANCHOVY FILLETS). STIR WELL. MIX PASTA WITH SAUCE AND SERVE!
SERVES 2-4 PEOPLE

---

CHRISTINE GOLDSCHMIDT
KAREN GOLDSCHMIDT
(312) 644-3020

300 W. GRAND AVE. SUITE 400
CHICAGO, IL 60610

# Tootsie Roll Industries, Inc.
7401 SOUTH CICERO AVENUE • CHICAGO, ILLINOIS 60629 • (312) 838-3400
910-221-4070 TWX

```
        T O O T S I E
           R O L L
      C H E E S E C A K E
```

1 1/3 cups graham cracker crumbs
1 1/2 cups sugar, divided
1/4 cup butter, softened
2 pounds cream cheese, softened
6 eggs
1 cup dairy sour cream
Juice of 1 lemon
1 teaspoon vanilla
8 oz. Tootsie Rolls
1/3 cup whipping cream

Combine graham cracker crumbs, 1/4 cup of the sugar, and the butter; mix well. Lightly butter a 10-inch round, 2-inch deep cake pan. (Don't use springform pan as the batter is too thin.) Press crumb mixture evenly into bottom of pan.

Beat cream cheese with remaining 1 1/4 cups sugar until smooth, scraping sides of bowl often. Add eggs, one at a time, beating well after each addition. Add sour cream, lemon juice and vanilla, beating well until smooth.

Melt Tootsie Rolls in top of a double boiler; stir in cream, then add to cream cheese mixture, mixing well. Pour over crust. Place cake pan in another large, deep pan; pour water around cake pan to a depth of about 1 1/2 inches. Bake in a 300-degree oven for about 2 hours or until center is set and a toothpick inserted near the center comes out clean. Cool, then chill several hours or overnight. To remove from pan, heat outside of pan slightly and cake will drop out. Re-invert onto serving platter.

Makes 16 servings.                    It is delicious!

                                      Sincerely,

                                      TOOTSIE ROLL INDUSTRIES, INC.

                                      *Melvin J. Gordon*

                                      Melvin J. Gordon,
                                      Chairman of the Board

## CAPTAIN GORSTAYN'S LAKE TROUT

Arrange for one day off.

Carefully select food and beverage for the fishing trip. Selection is of the utmost importance. (Will effect the Catch of The Day).

Manage to arrive at dockside before the boat leaves.

Once Captain and Crew are aboard leave for fishing grounds.

Fish until 12:00 noon; return with 15 fish and <u>never</u> say where or how you caught them.

Photograph any fish available.

Return to the hotel and have kitchen staff clean, filet and cryovak all fish.

Drive home with cleaned fish on ice. Present to wife Susan with a proud smile and spark up the barbecue!

## THE MONTEREY VINEYARD

**CARY GOTT**
Executive Vice President
and Winemaster

A friend of mine, Frank Alviso, is an excellent cook, especially when it comes to Mexican food and creating new dishes. He also is an outstanding grape grower in the Sierra Foothills.

Years ago, when we arrived for dinner at Frank's, he was standing in the middle of his vast kitchen pondering a collection of refrigerator odds and ends. He had forgotten to purchase the makings of an hors d'oeuvre, so he used what he had on hand to create:

### FRANK'S DIP

1 cup of each of the following:
    Mayonnaise
    Sour cream
    Low fat small curd cottage cheese - because it is firmer

3 to 4 small cans of chopped black olives
2 cloves of finely chopped garlic
1 bunch of finely chopped green onions (5-6)
1 bunch of fresh coriander leaf chopped, or about 1 cup
Lemon juice to taste

Mix the above and refrigerate to chill.
Serve with a sprinkle of Crystal hot sauce for color and taste.

Serve with these great chips:

   1 package each _fresh_ corn and flour tortillas.

   Cut tortillas into pie-shaped 'chips' and fry in lard (don't use anything but lard) until golden brown.

   Drain on paper, dust with salt, keep warm in oven until served.

A few months ago, we entertained Frank at our home and we served The Monterey Vineyard 1986 Petite Fume with Frank's Dip. The combination was great, since the flavor of the Sauvignon Blanc grape goes particularly well with the flavor of olives, garlic, and chips.

Cary Gott

800 SOUTH ALTA STREET • POST OFFICE BOX 780-GONZALES, CALIFORNIA 93926 • (408) 675-2316

# Crickettes

**THE LADIES WHO LUNCH**

ZARADA GOWENLOCK

*Meringue Cake with Fresh Exotic Fruits and Flowers*
*Serves 6 to 8*

This cake has a lovely, crunchy meringue base and is topped by folds of whipped cream and flavoured with fresh fruits and flowers. You can let your imagination run wild and make the creamy top into a dazzling picture combining exotic, different fruits with whatever wonderful flowers are available. Serve it as a stunning dessert decorated with a garland of fresh flowers around the plate.

3 large egg whites
3/4 cups sugar
light oil for the baking sheet
1 cup of heavy whipping cream
fresh fruits —— kiwi, passion fruit, pineapple, banana, peach, pear, grapes or oranges.
fresh flowers —— borage, mint, honeysuckle, English cowslip, primroses, pansies or rose petals.

Heat oven to 300 Farenheit.

In a large clean bowl, whisk the egg whites, until they form stiff peaks. Whisk in the sugar, a tablspoon at a time, until the mixture is fairly stiff. Oil a large baking sheet and line it with oiled parchment paper. Spoon the meringue mixture onto the paper in a large, even circle. Bake in the oven for 5—10 minutes, then reduce the temperature to 275 Farenheit and continue baking for 50 minutes. Turn off oven and leave the meringue in the oven for a few hours to dry out completely.

When the meringue is cool whip the cream until it forms peaks and pile it on top of the meringue. Add the fruits and flowers in an attractive pattern and serve serve this exotic picture cake to your delighted guests.

I prefer using kiwi fruit and rose petals, surrounding the cake with rose buds for a romantic look.

*Zarada J. Gowenlock*

The above can also be made up in individual size cakes, serve it to your favorite gentleman with a bottle of Crystal Champagne in Lalique Angel glasses —— and have a wonderful evening.

# THE THEOSOPHICAL SOCIETY IN AMERICA

1926 N. Main Street
P.O. Box 270
Wheaton, IL 60189
312/668-1571

This recipe is adapted from TOFU COOKERY by Louise Hagler and is a favorite with many of our staff members.

## TOFU LOAF

Preheat oven to 350 degrees

Mix together:

1 1/2 pounds of firm tofu, mashed
1/3 cup ketchup
1/3 cup tamari (a natural soy sauce)
2 Tbsp. dijon mustard
2 Tbsp. dried parsley (or 1/2 cup of fresh parsley, chopped)
1/4 tsp. black pepper
1 medium onion, chopped fine
1/4 tsp. garlic powder
1 cup rolled oats

Mix all ingredients together. Put 1/4 cup oil in a loaf pan, then press the mixture into the pan. Bake for about 1 hour. Let cool 10-15 minutes before trying to remove from pan. Flip it out, top down, and garnish with fresh parsley.

Best wishes,

*Jeff Gresko*

Jeff Gresko

INTERNATIONAL HEADQUARTERS • ADYAR, MADRAS, INDIA 600020

From the face of

# Skip Griparis

The main benefit of a Greek upbringing is the food. Greeks have to be good cooks--it's the <u>law</u>. Your mother is the best cook in the world--it's the <u>law</u>.

Yeah, alright, Baklava is the most popular Greek pastry, but if you really want to know what Zeus and Athena would kill and die for, try Loukoumathes (luke-oh-mah-thess). These deep fried fritters are not as prevalent, because they should be eaten fresh and hot, so they're usually found only at food fests, where an assembly line of matronly Greek ladies dish them up with remarkable skill and modest authority.

## LOUKOUMATHES

- 5 cups flour
- 1 Tabls sugar
- 1 Tabls melted butter or margarine
- 1½ teas salt
- 1 egg
- 2 cups warm milk
- ½ cup warm water
- 1 pack dry yeast
- ¼ cup water
- 1 qt hot oil
- 2 cups warm honey
- 1 cup warm water
- ground nuts
- cinnamon

Take 5 cups of flour and add 1 Tabls sugar and 1 Tabls melted butter or margarine and 1½ teas salt and 1 beaten egg. Warm 2 cups of milk and ½ cup of water and add to the flour mixture. Dissolve 1 package of dry yeast in ¼ cup of water and add to mixture. Beat till smooth. Let it rise 1 hour.

Drop the dough by the rounded teaspoonful into 1 quart of hot oil (about 375°--do not check with finger) until golden brown (The consummate Loukoumathes chef will grab a fist full and <u>squeeze</u> the proper sized glob out through the thumb and forefinger). Drain for a few minutes in a colander. Heat but don't boil 2 cups of honey and 1 cup of water. Quickly dip the Loukoumathes into the honey, drain, and then sprinkle with ground nuts and a little cinnamon. Serve hot.

Your only problem now is how to <u>stop</u> eating Loukoumathes. You'll have to deal with it in your own way. I just eat till I pass out.

# ENCYCLOPÆDIA BRITANNICA

*Chairman of the Board*

The following is a recipe which I find very tasty.  I hope it is enjoyed by others:

### QUAIL IN WINE

Salt & pepper to taste
6-8 quail, split in half
1 stick of butter
1 carrot, diced
1 small onion
1/2 cup mushrooms (stems & pieces)
2 tablespoons bell pepper, chopped
1 tablespoon flour
1 cup of chicken stock (or chicken broth)
1/2 cup white wine or sherry

Salt and pepper birds.  In skillet, lightly brown birds in butter.  Remove to a buttered casserole dish.  In same skillet, saute' vegetables for five minutes.  Stir in flour and gradually add stock or broth.  Simmer 10 minutes.  While sauce is simmering, pour wine over birds.  Pour the sauce over the birds, cover and bake for 1-1/2 hours at 350 degrees. Serves three to four.

Sincerely,

Robert P. Gwinn

mec

**BRITANNICA CENTRE**
310 SOUTH MICHIGAN AVE.  CHICAGO, IL 60604

# P·A·D·I INTERNATIONAL

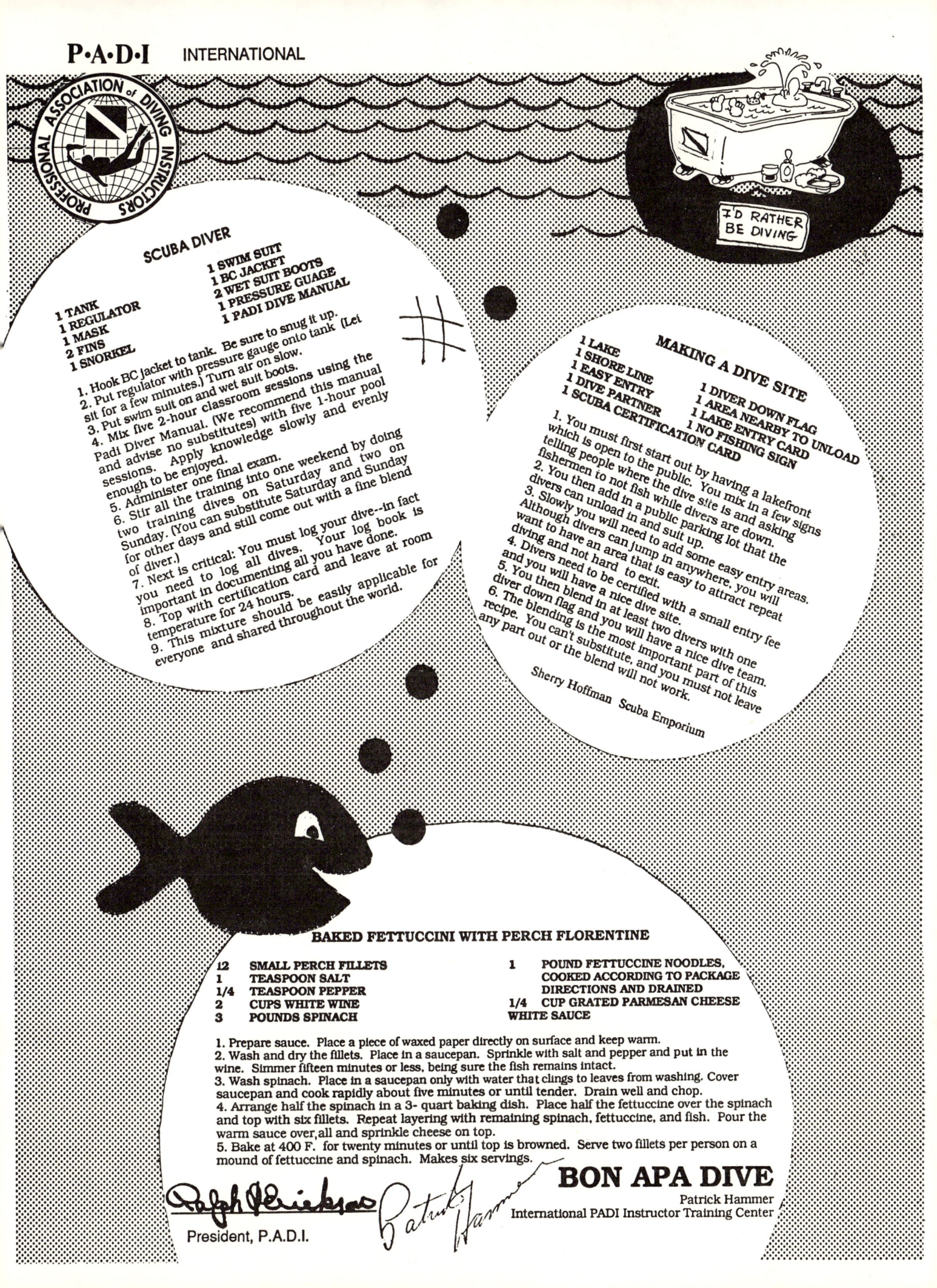

## SCUBA DIVER

- 1 TANK
- 1 REGULATOR
- 1 MASK
- 2 FINS
- 1 SNORKEL
- 1 SWIM SUIT
- 1 BC JACKET
- 2 WET SUIT BOOTS
- 1 PRESSURE GUAGE
- 1 PADI DIVE MANUAL

1. Hook BC jacket to tank. Be sure to snug it up.
2. Put regulator with pressure gauge onto tank (Let sit for a few minutes.) Turn air on slow.
3. Put swim suit on and wet suit boots.
4. Mix five 2-hour classroom sessions using the Padi Diver Manual. (We recommend this manual and advise no substitutes) with five 1-hour pool sessions. Apply knowledge slowly and evenly enough to be enjoyed.
5. Administer one final exam.
6. Stir all the training into one weekend by doing two training dives on Saturday and two on Sunday. (You can substitute Saturday and Sunday for other days and still come out with a fine blend of diver.)
7. Next is critical: You must log your dive--in fact you need to log all dives. Your log book is important in documenting all you have done.
8. Top with certification card and leave at room temperature for 24 hours.
9. This mixture should be easily applicable for everyone and shared throughout the world.

## MAKING A DIVE SITE

- 1 LAKE
- 1 SHORE LINE
- 1 EASY ENTRY
- 1 DIVE PARTNER
- 1 SCUBA CERTIFICATION CARD
- 1 DIVER DOWN FLAG
- 1 AREA NEARBY TO UNLOAD
- 1 LAKE ENTRY CARD
- 1 NO FISHING SIGN

1. You must first start out by having a lakefront which is open to the public. You mix in a few signs telling people where the dive site is and asking fishermen to not fish while divers are down.
2. You then add in a public parking lot that the divers can unload in and suit up.
3. Slowly you will need to add some easy entry areas. Although divers can jump in anywhere, you will want to have an area that is easy to attract repeat diving and not hard to exit.
4. Divers need to be certified with a small entry fee and you will have a nice dive site.
5. You then blend in at least two divers with one diver down flag and you will have a nice dive team.
6. The blending is the most important part of this recipe. You can't substitute, and you must not leave any part out or the blend will not work.

*Sherry Hoffman Scuba Emporium*

## BAKED FETTUCCINI WITH PERCH FLORENTINE

- 12 SMALL PERCH FILLETS
- 1 TEASPOON SALT
- 1/4 TEASPOON PEPPER
- 2 CUPS WHITE WINE
- 3 POUNDS SPINACH
- 1 POUND FETTUCCINE NOODLES, COOKED ACCORDING TO PACKAGE DIRECTIONS AND DRAINED
- 1/4 CUP GRATED PARMESAN CHEESE WHITE SAUCE

1. Prepare sauce. Place a piece of waxed paper directly on surface and keep warm.
2. Wash and dry the fillets. Place in a saucepan. Sprinkle with salt and pepper and put in the wine. Simmer fifteen minutes or less, being sure the fish remains intact.
3. Wash spinach. Place in a saucepan only with water that clings to leaves from washing. Cover saucepan and cook rapidly about five minutes or until tender. Drain well and chop.
4. Arrange half the spinach in a 3- quart baking dish. Place half the fettuccine over the spinach and top with six fillets. Repeat layering with remaining spinach, fettuccine, and fish. Pour the warm sauce over, all and sprinkle cheese on top.
5. Bake at 400 F. for twenty minutes or until top is browned. Serve two fillets per person on a mound of fettuccine and spinach. Makes six servings.

President, P.A.D.I.

## BON APA DIVE

Patrick Hammer
International PADI Instructor Training Center

**Paul Harvey News**

WILD RICE SOUP

Twelve slices bacon diced and fried with onion (drain grease).

Add: 3 cans cream of potato soup (do not add water to soup)
1 pint half & half
1 pint milk
1 cup grated American cheese
1 cup grated Cheddar cheese

Cook: 1/2 cup wild rice uncovered -- drain and add to above and simmer till cheese melts.

*Paul Harvey*

PAUL HARVEY NEWS
360 North Michigan Avenue
Chicago, Illinois 60601

## TV DINNER FRIED RICE

5 cups cold cooked rice
1 cup small raw shrimp split in half, lengthwise
1 tsp baking soda
1 tsp salt
5 tbsp oil
2/3 cup diced ham (or 2 slices cooked bacon)
3 eggs
1/2 cup frozen peas
2 tbsp shrimp cocktail sauce
1 cup bean sprouts
1/2 cup chopped scallions

## TV DINNER FRIED RICE RULES

1. Combine the shrimp, baking soda and salt. Let stand for 15 minutes, while watching the TV News. Rinse and pat dry.
2. Heat the oil. Don't spatter on the radio. Use a wok, if possible.
3. Cook the shrimp until pink (about a 30-second commercial).
4. Remove from heat and drain. Return the oil and juices to the wok.
5. Add the ham (you _knew_ there was a ham, right?) and cook until heated through.
6. Add the rice and cook quickly, until heated.
7. Do the following steps quickly: (Like the fast-talking Federal Express Man)
   Make a well in the center of the rice and add the beaten eggs, stirring constantly. When they have a soft, scrambled consistency, start incorporating the rice. Stir in a circular fashion -- like the CBS "Eye." When the rice and eggs have blended, add the peas and salt to taste. Stir in the cocktail sauce and shrimp. Add the bean sprouts and scallions; cook for another 30-second commercial. Remove from heat and serve immediately! You've almost missed "Wall Street Week!"

This serves 8-10 TV viewers and takes 15 minutes to make. The cocktail sauce is the main ingredient. And the passion for television.

Peter Hawley
Deputy Program Director

Museum of Broadcast Communications
at River City · 800 South Wells Street
Chicago, Illinois 60607   (312) 987-1500

# down beat
### For Contemporary Musicians

222 W. Adams  
Chicago, Illinois 60606

312 346-7822

MOTHER TUCKER'S PUNCH

Ingredients:
- One large can of frozen orange concentrate
- One quart of grapefruit juice
- One pint of cheap brandy
- Two bottles of cheap champagne
- One quart sparkling water or ginger ale
- Handfull of citrus fruit chunks/no Technicolor cherries

1/ Morning of the party, stick the brandy in the freezer and the orange concentrate in the frig with the other ingredients.

2/ When the first guest arrives, hang up their coat and hand them a knife and the fruit.

3/ Mix the orange concentrate with the brandy and grapefruit juice.

4/ Pour in the rest of the ingredients.

5/ Have your guest toss in the fruit.

A delicious way to get your daily requirement of Vitamin C. I served it at my college graduation party and the president of that Big ten school, now head of a major Chicago cultural institution, had several cups and was, I was told, the unexpected hit of a faculty party later that evening.

PS--If you double the recipe, triple the brandy.

*Dave Helland*

**Dave Helland**  
Associate Editor

DISTRICT OFFICE:
108 MAIN STREET
P.O. BOX 70
WEST CHICAGO, ILLINOIS 60185
312/293-1234

CAPITOL OFFICE:
ROOM 2127 STRATTON BUILDING
SPRINGFIELD, ILLINOIS 62706
217/782-8020

STATE OF ILLINOIS
HOUSE OF REPRESENTATIVES
**DONALD N. HENSEL**
FIFTIETH DISTRICT

COMMITTEES:
REGISTRATION AND REGULATION SPOKESMAN
APPROPRIATIONS I
COUNTIES AND TOWNSHIPS
FINANCIAL INSTITUTIONS
SELECT COMMITTEE ON SMALL BUSINESS
SELECT COMMITTEE ON HOUSING

PECAN PULLAPART

INGREDIENTS

2 cans of Pillsbury crescent rolls

1 cup sugar

1 1/2 teaspoons cinnamon

1/2 cup chopped Pecans

1/2 cup melted butter

---

Separate each can into four rectangles (8 total). Slice each 1/2 inch lengthwise. Roll each strip into a rope shape about 12 inches long.

Dip each in butter then roll them in the sugar, cinnamon and nut mixture.

Place on a pizza pan in a spiral fashion (starting in the center of the pan).

Bake at 375 degrees for 20 to 25 minutes.

*Donald N. Hensel*

RUSH–PRESBYTERIAN–ST. LUKE'S MEDICAL CENTER   1653 WEST CONGRESS PARKWAY, CHICAGO, ILLINOIS 60612-3864

LEO M. HENIKOFF, M.D.
PRESIDENT

## AFTER THE HUNT

### STUFFED WILD QUAIL WITH COGNAC SAUCE ON CROUTON WITH PHEASANT LIVER PATÉ

(Any relationship with the 1988 Presidential campaign is purely coincidental)

NOTE: Domestic quail may be substituted for the wild variety and will have less flavor but a pleasantly plumper body and will be juicier. Chicken livers may be substituted for pheasant liver in the paté portion of the recipe, but duck or goose liver would be preferred, if available.

Preparation of the quail:

Ingredients:
8 quail (two per person for entree, one per person for appetizer)
   (preferably cleaned by splitting down the back)
1 bunch parsley
1 bunch green onions
2 shallots
1 clove garlic
Butter
Salt
Pepper
Cognac
6 strips bacon
Lemon

The green onions, shallots, garlic, and parsley should be chopped moderately fine. Salt and pepper body cavities of the birds – throw in a dab of butter and stuff with mixture of chopped greens. Sprinkle 1/2 teaspoon of good cognac and a few drops of lemon juice onto the stuffing in each bird.

Turn birds breast up on a sheet of tin foil in a baking pan. Cut bacon strips into thirds and cover each breast with 2 of the resulting pieces of bacon, one on each side.

Preheat oven to 550° and roast the birds for 11 to 13 minutes (until the edges of the bacon brown and curl).

Preparation of pheasant liver paté:

Ingredients:
　　1/2 pound pheasant livers
　　One-third as much (by volume) pheasant fat
　　(Chicken livers and chicken fat can be substituted for above)
　　　(Duck or goose livers preferred)
　　2 large shallots
　　1 large clove of garlic
　　1/8 tsp thyme
　　1/4 tsp salt
　　Pepper
　　1 bay leaf
　　1/4 cup cognac
　　1 oz butter

Chop the pheasant liver and pheasant fat finely and mix together thoroughly. In butter over low flame briefly sauté the shallots (finely minced) and the garlic (pressed) until soft. Break bay leaf into three pieces and add along with the combined pheasant liver and fat and sauté over a medium fire for a few minutes, stirring frequently until the liver pieces are just barely cooked. Add the cognac and mix thoroughly, sautéing for several more minutes until all alcohol has been burned off and the mixture is no longer runny. Add salt, pepper, and thyme, seasoning to taste. Set mixture aside and allow to cool, removing the bay leaf pieces.

Preparation of the crouton:

Sauté rounds of white french bread (crust removed) in butter on both sides until golden brown. Set aside.

Preparation of the sauce:

Pheasant stock is ideal for this recipe (but not possessed by most people). Any poultry stock will do.

Combine 3 cups poultry stock with 1 cup beef stock (or beef bouillon) and reduce to half volume over high heat. Add 1/2 cup white vermouth and 1/4 cup cognac and continue simmering until all alcohol has been removed.

　　NOTE — OPTIONAL:
　　　Black truffles sliced into the sauce at this point are a wonderful although expensive addition. Don't forget to use the juice from the can!

Combine 4 tablespoons cornstarch with 1/3 cup of water and mix thoroughly. Slowly add this mixture to the vigorously simmering sauce while stirring until the desired consistency is achieved. The entire cornstarch/water mixture may not be used.

Assembly:

Spread the pheasant paté on the crouton. Place the bird breast up and cover with sauce. Serve with a light Bordeaux or Burgundy.

# Voyageur
## Outward Bound School

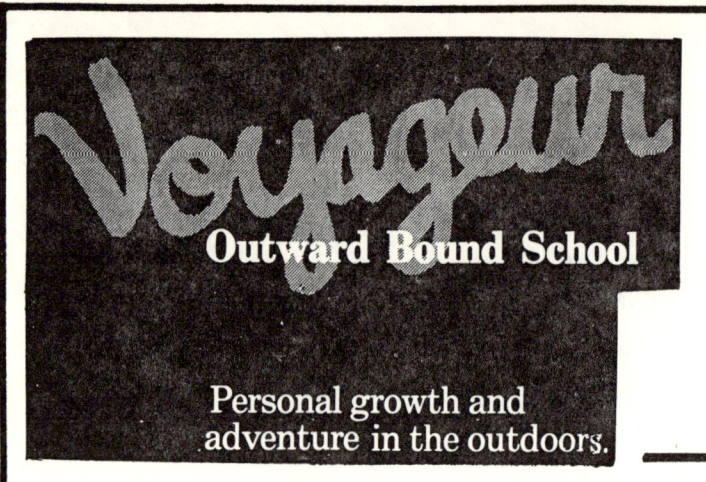

Personal growth and adventure in the outdoors.

### EVER CHANGING VOYAGEURS SOUP

| | |
|---|---|
| 2.5 gallons of water | 1/2 cup chicken base (optional) |
| 3-4 jumbo diced onions | 6oz wild rice (long grain) |
| 1/2 pound small brocolli chunks | 3-4 diced celery stalks |
| 1 whole chicken | 3 1/4 large sliced carrots |

Add everything together and boil chicken until tender. Then de-bone chicken, chop meat and add back into the soup... serve.

*This is a good soup mixture, but over time the voyageurs, trappers and other travelers have discovered that changing the amounts and types of ingredients provides variety and a personal touch.*

*As with any traveler, the voyageur had to survive off the land or with whatever staples were available during their time. Most travelers in the north country packed spices and dried beans & peas which are rich in plant protein. The wilderness offered the opportunity for variety in the form of bear, deer, beaver, squirrel, rabbit, fresh walleye & trout, and many types of fowl.*

*Also in the north country is a delicacy that is now popular nationwide... wild rice.\* One of the easiest meals on the trail has always been to just add everything into one pot and boil. The basic idea beginning with either rice, potatoes or beans, adding fresh vegetables, spices and on special occasions some form of meat. A true voyageur allows the mixture to boil all night long, allowing the rice to thicken the dish and the beans to make it just right!!!*

\* *Wild rice is not really a rice but a seed of aquatic grass.*

**An Unequalled Wilderness Adventure In Self-Discovery**

Wishing you a healthy appetite,

*Larry Hill*

Larry Hill
OFFICIAL CHEF VOYAGEUR OUTWARD BOUND SCHOOL
HOMEPLACE: ELY, MN 55731

Voyager Outward Bound School now has a CHICAGO office:
500 West Madison, Suite 2100
Chicago, Illinois 60606
(312) 715-0550

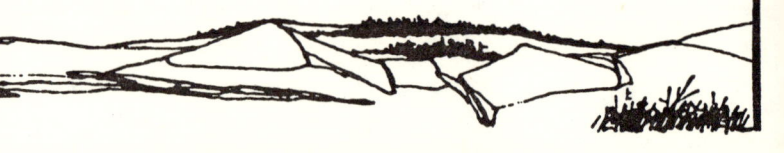

Marcella Hazan dropped by one Saturday morning to talk about her book, MARCELLA'S ITALIAN KITCHEN. Her recipe for a terrific dessert has become a favorite in our household. One tip for you...make a double batch!

## Semifreddo al Cioccolato

### CHOCOLATE SEMIFREDDO

ONE of the simplest of *semifreddi* whose disarmingly homey flavor makes it one of our own family favorites. It is nothing more complicated than whipped cream and grated chocolate frozen into a loaf.

*8 to 10 portions*

2 cups heavy cream, kept very cold
1¼ cups confectioners' sugar
4 ounces semisweet baking chocolate, grated

6 egg whites
A 1½- to 2-quart loaf pan

1. Whip the cream. Before it stiffens, while it is still the consistency of buttermilk, add the confectioners' sugar a little at a time and continue whipping.

2. When all the sugar has been incorporated, and you have whipped the cream until it is stiff enough to form peaks, add the grated chocolate, mixing it in thoroughly.

3. Beat the egg whites. When they are stiff fold them into the cream and chocolate mixture.

4. Line the loaf pan with wax paper, and pour the mixture into the pan. Place in the freezer overnight. To serve, unmold it over a flat platter and slice it, as though it were meat loaf, into individual portions.

*Mark C Hilon*
*News Director/*
*"Morning Show"*
*Host*

WNUA-FM 95.5
444 N. Michigan Avenue
Chicago, Illinois 60611
312-645-9550

**City of Chicago
Department of Planning**

Elizabeth L. Hollander
Commissioner

A prize winning recipe from my Father in law.

Avacado Soup

    1 can Campbell's Consomme
    (w) gelatine
    ½ pt. sour cream
    2 or 3 ripe avacados
    Spice Island Chili Con Carne
    seasoning

    Put avacados through food mill
    or ricer, mix with sour cream,
    <u>fold</u> in Consomme, but mix
    completely.  Add ½ T seasoning
    (taste) Chill.  Serve cold.

*Liz Hollander*

**International Polka Association**
4145 SOUTH KEDZIE AVENUE • CHICAGO, ILLINOIS 60632 • (312) 254-7771

## LAZY PIEROGI

1 lb. bag Kluski noodles
2 lbs. Sauerkraut
1 lb. Bacon
1 large Onion
1 can Mushrooms (save liquid)
Season to taste-salt-pepper-garlic

Fry Bacon crisp - set aside. Fry Onion (chopped or grated) in Bacon grease. Chop Mushrooms and put with Onions. Rinse Sauerkraut once and put in pot with Onions and Mushrooms. Stew for 1/2 hour. Cook 1 lb. Kluski noodles for 15 min. drain noodles and add to above mixture. Stew for 15 min. adding liquid from Mushrooms. Do not scorch. Add crumbled Bacon last.
Better the next day.

Submitted by:
Fred Hudy
President

*Fred Hudy*

— A NOT FOR PROFIT ORGANIZATION —

**WBBM-TV**

## Spiced Shrimp with Sweet Onions
### Served on a bed of Spinach

- 1 lb large shell-on shrimp (24)
- 2 teaspoons cider vinegar
- ½ " each: cayenne pepper
                ground cumin
- ½ " salt
- 2 medium sweet onions (14 oz total) peeled
- ¼ cup light olive oil
- 2 teaspoons oriental sesame oil
- ½ cup orange juice
- Spinach

Peel shrimp, leaving tail intact. Rinse and pat dry. Mix vinegar, cayenne, cumin and ¼ teaspoon salt to a smooth paste. Put shrimp in a plastic bag and add spice mixture. Working through the bag, coat shrimp with spice mixture. Let marinate while cooking onions

**WBBM-TV**

CBS Television Stations
A Division of CBS Inc.
630 North McClurg Court
Chicago, Illinois 60611
(312) 944-6000

Cut onions into thin slices. Heat olive oil and sesame oil in a 10" skillet. When it's hot, add the onions and remaining ¼ teaspoon salt and cook over high heat until they are very soft and light brown, about 6 minutes. Add orange juice and cook until most of it has evaporated.

Add shrimp and cook, stirring several times, until they turn opaque, about 3 minutes. Serve warm or at room temperature on bed of spinach.

Do not overcook (especially the spinach).

Walter Jacobson

HEART OF AMERICA
CHALLENGE

**CAPER CASSEROLE**

8 oz. noodles
Butter or olive oil
1 lb. ground round steak
1/2 cup diced scallions
1 large green pepper, chopped
1 lb. small curd cottage cheese
1 large package cream cheese, softened
1 c. sour cream
1 tsp. Worcestershire sauce
16 oz. tomato sauce (Ragu)

Cook noodles and set aside. Brown beef, scallions, and green pepper. Pour off any excess fat. Mix together the softened cream cheese, sour cream and Worcestershire sauce. In a large flat casserole, alternate layers of noodles, cottage cheese, meat sauce, and mixture of cream cheese and sour cream. Top with tomato sauce. Bake in 350° oven for 1 hour.

> This has been a great favorite with the crew on the 18 races we made from Chicago to Mackinac Island. For a hungry crew of six or seven, all ingredients were tripled -- and there were never any leftovers. The casseroles were frozen at home and heated up on the boat. Escapade had an oven, and so there were two casseroles, one for each watch. Caper had no oven, so the casseroles were divided into six equal portions and put in Seal-A-Meal bags, which could be warmed up in boiling water.

Alan R. Johnston

J. Joho
Chef de Cuisine

The Everest Room

440 South LaSalle, 40th Floor
Chicago, Illinois 60605

(312) 663-8900

TURBOT AND CABBAGE TERRINE
WITH BEURRE BLANC

6 Servings:

1 pound green cabbage, very thinly sliced
1 tablespoon butter
1¼ pounds turbot or flounder fillets, well chilled
  salt and freshly ground pepper
2 eggs
3/4 cup whipping cream, well chilled
1 cup dry white wine (preferably Alsatian)

Beurre Blanc:

1½ cups dry white wine (preferably Alsatian)
3/4 cup white wine vinegar
2 teaspoons minced shallot
1 cup plus 2 tablespoons (2¼ sticks) well-chilled unsalted butter
  cut into 19 pieces


Blanch cabbage in boiling water 45 seconds. Drain well; pat dry. Melt 1 tablespoon butter in heavy large skillet over medium heat. Add cabbage and cook until very limp, stirring frequently, about 10 minutes.

Puree ½ pound turbot in processor. Season with salt and pepper. Blend in egg 1 at a time. Transfer to stainless steel bowl set over large bowl filled with ice. Gradually add cream, beating with wooden spoon until thick.

Generously butter six 3/4 cup oval molds. Divide cabbage among molds, pressing down firmly. Top with turbot mousse. Cut remaining turbot to cover molds and place atop mousse. Chill until firm, at least 1 hour.

Generously butter heavy large skillet. Run tip of knife around edge of molds and unmold unto skillet. Pour 1 cup wine around molds. Cover with buttered parchment. Adjust heat so wine barely simmers. Cook until metal skewer inserted in center of mousse comes out hot, 8 to 10 minutes.

Meanwhile, prepare beurre blanc: Boil wine and vinegar with shallot in heavy small saucepan until reduced to 1½ tablespoons, about 10 minutes. Remove from heat and whisk in 2 pieces of butter. Set pan over low heat and whisk in remaining butter 1 piece at a time, removing pan from heat briefly if drops of melted butter appear. (If sauce breaks down at any time, remove from heat and whisk in 2 pieces of cold butter). Strain sauce into small bowl.

Transfer fish molds to plates, using slotted spoon. Spoon sauce over each.

**m-i**

MUSEUM OF SCIENCE AND INDUSTRY • FOUNDED BY JULIUS ROSENWALD

AUNT IRMA'S MEXICAN QUICHE

3 eggs, beaten

1 cup sour cream

1 - 7-ounce can diced green chilies

1/4 teaspoon cumin

1 1/2 cup shredded Jack cheese

1 cup sharp cheddar cheese, grated

Put two largest size flour tortillas in greased 9" pie plate. Pour in mixture and bake at 350 degrees for 45 minutes.

JAMES S. KAHN
PRESIDENT AND DIRECTOR

Aunt Irma is an adopted relative my family and I met in Maui, Hawaii in 1978. One evening while watching the sun set over island "beverages," Irma surprised us with this delicious heavy pupu. It was a delightful dish then, and remains so today.

## CHICAGO ARCHITECTURE FOUNDATION

1800 South Prairie Avenue
Chicago, Illinois 60616

(312) 326-1393


Dear Cookbook Editor:

I have just received your request for a recipe and the following is a recipe that might have been known and used by Caroline Clarke, mistress of what is today the Clarke House Museum, the oldest surviving building in Chicago (1836).

Hasty Pudding

Boil water, a quart, three pints, or two quarts, according to the size of your family; sift your meal, stirrfive or six spoonfuls of it thoroughly into a bowl of water; when the water in the kettle boils, pour into it the contents of the bowl; stir it well, and let it boil up thick; put in salt to suit your own taste, then stand over the kettle, and sprinkle in meal, handful after handful, stirring it very thoroughly all the time, and letting it boil between whiles. When it is so thick that you stir it with great difficulty, it is about right. It takes half an hours cooking. Eat it with milk or molasses. Either Indian meal or rye meal may be used. If the system is in a restricted state, nothing can be better than rye hasty pudding and West India molasses. This diet would save many a one the horrors of dyspepsia.

This recipe appears in Modern Cookery by Eliza Acton, published in Philadelphia in 1852.

Sincerely,

Lauren Kaminsky
Clarke House curator

# COPERNICUS FOUNDATION

5216 WEST LAWRENCE AVENUE - CHICAGO, ILLINOIS 60630

(312) 777-8898

## HELIOCENTRIC PORK CHOPS

INGREDIENTS:

3 tblsp oil for frying
1 large onion
8 to 12 medium thick pork chops
1 bay leaf
salt, pepper
3 chicken cubes
3 tblsp worchestershire sauce
1 cup sour cream or 3 tblsp flour

Put oil in large frying pan. Saute onion until lightly browned. Set aside. Saute pork chops on both sides in oil, adding more if necessary. Put onion, pork chops, bay leaf, chicken cubes, salt, pepper, and worchestershire sauce in dutch oven. Add 4 cups water. Bring to a boil. Reduce to medium heat and cook, covered, until tender, about 1 hour. The water level should be reduced to about half. Add water during cooking however, to make 2 cups gravy if necessary. Thicken sauce with sour cream or flour just before serving. Serves 4 to 6.

The sun might not necessarily stand still when you taste these pork chops, but you might wish that it would, so that you could perpetually enjoy the flavor of this old Polish recipe, one that Nicholaus Copernicus might have enjoyed himself!

SMACZNEGO! ENJOY!

Zofia Sadlinska-Kaspar
Executive Director
COPERNICUS FOUNDATION

**THE COPERNICUS CULTURAL & CIVIC CENTER**

# Yoshi's Café

3257 N. Halsted • Chicago, IL 60657
(312) 248-6160

<u>BRAISED TURBOT ON A BED OF DAIKON WITH WHOLE GRAIN MUSTARD SAUCE</u> – Serves 4


2 lbs. Daikon – Peeled and cut crosswise into thirds
1 c. milk
½ lemon

8 – 3 ounce turbot fillets
8 large sea scallops, sliced thin crosswise
finely chopped shallots
butter
dry white wine

1 T. wholegrain mustard
1 c. heavy cream
salt & pepper


Blanche daikon for 20 minutes in boiling water to which milk and lemon have been added. (to keep the daikon white.) Slice into thin rounds.

Butter four individual baking dishes. Layer the daikon in the bottom, slightly overlapping. Top with two fish fillets per dish. Top fillets with thin-sliced sea scallops.

Sprinkle dishes with shallots, dot with butter and pour white wine around fish, almost to cover. Cover with aluminum foil and braise in the oven at 425° for approximately 12-15 minutes.

Strain cooking liquids into a saucepan. Add 1 c. heavy cream and reduce until slightly thickened. Add 1 T. mustard and salt & pepper to taste.

Remove fish from baking dishes to warm plates. Circle the fish with the mustard cream sauce.

Suggested accompaniments: Rice Pilaf, Saffron Rice or Boiled Potatoes


Chef Yoshi Katsumura
Yoshi's Café

CAPITOL OFFICE

ROOM M-2, STRATTON BUILDING
SPRINGFIELD, ILLINOIS 62706
TELEPHONE: (217) 782-8127

DISTRICT OFFICE

10231 S. WESTERN
CHICAGO, ILLINOIS 60643
TELEPHONE: (312) 881-0306

**JAMES F. KEANE**
STATE REPRESENTATIVE - 28TH DISTRICT

CHAIRMAN
  LEGISLATIVE AUDIT COMMISSION
  LOCAL ACCOUNTING TASK FORCE

VICE CHAIRMAN
  REVENUE COMMITTEE

MEMBER
  HIGHER EDUCATION COMMITTEE
  COUNTIES AND TOWNSHIPS COMMITTEE
  ECONOMIC & FISCAL COMMISSION
  ECONOMIC RECOVERY COMMITTEE
  INTERGOVERNMENTAL COOPERATION
  COMMISSION

HEARTY HODGEPODGE

(a homemade stick-to-your ribs soup)

6 slices bacon
1 medium onion, thinly sliced
1-pound beef shank
3/4-pound ham hock
6 cups water
2 teaspoons salt
2 15-ounce cans (3½ cups) garbanzo beans
3 cups diced potatoes (4 medium)
1 clove garlic, minced
1 4-ounce link Polish sausage, thinly sliced
Toasted and buttered French bread

In Dutch oven, cook bacon till crisp; drain, reserving 2 tablespoons drippings. Crumble bacon and set aside. Add sliced onion to reserved drippings in pan. Cook till tender but not brown. Add beef shank, ham hock, water, and salt. Cover and simmer 1½ hours. Remove meat from beef shank and ham hock and dice; discard bones. Carefully skim fat from broth. Return diced meat to soup; add undrained beans, potatoes, and garlic. Simmer, covered, for 30 minutes more. Add sausage and the crumbled bacon. Continue simmering, covered, for 15 minutes. Serve with toasted French bread, if desired. Makes 8 to 10 servings.

This is a prize winning recipe of Mr. and Mrs. Noble of Minneapolis, Minnesota.

Pennsylvania Shoo-Fly-Pie

1½ cups unbleached flour
¼ cup butter — Mix
In seperate bowl mix
½ tsp. baking soda
¾ cup boiling water

½ cup brown sugar
together to make crumbs
together.
¾ cup dark molasses

Put ⅓ molasses mixture into unbaked 9" pie shell and add layer of crumb mixture — continue this, ending with crumb mixture

Bake at 425° for 15 minutes and reduce heat to 350° and bake for 40 minutes

**CHAS. LEVY COMPANY**

**Barbara L. Kipper**
Chairman of the Board

1200 N. North Branch Street
Chicago, Illinois 60622
312-440-4401

## LEMON CHICKEN

8 pieces boneless chicken breast with skin
1 large, whole lemon
1/3 cup flour
1 1/2 teaspoons salt
1/2 teaspoon grated fresh ginger root (optional)
1/4 cup salad oil
2 tablespoons brown sugar
2 lemons, thinly sliced
3/4 cup regular strength chicken broth

1. Wash and drain chicken on paper towels.
2. Grate the peel from first lemon and set aside.
3. Squeeze juice from first lemon and pour over chicken. Rub into each piece.
4. Drudge with flour and salt.
5. Brown chicken slowly in salad oil until deep golden color.
6. Arrange in casserole.
7. Sprinkle grated lemon peel, ginger and brown sugar over chicken.
8. Place thinly sliced pieces of lemon on top of chicken.
9. Carefully pour broth into casserole.
10. Cover and bake at 375° until tender (40-45 minutes).
11. Serves 8.

*Barbara L Kipper*

# Chicago Sun-Times

## DR. BRATWURST'S THE WAY-IT-SHOULD-BE-DONE BRATS

### By Henry (Dr. Bratwurst) Kisor
### Book Editor, Chicago Sun-Times

INGREDIENTS:

* One to two dozen Sheboygan-style pork bratwursts (veal or turkey brats can be substituted, but won't taste quite like the real thing)
* Two bottles Heineken beer (or your preference, but make sure it's a DECENT beer -- if you use Old Style, you're gonna have brats with an Old Style aftertaste)
* One to two dozen decent bakery wiener rolls, not the godawful supermarket kind.  In a pinch hard or Italian rolls will do, but use only if your guests are fairly young and have vigorous jaws.
* Weber charcoal grill, the older and rustier the better
* Aluminum drip pan about 12 by 7 inches by 2 inches deep; the Weber-brand drip pans are perfect.
* Charcoal (use mesquite if you're a yuppie)

1. In grill, prepare two beds of coals, one on either side of an area large enough to hold the drip pan.
2. Pierce brats with fork (keeps them from exploding and putting your eye out), then brown over the coals for approximately 7 to 10 minutes, turning once, and keeping the grill cover on.  It is OK if you char an edge or two --makes for a more interesting eating experience.  Much smoke will be produced; with practice, you can send signals to the brat expert in the next neighborhood.
3. Remove brats from grill.
4. Place drip pan between coals.  Pour the contents of the two Heineken bottles in the drip pan.
5. Place brats in drip pan.  Let boil for 20 minutes.
6. Slather with condiments of your choice (mine are mustard and garden relish).
7. Eat.

(This recipe reverses the ordinary process of boiling first, then browning.  That way is for faint-hearted suburbanites and other white-bread people.  The Dr. Bratwurst way gives you a moister, tastier brat.)


Sincerely,

*Henry Kisor*

Henry Kisor
Book Editor

CHICAGO SUN-TIMES, INC.
401 N. WABASH AVENUE  •  CHICAGO, ILLINOIS 60611  •  (312) 321-3000

## THE MONTEREY VINEYARD®

### PORK CARNITAS

Living and working around a Hispanic population has tended to influence my style of cooking. This dish can be served with eggs for breakfast, wrapped in tortillas for lunch, or the main course for a Mexican dinner.

    1 pork butt or shoulder roast (approximately 4 lbs)
    1 Tbsp. ground cumin
    1 tsp. ground black pepper
    4 cloves crushed garlic or 1 Tbsp. powdered garlic
    Vegetable oil

Slowly roast the uncovered pork in a cooking rack at 225° for 6 to 8 hours. Allow to cool down so that it is still warm but will not burn your hands when you handle it. Separate and discard the fat and bone from the now-tender cooked meat. Chop the meat into chunks approximately one inch square. Heat a tablespoon or two of vegetable oil in a large frying or sautee pan and evenly brown (approximately 10 minutes) all sides of the chunks of pork. Add spices just prior to removing from heat, and serve with the sizzle still in it.

The great flavor of the pork comes out in the searing of the sides of the chunks. These pieces should be crispy brown on the outside, and juicy and tender inside.

Enjoy.

Jeff Koligian
Grower Relations/Vineyard Manager

ARDIS KRAINIK
GENERAL DIRECTOR

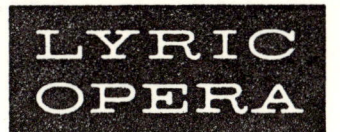

**LYRIC OPERA**

CABLE LYRTH—CGO
TELEX: 190252
312-332-2244

OF CHICAGO

20 NORTH WACKER DRIVE
CHICAGO, ILLINOIS 60606

# A Note from Ardis Krainik

MEAT LOAF

| 1½ pds. | ground beef ground sirloin is best |
| --- | --- |
| 1 cup | V-8 juice |
| ¼ cup | milk |
| ¾ cup | breadcrumbs |
| 1 lg. | egg |
| 1 pkg. | onion soup mix |
| salt | |
| pepper | |

Put in greased breadpan

350° for 1 hour

*Ardis Krainik*

IRV KUPCINET

# Individual Chicken Pot Pies

4 chicken breasts or 1 whole chicken
5 cups water to make broth
1 onion chopped
2 carrots diced
1/2 cup peas
1/2 cup celery chopped
1/4 cup pimento chopped

Place chicken, celery, onions, carrots, salt & pepper in pot. Cover & simmer for 1 hour. Remove chicken only. Cut up in bite size pieces. Add to broth peas & 2 Tbs. flour. Mix with 1/2 cup water until slightly thickened. Add cut-up chicken. Fill individual bowls.

## Pie Crust

1 1/2 cups flour
1/2 tsp. salt
3/4 cup shortening
4-5 tsp. water
2 Tbs. sugar

Mix & press together to form 6 balls and roll out to cover individual cooking bowls. Bake until crust is brown. 350 degrees.

*We love this one-dish dinner, of course, accompanied by a salad — Irv loves it & says it's so much better than the world famous Chasen's Chicken Pot Pie. Sincerely, Essee and Irv*

*Irv Kupcinet*

CHICAGO SUN-TIMES • NEWS GROUP CHICAGO, INC.
401 N. WABASH AVENUE • CHICAGO, ILLINOIS 60611 • (312) 321-2587

*Ann Landers*
*Chicago Tribune*
*435 North Michigan Avenue*
*Chicago, Illinois 60611*

### Best-Ever Lemon Pie

1 baked pie shell
1 1/4 cups sugar
6 tablespoons cornstarch
2 cups water
1/3 cup lemon juice
3 egg yolks
1 1/2 teaspoons lemon extract
2 teaspoons vinegar
3 tablespoons butter

Mix sugar, cornstarch together in top of double boiler. Add the two cups of water. Combine egg yolks with juice and beat. Add to rest of mixture. Cook until thick over boiling water for **25 minutes**. This does away with starchy taste. Now add lemon extract, butter and vinegar and stir thoroughly. Pour into deep **9-inch** pie shell and let cool. Cover with meringue and brown in oven.

### Never-Fail Meringue

1 tablespoon cornstarch
2 tablespoons cold water
1/2 cup boiling water
3 egg whites
6 tablespoons sugar
1 teaspoon vanilla
pinch of salt

Blend cornstarch and cold water in a saucepan. Add boiling water and cook, stirring until clear and thickened. Let stand until **COMPLETELY** cold. With electric beater at high speed, beat egg whites until foamy. Gradually add sugar and beat until **STIFF**, but not dry. Turn mixer to low speed, add salt and vanilla. Gradually beat in cold cornstarch mixture. Turn mixer again to high speed and beat well. Spread meringue over cooled pie filling. Bake at **350 degrees** for about **10 minutes**.

**UIC**

The University of Illinois at Chicago

Office of the Chancellor (M/C 102)
Box 4348, Chicago, Illinois 60680
(312) 413-3350
BITNET: U45115@UICVM

*Poppy Seed Cake has been the most popular birthday request not only of my husband, but also of our four children, over some twenty years. I have baked this cake wherever we happened to be, in Philadelphia, our home before Chicago, on sabbatical leave in Paris and in Munich — maybe thirty cakes in all.*

*POPPY SEED CAKE*

*Cake:*
*1/3 cup poppy seeds*
*3/4 cup milk*
*3/4 cup butter*
*1-1/4 cups sugar*
*1 tsp. vanilla*

*1/8 tsp. almond extract*
*2 cups cake flour, sifted*
*2 tsp. baking powder*
*1/2 tsp. salt*
*4 egg whites*

*Soak poppy seeds in milk about two hours. Cream butter and add sugar, beating until light and fluffy. Add extracts. Add sifted dry ingredients alternately with the milk and poppy seed mixture. Beat egg whites to soft peaks and fold into batter. Pour into 3 greased 8 inch diameter cake pans, and bake in a moderate (350) oven 30 to 35 minutes. Cool. Spread filling between layers, and chocolate glaze on top only.*

*Filling:*
*1-1/2 cups milk*
*1/2 cup sugar*
*2 tblsp. cornstarch*

*1/4 tsp. salt*
*4 egg yolks*
*1/2 cup chopped walnuts*

*Scald milk in heavy saucepan. Mix sugar, cornstarch and salt, and add to milk. Cook, stirring constantly until thick; boil several minutes. Beat egg yolks and add a few spoonfuls of the hot mixture to warm the eggs. Stir egg mixture into the hot mixture in the saucepan and cook until very thick (a few minutes). Cool completely and add nuts just before assembling the cake.*

*Chocolate glaze:*
*Melt 5 oz. good quality semi-sweet chocolate (Hershey's Special Dark, Ghirardelli or Lindt are good). Beat in bit by bit 3 oz. butter.*

*Pat Langenberg*

**Fermilab**

Fermi National Accelerator Laboratory
P.O. Box 500 • Batavia, Illinois • 60510

Hundreds of visitors from all over the world visit Fermilab each year to carry on high energy physics research. They work hard, long hours and it can be grueling.

Imagine our delight a few years ago when Tita Jensen, a wife of one of our visitors, brought us her talent for preparing elegant cuisine. She prepares one lunch and one dinner each week for Fermilab people. Our hard working visitors look forward eagerly to these wonderful meals. We'll never let her leave!

Here is a menu and recipes that Tita might serve. Enjoy!

Leon M. Lederman, Director
Fermi National Accelerator Laboratory

## Pescado con Salsa de Coco
### Red Snapper with Coconut Sauce

Yield 6

3 lbs. Red Snapper Fillets
4 cloves garlic - mashed
2 1/2 teaspoons salt
Juice of 2 limes
1 1/2 teaspoons dried oregano
1/4 teaspoon fresh ground pepper

Wash and dry fish. Mash the rest of the ingredients and marinate for at least 1 hour. Pat dry, dredge in flour and saute in hot olive oil for about 4 minutes on each side. Serve with following sauce.

### Coconut Sauce

1/4 cup olive oil
1 large onion sliced very thin
3 cloves of garlic sliced thin
1 bay leaf
1 teaspoon dried oregano
1/4 teaspoon crushed red pepper - (dried & hot)
14 oz. can <u>unsweetened</u> coconut milk
1/2 cup chopped peeled tomatoes
Juice of half of a lime
1/4 teaspoon salt

Heat olive oil and saute onion, garlic, bay leaf, oregano and pepper until golden. Add coconut milk, tomatoes, lime juice and salt and reduce until it coats a spoon. Serve with fish. Garnish with coriander and sliced limes.

NOBEL LAUREATE, PHYSICS 1988

## Sopa de Plátanos
### Plantain Soup

Yield 6 to 8

2 Plantains - cut in 1" circles
3 teaspoons of olive oil
1 large onion - small chunks
6 cloves of garlic - minced
6 cups chicken stock
2 teaspoons white vinegar
2 teaspoons chopped coriander leaves

Peel plantains and rub with olive oil. Place on baking pan in preheated 350°F. oven for about 30 minutes.

Saute onions and garlic in olive oil until golden brown. Crush the cooked plantains and add to this mixture. Add stock, vinegar and half of fresh coriander. Let simmer for 30 minutes. Correct seasonings and serve with fresh coriander.

## Flan de Piña
### Pineapple Flan

Yield 6

1 cup sugar
3 teaspoons water
To make a caramel, combine sugar and water, melt slowly and let brown until dark. Remove from heat. Put into 6 small souffle dishes. When cool, butter the sides.

4 eggs
2 egg yolks
1 can (14 oz.) condensed milk
1 can (14 oz.) unsweetened pineapple juice
1 teaspoon pure vanilla extract

Whisk eggs and yolks until creamy. Add condensed milk, pineapple juice and vanilla extract. Whisk until well mixed. Pour into caramelized dishes. Place in a shallow pan. Fill pan with one inch of water. Cover tightly with foil and place in the middle rack of the <u>preheated oven</u> 325°F. for one hour until firm to the touch. To unmold, wait until cool, release with a knife around the edge and invert. Serve very cold.

COMMITTEES:
  CHAIRPERSON,
    PUBLIC UTILITIES
  CO-CHAIRPERSON,
    JOINT COMMITTEE ON
    MINORITY ACCESS TO
    HIGHER EDUCATION
  JUDICIARY I
  SELECT COMMITTEE ON AGING
  SELECT COMMITTEE ON HOUSING

COMMISSIONS:
  ADMINISTRATIVE RULES
  LONG TERM CARE INSURANCE

STATE OF ILLINOIS
**ELLIS B. LEVIN**
STATE REPRESENTATIVE • 5TH DISTRICT

DISTRICT OFFICE:
3733 N. CLARK
CHICAGO, ILLINOIS 60613
312/975-0800

CAPITOL OFFICE:
2073 STRATTON BUILDING
SPRINGFIELD, ILLINOIS 62706
217/782-8062

## Chocolate Mousse Cake

6-8 serving
Preparation time: 25 minutes
Cooking time: 30 minutes (pre-heat oven 350)

6 oz. good quality dark sweet chocolate
2 tablespoons strong coffee
6 eggs, separated at room temperature
2/3 cup sugar
1/4 teaspoon salt
1 cup chilled whipping cream

1) Melt chocolate and coffee in top of double boiler. Remove from heat, stir until smooth and set aside.

2) Whip egg whites with salt until stiff peaks form. Beat 6 egg yolks with 2/3 cup sugar (add slowly) until thick and fluffy. Mix chocolate and egg yolks together. Fold chocolate mixture into egg whites.

3) Transfer 1/3 batter into small bowl and refrigerate. Pour remaining batter into buttered 9" spring form pan.

4) Bake 350 for 25 minutes. Turn off heat and leave in oven for 5 minutes more (center will fall and a rim will form--cake will only be 1-1 1/2" high, don't be alarmed).

5) While cake is still hot, place on serving platter.

6) Spread chilled uncooked batter over chilled cake and refrigerate for 1 hour.

7) When ready to serve, whip cream until it begins to thicken, add 1 teaspoon of vanilla and two teaspoons of sugar, and beat until firm peaks form. Spread on top and around edges. Serve.

*A Passover & Thanksgiving favorite of the Levin family. It's super rich so you need to slice small pieces. But it's wonderful if you are a chocoholic like everyone in our family.*

*Ellis B. Levin*

**Chicago Tribune**
435 NORTH MICHIGAN AVENUE
CHICAGO, ILLINOIS 60611

## B.O. PLENTY'S CHUCK WAGON CASSEROLE

1½ lbs. GROUND BEEF
1 CUP CHOPPED CELERY
1 GREEN PEPPER CHOPPED
1 MEDIUM ONION, FINELY CHOPPED
1 CAN TOMATO SAUCE
1 TBSP. CHILI POWDER
1 TSP. EACH SALT, PAPRIKA
1 SMALL CAN PORK & BEANS
1 CAN REFRIDGERATED BISCUITS
10 HALF INCH CUBES CHEESE

BROWN MEAT. POUR OFF DRIPPINGS. ADD CELERY, GREEN PEPPER, ONIONS, TOMATO SAUCE AND SEASONINGS. SIMMER FOR 20 MINUTES. ADD PORK & BEANS. TURN INTO 2½ qt. CASSEROLE. PLACE A CUBE OF CHEESE ON EACH BISCUIT; FOLD IN HALF. PLACE ON MEAT MIXTURE. BAKE 400° FOR 15 MINUTES.

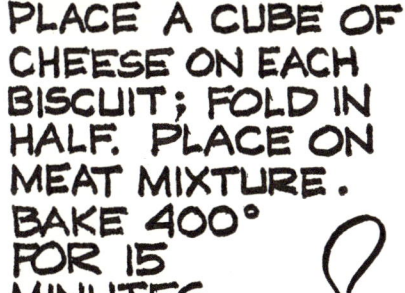

AN' WATCH WHERE YOU SPIT!

PTOO

# LOHAN ASSOCIATES

Architecture  
Planning  
Interior Design

225 North Michigan Avenue  
Chicago, Illinois 60601  
Telephone 312.938.4455

Dirk Lohan FAIA

## MY MOTHER'S HAZELNUT CAKE

1 POUND Grated Hazelnuts  
1 POUND Cream of Wheat (not too fine)  
1 POUND Sugar (or a little less)  
Small Package of Baking Soda  
2 Cups of Milk

Mix ingredients.

Pour into large spring form after wiping surfaces with butter and powdering with cream of wheat.

Bake for an hour.

After cooling, glaze with mixture of powdered sugar and rum or lemon juice.

Decorate with single hazelnuts on top.

The cake tastes best after several days, and especially so when returning from the Mackinac Race.

*Dirk Lohan*

**CHICAGO WHITE SOX**
324 W. 35th STREET
CHICAGO, ILLINOIS 60616
(312) 924-1000

## LUSTFUL CHEESECAKE

INGREDIENTS:
- 3 pkgs. 8-oz. cream cheese
- 1 c. sugar
- 5 eggs
- 1-1/2 tsp. vanilla

Top of cake:

- 1 pt. sour cream
- 1/4 c. sugar
- 1/4 tsp. vanilla

DIRECTIONS: Soften cheese (first with fork, then with mixer). Add 1 egg at a time, and beat after each egg. Add sugar, vanilla. Bake at 300 degrees for 40 minutes in a greased 13x9 Pyrex dish. Remove from oven, cool (1/2 hour). Do not turn oven off.

TOP: Mix together sour cream, sugar and vanilla and spread over cheesecake. Return to oven for 5 minutes at the same temperature. Cool and refrigerate until serving time.

CRUST (Optional):
- 1 stick butter or margarine
- 8 graham crackers rolled finely
- 1/4 cup confectioners sugar

Mix together graham crackers and sugar. Spread in bottom of dish.

MAGGIE PHELAN-LONG

WILLIAM D. LONG

**ASCO**

*Association of Sheridan Condo-Coop Owners    6121 N. Sheridan Road, Chicago 60660*

Potato-Onion Soup

(keep on hand in freezer for use during
bone-chilling Lake Michigan storms)

3 large potatoes, peeled and sliced
4 cups vegetable stock or water
1 large onion, sliced thin
½ cup diced celery
2 Tbs. butter or margarine
Nutmeg, salt, pepper to taste
1 cup milk
handful defrosted frozen peas
grated Romano or Parmesan cheese

Put potatoes in soup pot with stock or water and bring to boil. Simmer until soft and remove from flame. Mash with potato masher in pot and set aside.

Saute onion and celery in butter until clear and soft. Add to potato mixture. Replace soup pot on stove. Add milk slowly while stirring and season to taste.

Heat thoroughly without boiling. Garnish with peas and cheese. Serves 4.


Submitted by
Sheli A. Lulkin
President

## CHEF JOHANN LUSTENBERGER'S CHICKEN BREAST BAKED IN PHYLLO DOUGH

6 CHICKEN BREASTS (APPROX. 8 OZ. EACH)
2 BUNCHES FRESH SPINACH LEAVES
8 OZ. RICOTTA CHEESE
2 EGGS
1 LB. FRESH MUSHROOMS
1\4 LB. BUTTER
1 PACKAGE PHYLLO DOUGH
SALT, PEPPER, THYME, OREGANO (TO TASTE)

BONE AND SKIN THE CHICKEN BREASTS. POUND CHICKEN BREASTS BETWEEN TWO PIECES OF WAX PAPER TO 1/4 INCH THICK. BLANCH SPINACH LEAVES FOR ONE MINUTE, THEN DRAIN AND CHOP. CHOP MUSHROOMS AND SAUTE. ALLOW TO COOL.

MIX MUSHROOMS, SPINACH, RICOTTA CHEESE, AND EGGS. SEASON WITH SALT, PEPPER, OREGANO, AND THYME TO TASTE. LAY CHICKEN BREAST OUT FLAT AND PUT APPROXIMATELY 2 TABLESPOONS OF THE MIXTURE IN THE MIDDLE. ROLL THE CHICKEN BREAST KEEPING THE FOLD AT THE TOP. SET ASIDE. CUT DOUGH TO 9X9 INCH SQUARES--ENOUGH SQUARES FOR 3 LAYERS OF DOUGH PER CHICKEN BREAST (18 SQUARES). BRUSH ONE SIDE OF EACH PHYLLO SQUARE WITH BUTTER AND LAYER, MAKING THREE LAYERS. PLACE BREAST IN MIDDLE OF PHYLLO SQUARES AND FOLD. (FOLD-TOP TO BOTTOM AND END TO END--MEETING IN THE MIDDLE). PLACE FOLD ON BOTTOM AND BRUSH TOP WITH MELTED BUTTER. BAKE AT 350 DEGREES FOR 40 MINUTES.

*NOTE--PHYLLO DOUGH DRIES OUT VERY QUICKLY. COVER WITH DAMP CLOTH WHEN NOT WORKING WITH DOUGH.

## Palmer House and Towers

A Hilton Hotel
17 East Monroe   Chicago, Illinois 60603-9990   312/726-7500

### PALMER HOUSE GRIDDLE CAKE WITH STEWED RED CHERRIES          6 SERVINGS

```
    2     Cups of sifted all purpose flour
2 1/2     Tablespoons of sugar
    2     level tablespoons of double action baking powder
  1/2     teaspoon of salt
    5     tablespoons of granulated sugar
2 1/2     cups of milk
    2     egg yolks, beaten
    2     egg whites, stiffly beaten
  1/8     cup of melted butter
  1/2     lemon
          melted butter for the griddle cakes
```

Sift the flour, add 2 1/2 tbsp. of sugar, baking powder and salt together, make a well in the center of the dry ingredients, combine the milk and egg yolks, add slowly to dry ingredients, stirring continually until free from lumps.  Stir in 1/4 cup of the melted butter, fold in egg whites, allow the batter to stand for a few minutes.  Heat an 11 inch griddle, brush with melted butter pour in slightly less than 1 cup of batter.  Cook over medium flame until side is golden brown, about 3 to 4 minutes, turn and brown second side, about 2 or 3 minutes.  Remove from the griddle and brush second side with melted butter, sprinkle with sugar and lemon juice, spread with stewed red cherries, using half the amount on inside of pancakes.  Fold edge of pancake one fourth way over, then roll as for jelly roll.  Sprinkle top of each pancake with remaining sugar.  Place pancakes on oven proof platter and broil until sugar dissolves, serve with remainder of hot stewed red cherries.

### STEWED RED CHERRIES

```
    2     ( 10 oz. ) packages of frozen sour red cherries
    1     ounce of kirschwasser of cherry liquor
    3     tablespoons of granulated sugar
    4     teaspoons of cornstarch
```

- page 2 -

    Thaw and drain the cherries, measure 2 cups of drained juice, combine cornstarch and sugar in a sauce pan, stir in drained cherry juice gradually. Cook, stirring constantly until thickened Reduce flame, add the cherries and bring to boiling point and let simmer for 5 minutes. Add 2 ounces of Kirschwasser or Cherry Liquor and serve hot.

    Yield 2 cups of stewed red cherries.


The Palmer House griddle cake has been in existence at the Palmer House since 1954. It is a favorite now as it has been for 34 years. The recipe has not changed in all this time. As Chicago has many traditional aspects which the Palmer House is a part so do its griddle cakes - Bon Appetite !

**VIRGINIA B. MACDONALD**

STATE SENATOR - 27TH DISTRICT
ROOM 111 STATE HOUSE
SPRINGFIELD, ILLINOIS 62706
217/782-8187

DISTRICT OFFICE:

120 WEST EASTMAN, SUITE 102
ARLINGTON HEIGHTS, ILLINOIS 60004
312/253-4500

COMMITTEES:
  MINORITY SPOKESMAN
    ENERGY & ENVIRONMENT
MEMBER:
  ELECTIONS & REAPPORTIONMENT
  JUDICIARY

# GENERAL ASSEMBLY
## STATE OF ILLINOIS

NUSSKUCHEN (Nut Cake)

```
1     cup softened butter
2     cups sugar
5     eggs, seperated
1     teaspoon vanilla
1     cup each:  mini-semisweet chocolate pieces, chopped walnuts
2½    cups flour
1     teaspoon each:  baking soda and baking powder
3     tablespoons chocolate flavored beverage mix (such as Nestles)
1     cup buttermilk
```

In large bowl, beat butter, sugar, egg yolks and vanilla until well blended. Stir in chocolate pieces and nuts. Sift dry ingredients together and blend into creamed mixture. Stir in buttermilk. Fold in stiffly beaten egg whites. Turn into 2 greased and floured 9" x 5" x 3" loaf pans. Bake at 350° for one hour or until cake tests done. Cool; dust with confectioner's sugar.

This German recipe for "nusskuchen" (meaning nut cake) was given to me by a German neighbor several years ago, and it is a family favorite - especially at Christmastime.

*Virginia Macdonald*
Virginia B. Macdonald

**GENERAL ASSEMBLY**
STATE OF ILLINOIS

MICHAEL J. MADIGAN
SPEAKER
316 CAPITOL
SPRINGFIELD, ILLINOIS 62706

HOUSE OF REPRESENTATIVES
EX OFFICIO MEMBER
ALL HOUSE COMMITTEES

PASTA CON BROCCOLI

1 STICK OF BUTTER
2 CUPS OF HALF AND HALF
1/2 POUND OF PASTA SHELLS
1/2 POUND OF MUSHROOMS
1/2 POUND OF BROCCOLI
8 OUNCE CAN OF TOMATO SAUCE
1 CUP FRESHLY GRATED PARMESAN
4 CLOVES OF CRUSHED GARLIC
SALT AND PEPPER TO TASTE

Boil and drain pasta. Boil broccoli. Saute' mushrooms in butter and garlic. Mix all ingredients together. Simmer for several hours before serving. Watch closely and stir often; mixture burns easily. Makes about 5-6 servings.

*Michael J. Madigan*

# SPIAGGIA

### PIZZA DOUGH

```
4 Cups    Flour                1/2 - 1 Qt. Lukewarm Water
2 oz.     Whole Wheat Flour    1/4 oz.     Salt
1/4 oz.   Yeast                1/4 oz.     Honey
3/4 oz.   Olive Oil
```

Place lukewarm water in bowl with honey, yeast and olive oil. Whisk all together until yeast and honey are dissolved.

Proof.

Add flours and salt in large mixing bowl with dough hook.

Mix flour to assure equal distribution.

Add yeast mixture. Mix, then add water. Work until smooth, soft and elastic. Proof at room temperature for 1-2 hours.

Knock down and refrigerate.

Yield: 2 pounds of pizza dough.

NOTE: Variances in volume of water:
　　　　High humidity --- less water
　　　　Low humidity --- more water

Prepared by: Chef Anthony Mantuano

---

ONE MAGNIFICENT MILE    980 NORTH MICHIGAN    CHICAGO 60611    312 280-2750

SPIAGGIA
*A signature of The Levy Restaurants*

# SPIAGGIA

## PIZZA AL QUATTRO FORMAGGI

| | | | |
|---|---|---|---|
| 3 oz. | Prepared Pizza Dough | 3/4 oz. | Grated Romano |
| 3/4 oz. | Diced Gorgonzola | 2 Tbsp. | Minced Sun-Dried Tomatoes |
| 3/4 oz. | Diced Mozzarella | 1 oz. | Olive Oil |
| 3/4 oz. | Diced Provolone | | Cornmeal |

Preheat oven to 475°. Line oven with pizza tiles.

Roll pizza dough as thin as possible. Transfer to pizza peel that has been liberally dusted with cornmeal.

Top pizza dough alternating ingredients, except sun-dried tomatoes and olive oil. Then sprinkle with sun-dried tomatoes and drizzle with olive oil.

Slide off peel onto tiles in oven.

Cook until golden brown 10-12 minutes. Remove from oven with peel.

Slice and serve.

Prepared by: Chef Anthony Mantuano

ONE MAGNIFICENT MILE    980 NORTH MICHIGAN    CHICAGO 60611    312 280-2750

SPIAGGIA
*A signature of The Levy Restaurants*

*Jacki Mari*

**PROFESSIONAL PSYCHIC CONSULTANTS**
312-636-4578

*Alyn Richard*

JACKI MARI & ALYN PRESENT

"The Honeymoon Cake"

Ingredients: 1 Box Dromedary Cake Mix
3 Whole eggs
1/2 cup Half & Half cream
1/4 cup milk
1/4 cup Puritan Oil
1 pkg. of Philadephia Cream Cheese

Spoon mix all of the above ingredients, then beat with an electric beater for 4 minutes.

Cut up (small) peaches, or apricots, you can use drained Maraschino cherries, or blueberries. Be sure to wash them and drain them well, ADD to the above batter. Be sure you have ALL of the lumps out, smooth, before you FOLD in the fruit.

Bake in a square pan or loaf pan, be sure to GREASE the BOTTOM of the pan. Be sure to PREHEAT the oven at 325 degrees, and bake this cake for 75 minutes. Set a timer and you can watch a Soap Opera, get dressed up or...do whatever you want to, you will have plenty of time!

Your TOPPING can be sifted powdered sugar or whipped-cream. This is actually a very light cake! Wonderful to serve for your ROMANTIC dinner with the one you love.

JACKI MARI            *Jacki Mari*

Your Professional/Personal Psychic-Astrologer, using the new 4TH DIMENSION ASTROLOGY. Confidentiality assured! Self-Help Tapes and Hypnotherapy are available to you. Write to me at P.O. Box 802, Oak Lawn, Il. 60454...or you can call me at (312)636-4578. Services by phone or mail available.

# HB McC

As I do not know where THE KITCHEN is - I always call Zarada Gowenlock at George Jewel Catering. She brings me some of my favorite things such as ----

*Short and fun from Alexandre Dumas' Dictionary of Cuisine 1870.*

### Quail

This is the most darling and lovable of game. A fat quail gives equal pleasure by its flavor, color and form. It is an act of culinary ignorance to prepare quail in any way except roasted in buttered paper, for when they are in contact with a liquid their flavor is dissolved, evaporated, and lost.

### Larks
(not the cigarettes)

They have the double distinction of being loved by both poets and gourmets. The lark is very delicate and highly esteemed for its flavor. It is only really good from November until February. It fattens with suprisingly rapidity in foggy weather.

### Larks in a Casserole

Take 12 to 24 larks, depending on the number of your guests, pluck them (the larks, not the guests). Singe them. Put them in a pot and cook them with butter until half done. Take them off the fire, drain them and draw them. Crush some goose livers and truffles. Season with salt and pepper and nutmeg. Fill your birds with this stuffing. Put the left over stuffing on the bottom of a casserole and bury the stuffed larks in it so they can scarcely be seen. Cover with a slice of bacon and a piece of buttered paper. Bake 1/2 hour. Just before serving remove the bacon and paper, drain the platter, sprinkle the dish with fresh bread crumbs, and rest easy over the results.
"This divine dish may be eaten with any sauce you desire. I have often feasted on it with currant jelly, taking a half a mouthful of each to a bite."

*Hope McCormick*

# WHERE
·CHICAGO·

1165 N. Clark Street, Chicago, Illinois 60610 (312) 642-1896

Salmon Spread

After a hectic work week, my husband and I look forward to cocooning on the weekends. Our idea of an absolutely wonderful evening is creating something special in the kitchen. Quite often, we'll whip up something to nosh on while we cook. This salmon spread is easy to prepare and quite delicious. We like it best with a chilled glass of champagne.

Ingredients

1 large package cream cheese -- softened
¼ lb. Nova lox -- thinly sliced
4 tbs. finely chopped onions -- or to taste
3 tbs. capers -- or to taste
Juice of ½ fresh lemon
Boudin sourdough bread -- thinly sliced and toasted

Squeeze the juice of ½ lemon over thinly sliced salmon and let marinate for at least ½ hour. Mix together softened cream cheese, chopped onions and capers. Add marinated salmon and gently mix together.

Serve with thin slices of toasted Boudin sourdough bread.

Enjoy!

*Karen McKay*
Karen McKay
Publisher
WHERE CHICAGO Magazine

# bloomingdale's

## BLOOMIE'S BAKED APPLES WITH SHERRY PORK CHOPS

4 PORK CHOPS
3 COOKING APPLES
1/2 CUP BROWN SUGAR
1 TBS. CINNAMON
3 TBS. BUTTER OF MARGARINE
SALT AND PEPPER
1/2 CUP SHERRY

Brown the pork chops in a skillet and season with salt and pepper to taste. Wash and thinly slice the apples, leaving the peel on. Spread the apples in a greased 8 by 12 inch baking dish. Dot with butter. Then arrange the pork chops over the apples and pour the sherry over the chops. Cover the dish with tin foil and bake at 400° for one hour. Nice when served with rice.

SERVES: 4

Public Relations   900 North Michigan Avenue, Seventh Floor   Chicago, Illinois 60611   312·440·4515

# THE FRANK LLOYD WRIGHT HOME AND STUDIO FOUNDATION

951 CHICAGO AVENUE    OAK PARK ILLINOIS 60302    PHONE: 312 848-1976

## FRANK LLOYD WRIGHT'S CHOCOLATE INDULGENCE

"Give me the luxuries of life and I'll
gladly do without the necessities."
Frank Lloyd Wright

Inspired by this often quoted remark, the following recipe produces a dessert that is indeed luxurious! Chocolate is used extravagantly and combines beautifully with Wright's favorite libation, Bushmill's Irish Whiskey. Bushmill's rich, complex bouquet and smooth, assertive taste adds a very special touch to this wonderful creation.

The dessert has three parts. A fudgey brownie is baked in an 11" by 7" jelly roll pan. When cool the brownie is cut into shapes to line a 2 quart round bowl or charlotte mold. A dense chocolate mousse is next and is used to fill the cake lined form. After a thorough chilling the dessert is unmolded and topped with a chocolate glaze laced with whiskey. Assembly of the dessert can be done a day in advance, making it an ideal finale for a party.

BROWNIE-CAKE:
1 C. flour
3/4 C. Hershey's cocoa
3/4 t. baking powder
1/4 t. salt
2 t. instant espresso powder
1 C. melted butter
2 C. sugar
2 1/2 t. pure vanilla
4 extra-large eggs, room temperature

MOUSSE FILLING:
4 extra-large eggs, separated
1/2 C. strong, hot coffee
3 T. sugar
1 lb. Ghirardelli's dark, semisweet chocolate
1/4 to 1/3 C. Bushmill's Irish Whiskey, to taste
pinch of cream of tartar
1/2 C. heavy cream, whipped

GLAZE:
5 oz. Ghirardelli's dark, bittersweet chocolate
2 T. corn syrup
4 T. melted, clarified butter
2 T. Bushmill's Irish Whiskey

## BROWNIE-CAKE

Butter an 11" X 17" jelly roll pan. Line with wax paper or parchment paper and then butter and flour the paper. Preheat the oven to 350 degrees.
In a separate bowl, sift together the flour, cocoa, baking powder, salt and instant espresso. Set to the side.
In a large mixing bowl, combine the melted butter, sugar and vanilla. Beat at medium speed for one minute. Add the eggs, one at a time, and beat an additional minute. Slowly add the dry ingredients and mix until smooth.
Pour the batter into the prepared pan and spread as evenly as possible. Bake in the middle of the oven for 20 to 25 minutes. Test with a tooth pick or wooden skewer. Be careful not to over bake the brownies.
Remove from the oven and cool the brownies in the pan for 10 minutes. Invert them onto a rack and remove the wax paper/parchment liner. Line the pan with new paper and return the brownies to the pan, right side up. Cover with wax paper to keep them from drying out. Proceed with the mousse.

## MOUSSE FILLING

Place the 4 yolks in a large mixing bowl -- the eggs should be room temperature. Beat until pale yellow. Slowly add the very hot coffee to the yolks, beating constantly with a wire whip. Add the sugar. Carefully melt the chocolate over very warm water and then add it to the eggs, beating constantly with the wire whip. Set to the side to cool. Beat the 4 egg whites with the cream of tartar to soft peaks. Add the whiskey to the cooled chocolate/egg mixture. Carefully fold in the whipped cream and then the beaten whites. Chill. The mixture should thicken though, not set. Proceed to line the form with brownies.

To line the bowl or charlotte mold with brownies, it is easiest to cut out paper patterns first. Cut a small circle for the bottom of the container; this will be the top of the unmolded dessert. Cut wedge shaped pieces to line the sides and finally a large circle to top things off. Use the paper patterns as a guide to cut out the brownie pieces. Line the container with plastic wrap, to facilitate unmolding, and then line with the brownie pieces, best side out. Press the brownie carefully to fit the container. Spoon in the chilled, thickened mousse. Place the large circle of brownie on top and press down lightly to seal the edges. Cover the container with plastic wrap and refrigerate for four hours or overnight. When firm, unmold the dessert onto an attractive plate and pour on the glaze.

## GLAZE:

To make the glaze, carefully melt the chocolate over very warm water. Add the corn syrup, melted butter and whiskey. Mix thoroughly. Pour the warm glaze over the cold dessert covering the top thoroughly and then drizzling down the sides. Refrigerate until ready to serve.
When preparing to serve, cut the dessert with a hot knife into slender pieces. Unsweetened whipped cream is an excellent accompaniment.

My friend and co-chef, Jan Kolar, and I worked on this recipe. The end result is a truly memorable dessert with a personal touch for Mr. Wright.

Regards,

Mary McLeod

# LWV
LEAGUE OF WOMEN VOTERS OF CHICAGO 332 S. Michigan Ave. #1142, Chicago, IL 60604 • 939-5935

Marion Meyerson
Member of the Shoreline Protection Commission
(Co-President - League of Women Voters of Chicago)

## Caviar Mousse (Appetizer)

1 envelope unflavored gelatin in 1/4 cup cold water. Dissolve over pan of boiling water. Cool.

Blend with:
- 1 cup sour cream
- 1 small cream cheese
- 1/4 cup mayonnaise
- juice of 1/2 lemon
- 1 scallion
- pinch of cayenne pepper

Fold in 2 oz. jar of caviar.
Refrigerate to thicken.
Unmold - decorate with grated hard boiled egg and caviar.
Serve with crackers or rye rounds

**LWV**

**LEAGUE OF WOMEN VOTERS OF CHICAGO** 332 S. Michigan Ave. #1142, Chicago, IL 60604 • 939-5935

A bottle of your favorite wine to share with soul mates on the shores of Lake Michigan as the sun slowly sets into the horizon will greatly enhance the flavor of this elegant dish.

Marion Meyerson

# THE LIRA SINGERS
## POPULARIZING POLISH MUSIC

*An ancient Polish recipe in my own interpretation*

## TRADITIONAL POLISH BIGOS    (HUNTER'S STEW)

- 2 lb. sauerkraut
- 1/2 lb. pork cut into small pieces
- 1/2 lb. veal cut into small pieces
- 1/2 lb. venison or rabbit cut into small pieces
- 1/2 lb. smoked polish sausage, cut into small pieces
- 1/2 lb. bacon, cut into strips
- any other leftover meat
- 3 med. onions chopped coarsely
- 1 sm. cabbage sliced, optional
- 2 lg. apples, peeled, cored, sliced optional
- 1 lb. fresh mushrooms, sliced
- 2 dried european mushrooms
- 3 sm. ripe tomatoes, peeled and sliced
- 2 bay leaves
- 1 T. caraway seeds
- 1/2 c. red or white wine
- salt and pepper to taste
- sugar to taste
- water as needed

Put sauerkraut with its water in large pot or slow cooker; if a less strong taste is desired, drain water and replace with fresh boiled water. Bring to boil on medium heat; turn down to simmer. Meanwhile brown pork, veal, venison or rabbit or any fresh meat in smoked bacon slices; cook until just about done, then add to kraut pot with bacon and all juices. Skin the sausage, cut into small cubes and add to kraut. Add any leftover ham or other smoked meat or any other cooked meat, all cut into small pieces. Soak dry european mushrooms in 1/2 c. water until soft; cut into small pieces and add to kraut with water they soaked in. Chop onions and brown in butter; add sliced fresh mushrooms and saute until just about done. Add entire contents of skillet to kraut pot; add tomatoes for color. Add bay leaves and apples for sweeter, less "wild" taste if desired. Simmer 3-4 hours, stirring often until all ingredients blend into a golden brown color. It is best to make bigos a day or two ahead and let it simmer an hour or two each day, adding ingredients each day if desired. Just before serving add wine and stir. Bigos is traditionally served with hard crust rye bread or parboiled potatoes.

Lucyna Migala

*Lucyna Migala, Artistic Director & General Manager, 561-9197*

6033 NORTH SHERIDAN ROAD #34H    CHICAGO, ILLINOIS 60660

The Lira Singers are a not-for-profit corporation of the State of Illinois.
Donations to the Lira ensemble are fully tax deductible as provided in the Federal Tax Code.

**MARSHALL FIELD'S**
111 NORTH STATE STREET
CHICAGO, ILLINOIS
60602

PHILIP B. MILLER
CHAIRMAN

# FRANGO RASPBERRY CHOCOLATE PECAN TORTE

*This sublime European-style dessert is heady with the aroma of raspberries, crunchy with buttery pecans, and bursting with dark chocolate flavor.*

## TORTE
- 1 cup plus 2 tablespoons (2 1/4 sticks) unsalted butter, cut up
- 15 Frango Raspberry Chocolates (5 1/2 ounces), chopped fine (about 1 cup)
- 5 large eggs, at room temperature
- 1 1/2 cups sugar
- 1 cup flour
- 4 ounces (about 1 cup) pecans, chopped fine
- 4 tablespoons framboise or raspberry-flavored liqueur
- 1 teaspoon vanilla extract
- 1/4 teaspoon salt

## GLAZE
- 2/3 cup heavy (whipping) cream
- 12 Frango Raspberry Chocolates (about 4 ounces), chopped fine (about 3/4 cup)
- 4 ounces bittersweet chocolate, chopped fine
- 3 ounces (about 2/3 cup pecans), chopped coarse

## GARNISH
Pecan halves (optional)

**Make the torte:**

1. Position a rack in the center of the oven and preheat to 350 degrees F. Butter the bottom and sides of a 9-inch round springform pan that is 2 inches deep. Line the bottom of the pan with a circle of waxed paper and butter the paper.

2. In a double boiler over hot--not simmering water, melt the butter. Add the chopped chocolates and melt, stirring frequently until smooth. Remove the pan from the water and cool until tepid.

3. In a large mixing bowl, whisk the eggs and sugar together just until blended. Do not overmix. Whisk in the cooled chocolate mixture just until smooth. Using a wooden spoon, stir in the flour, chopped pecans, 2 tablespoons of the framboise, the vanilla, and the salt just until smooth. Do not overmix. Spoon the batter into the prepared pan and spread evenly.

4. Bake until a toothpick inserted halfway between the center and edge of the torte comes out with a moist crumb, about 1 hour. <u>Do not overbake. The cake will appear underbaked.</u> Transfer the torte in the pan to a wire rack. Let cool for 10 minutes. Run a sharp knife around the inside of the pan to release the sides of the torte from the pan. Remove the sides of the springform pan. Invert the torte onto the rack and carefully peel off the waxed paper. Sprinkle the torte with the remaining 2 tablespoons of framboise. Let the torte cool completely.

Make the glaze:

5. In a small saucepan over medium heat, bring the cream just to the simmer. Remove the pan from the heat, add the chopped chocolates, and let the mixture stand for 1 minute. Whisk the mixture gently until smooth. Let the glaze cool until tepid.

*Josephine Baskin Minow*

## Tangy Salad Dressing

1 pint mayonaise
juice of ½ lemon
2 cloves of garlic (pressed)
2 cans of anchovies
1 head of parsley

Toss in food processor.
Great for salads, dips or sauce for fish.

*Jo and Newt Minow*

JOHNNY MORRIS' RECIPE
FOR "STEAK TARTARE"
OR AS I LIKE TO THINK OF
IT "BARE MEAT"

Serves 2 as a dinner
and 4 for an appetizer:

1 lb freshly ground tenderloin.
2 eggs
¼ C. minced onion
2 anchovie fillets (opt)
¼ C. capers, drained well
salt ,freshly ground pepper to taste
½ t. worcestershire sauce
1 t. olive oil
¼ C. chopped parsley
small onion chopped fine
cocktail ryes

Mix beef, salt, pepper, and eggs. Add mashed anchovies and worcestershire. Drizzle olive oil over and mix in minced onions. Mix thoroughly.
Shape into large patties and garnish with chopped onion, capers, and parsley. Serve with cocktail rye.
If for some reason yours doesn't taste so good, stop in and see Patrick at the Cape Cod Room and I'll guarantee a great Tartare.

## DEEP FRIED CARPACCIO OF SALMON, CHINOIS

Arnold J. Morton, Proprietor
Alexander S. Dering, Executive Chef
ARNIE'S RESTAURANT

**ARNIE'S MANAGEMENT GROUP**
1050 NORTH STATE STREET
CHICAGO, ILLINOIS 60610
(312) 266-0068

12oz. Salmon pounded approximately ½" thick, 5"x5" square
½oz. Shallots (minced)
½oz. Chives (minced)
1oz. Olive Oil
2 Scallions - large (5" long)
pinch of Salt and Pepper
2 sheets dried and pressed Seaweed

unit for deep frying, preferrably with peanut oil - 400°F

### METHOD

1. Place 2 pieces of salmon, after pounded and squared, on cutting board.
2. Prepare marinade with shallots, chives, olive oil and salt and pepper. Brush both sides of salmon fillets and let marinate for 10 minutes.
3. Place one scallion in center of each piece of salmon and roll into cigar shape.
4. Brush sheets of seaweed with marinade on both sides. Moisten slightly with a little water until pliable enough to work with.
5. Place salmon cigar on seaweed and wrap firmly in order to keep proper shape. Set aside.

May be prepared and kept refrigerated for up to 24 hours in advance.

### BATTER

6 Egg Whites (lightly beaten)
6oz. Cornstarch
1 t. Paprika (Spanish)
1 t. Sugar
1 t. Baking Powder
1 T. Chives minced
    Salt and Pepper to taste

### METHOD

1. Mix all ingredients well and let stand until needed. (covered)

### SAUCE

4oz. White Wine
½oz. Shallots (minced)
6oz. Heavy Cream
4oz. Butter (sweet)
2 T. Chives (chopped)
    Salt and Pepper to taste

### METHOD

1. Place white wine and shallots in saucepan and let reduce by 2/3. Add heavy cream and reduce until slightly thickened.

## DEEP FRIED CARPACCIO OF SALMON, CHINOIS

**Arnold J. Morton, Proprietor    Alexander S. Dering, Executive Chef**
**ARNIE'S**

2. Remove from heat and whip butter into sauce piece by piece until slightly thickened and smooth. Strain.
3. Add chopped chives and stir well. Season with salt and pepper and reserve until needed.

METHOD

1. Place the rolled cigar of salmon gently into batter, assuring that it is well coated and lower slowly into frying oil. (Don't drop into oil as the salmon will stick to the bottom). Let fry for 20 seconds and remove. Place into batter again in order to assure an even coat and place into frying oil for a second time for 40-60 seconds or until cigar is well browned and crispy. Remove and place on towel.
2. Slice each cigar into approximately 10 slices, discarding end pieces.

Take one leaf of flowering white savoy and place at the head of the plate. Put 5 whole chives on the leaf, being sure that approximately 4" of chives extends over the leaf. Take a slightly smaller piece of purple savoy and press onto white savoy so that the chives stand straight up.

Place sauce on plate, and arrange 4 pieces of carpaccio over sauce. Serve.

# The usa karate Federation

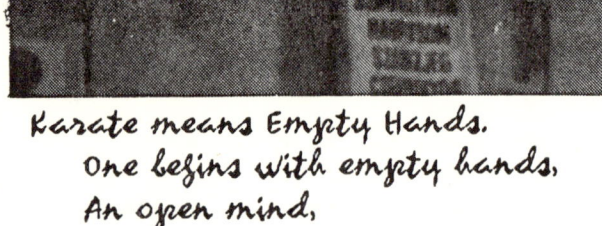

*Karate means Empty Hands.*
  *One begins with empty hands,*
  *An open mind,*
  *and a willingness to learn.*

*Mr. Nanay has coached the United States Children's Team to Victory in Europe in 1985, 1986, 1987 and 1988.*

## POPPY SEED CAKE

1 yellow cake mix
1 instant coconut cream pudding mix
4 eggs
1 cup hot water
1/4 cup poppy seed
1/2 cup oil

Mix all ingredients 4 minutes and pour in greased angel cake pan

Bake 1 hour at 350 degrees.

Poppy Seed Cake has been a favorite of mine since I was back home in Hungary. (I sure wish one of my students would bake this for me --'cause I can't cook!)

**CRESTWOOD KARATE CENTER**
14125 S. Cicero Avenue
Crestwood, IL 60445

Sensei John Nanay
Coach of the U.S. Karate Team

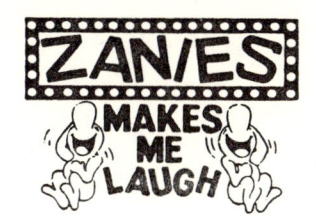

**ZANIES COMEDY NITE CLUB**

1548 NORTH WELLS, CHICAGO, ILLINOIS 60610
(312) 337-4027

## DOROTHY'S SPECIAL BEEF STEW

1 cup beef broth
1 15oz can tomato sauce
2 pounds of beef stew meat
3 tablespoons of instant tapioca pudding
5 medium carrots cut into pieces
2 medium onions chopped
2 cans of small potatoes-whole
5 medium fresh mushrooms-sliced
1 bay leaf
salt and pepper to taste

Place all ingredients in a covered dish or roasting pan and mix well.
Do not brown meat before placing with other ingredients.
Place bay leaf on top of stew and cover.
Bake 5 hours at 300 degrees.
**DO NOT PEEK!!**

This very easy stew is great for a cold winter day. A simple and delicious meal for the working individual- just set the oven timer and the stew is ready when you arrive home from work!

*Lauri Neal*
Lauri A. Neal
Manager
Zanies Comedy Nite Clubs, Inc.

MT. PROSPECT          NASHVILLE

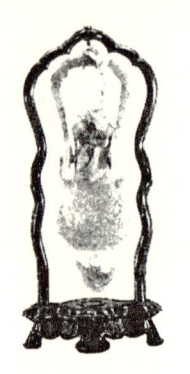

## Lizzadro Museum of Lapidary Art

*220 Cottage Hill    Elmhurst, Illinois 60126*

### SPINACH JADE SOUFFLE

1 small chopped onion
3 tablespoons butter
3 pkgs. chopped frozen spinach
1 can cream of mushroom soup
1/4 cup grated parmesan cheese
5 eggs
1/2 teaspoon salt
1/8 teaspoon black pepper
2 drops green food coloring

THAW    frozen spinach and drain well

SAUTE   onion and frozen spinach in butter - cool

BEAT    eggs, soup, cheese, salt, pepper, & coloring

ADD     spinach mixture

POUR    into greased ring mold

PLACE   in pan of water

BAKE    in moderate oven 45-60 min. until firm.

SUBMITTED BY:

DIANA NICHOLAS
CURATOR

LIZZADRO MUSEUM OF LAPIDARY ART
ELMHURST, IL

*312-833-1616*

# Nightingale-Conant Corporation

**World's Largest Producer of Audiocassette Programs**

Great Ideas for Successful Living

7300 North Lehigh Avenue
Chicago, Illinois 60648
Phone: 1-312-647-0300
1-800-323-5552

Earl Nightingale

Take a trip to one of the great game parks of Africa. Get up at 5:00 A.M. muscle down a bit of rusk and coffee, then get in the Land Rover for a deep tour of the bush and a view of the fabulous African animals in their natural setting.

Return to camp for a trencherman breakfast at 9:00 A.M. This will include eggs and everything in camp -- including slices, sauteed, of last night's . . .

Roast Impala

Here we have the finest, most delicious, most satisfying , most un-fouled-up, non-chemicalled, un-antibioticed tender meat on the face of old Mother Earth. And it was even better last night when it was cooked fresh, on the bone, over the camp fire.

Give me Roast Impala every time.

Formerly 1448 Lake Shore Drive in Beautiful Chicago

**WBEZ 91.5 FM** 1819 WEST PERSHING ROAD 6-EAST CHICAGO, ILLINOIS 60609 PHONE 312-890-8225

A simple, quick appetizer for
busy people to prepare at the last minute.

CAROLE'S PITA SURPRISE

Cut pita bread into 1/8" wedges

    1 cup mayonaise

    1 cup artichokes (chopped)

    1 cup parmesan cheese

    (process in food processor)

Spread on pita bread wedges.

Place under 350° broiler for 5 minutes and serve piping hot.

Makes about 64.

*Carole R. Nolan*
Carole R. Nolan
General Manager

MARTIN J. OBERMAN

856 W. Belden Avenue • Chicago, Illinois 60614

STEAK TARTARE

1 pound ground sirloin

1 raw egg yolk

½ bottle (2¼ ounce) capers, drained

2T chopped onion

anchovy paste--to taste

garlic powder--to taste

3T Durkee's sauce

1T (at least) worcesteshire sauce

tobasco sauce--to taste

Lawry's salt and freshly ground pepper--to taste

Mix ingredients, except meat, capers, and onions. After sauce is blended, fold in remaining ingredients.

*Marty Oberman*

# Brookfield Zoo

### OLGA'S DELIGHT

2 dozen clams (*Venus mercenaria*)
5 pounds squid (*Loligo pealei*)
4 dozen smelt
4 pounds Atlantic round herring (*Clupea harengus*)
6 handfuls Gulf mackerel (*Scomber scombrus*)

- Mix above ingredients in very large bucket.
- Chill 24 hours.
- Serve with 5 loving keepers and one friendly harbor seal.

I especially like the above recipe while relaxing in my outdoor pool on a nice cool morning at Brookfield Zoo.


Olga, the nation's oldest walrus in a zoo, arrived at Brookfield Zoo in 1961 when she was 6-months old. She weighs approximately one ton and eats between 45 and 60 pounds of fish a day, making her the zoo's most expensive animal to feed.

Olga does various behaviors including whistling, blowing kisses, and waving. She resides in the Seascape at Brookfield Zoo's new Seven Seas Panorama with her poolmate, Amy the harbor seal.

Brookfield, Illinois 60513   312.485.0263

## BILL'S FAVORITE APPLE CRISP

| | |
|---|---|
| 1 1/2 quarts apples (sliced) | 1 cup sugar |
| 1/2 cup sugar | 1/2 tsp. baking powder |
| 2 tsp. cinnamon | 1 tsp. salt |
| 1/3 cup butter (melted) | 1 egg (unbeaten) |
| 1 cup flour (do not sift) | |

Mix the apples, the 1/2 cup of sugar and cinnamon together. Place in a 8 x 12 inch pan. Mix the flour, sugar, baking powder and salt together. Add unbeaten egg. Stir well until blended. Sprinkle over the apples in the pan. Pour the melted butter over the top and bake at 350° for 30-35 minutes.

Bill Paar, Jr.
Station Manager

*Enjoy! Bill*

SARA PARETSKY

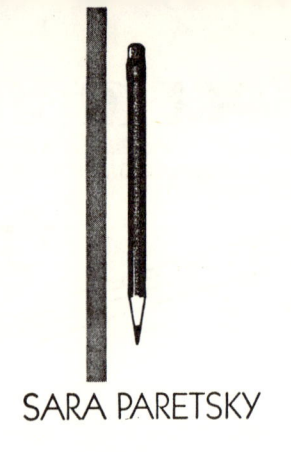

Artichokes in honor of Courtenay

For each person, use one whole fresh artichoke. Cut the stem so that the artichoke sits flat in a pan. Cut off the top half inch of spines. With kitchen scissors cut off the pointed ends of the leaves -- this will make the artichokes easier to eat.

Select a pan in which the artichokes will just fit comfortably -- not too much space around them, but not tightly packed. Fill the pan with about one inch of water (it should just cover the bottom-most layer of leaves). Add to the water:

2 whole peeled garlic cloves
6 peppercorns
1 tsp salt
1/2 tsp thyme
1/2 tsp oregano
1/4 tsp tarragon
1 bayleaf
4-6 thin slices of lemon
1 1/2 tbsps. olive oil

Put in the artichokes. Cover the pan and bring to a boil, then simmer over low heat until the artichokes are done, approximately 40 minutes. You know they are done when you can easily pull out a leaf.

Serve hot or cold with the following sauce:

1/4 tsp dry mustard
1/8 tsp dill
1/8 tsp tarragon
1/4 tsp thyme
1/4 tsp oregano
Mix with 2 tbsp sweet sherry
Add 1/2 mayonnaise and stir until lumps disappear
   (For lower-fat sauce, use 1/4 cup yogurt and 1/4 cup mayonnaise)

5831 South Blackstone • Chicago, Illinois 60637 • 312 947-9570

# CHICAGO NEW PLAYS

3023 North Clifton, Chicago, IL 60657  (312) 327-5046

**ARTISTIC DIRECTOR**
Nicholas A. Patricca

**BUSINESS MANAGER**
Robert Sturm

<u>Zuppa di Scarola</u>
(or <u>La Pozione d'Amore</u>)

for two (naturally)

1 lb of escarole
4 cloves of garlic (whole or diced)
4 cups of chicken broth (home made)
1 cup of white kidney beans (dried)
1/4 lb of mild, lean Italian sausage (optional)
2 tablespoons of olive oil

1. Prepare the white kidney beans and the chicken broth in advance. (The potion is not guaranteed to work if you use canned beans or canned chicken broth. If you do not know how to prepare these items, have your mother or a friend do it for you.)

2. Clean the escarole thoroughly with cold water, set in colander to drain.

3. Cut the sausage into bite size pieces, brown them in a skillet, drain off the fat.

4. Saute the escarole lightly and briefly in a stockpot with the garlic and oil. When the escarole is slightly softened, remove it from the stockpot, cut it into ribbons, then return it to the pot.

5. Add the chicken broth, the beans, and the sausage to the stockpot. Simmer for 30 minutes.

Serve immediately with fresh Italian bread and a robust Italian red wine. If you like to live dangerously, sprinkle the soup with crushed red pepper. (I assume no responsibility for your or your guest's behavior if you add the red pepper.)

I served this soup or love potion to my lover on the evening of our first encounter. The rest is legend.

Enjoy!

*Nicholas A. Patricca*

# STANLEY PAUL ORCHESTRA

### GREEN PEPPER GINGER BEEF WITH OYSTER SAUCE

1 1/2 lbs. flank steak
1 tablespoon soy sauce
1 tablespoon sugar
2 tablespoons bottled oyster sauce
1 tablespoon fresh ginger root, minced
1 small garlic clove, minced
2 tablespoons cooking oil

2 small onions - cut into cubes
1 teaspoon sesame oil
2 teaspoons dry sherry
1/4 cup chicken stock
1 green pepper, cut into cubes
1 tablespoon cornstarch mixed with
1 tablespoon water

Prepare ahead, 1 1/2 lbs. flank steak cut into two strips with the grain. Put the strips in the freezer until partially frozen (about 1/2 hour).

Take out of freezer and cut each strip across the grain into paper thin slices. (By partially freezing the meat, it makes it easier to cut into very thin slices.)

In a bowl combine soy sauce, sugar, oyster sauce. Place sliced beef in the marinade. This can be done several hours before it is to be used, and kept in the refrigerator.

Place wok or sauce pan over high heat and heat the two tablespoons cooking oil. When wok is hot, add the minced ginger and garlic and stir-fry for about 1/2 minute.

Add marinated beef and onions and stir-fry for about 2 minutes. Then add sesame oil, sherry, 1/4 cup chicken stock, green pepper and stir-fry until meat is browned -- about another 2 minutes.

Add the cornstarch mixture and mix together until everything is coated.

Remove from heat and place on platter.

You can sprinkle with toasted sesame seeds if you like.

P.S. It's delicious!!!

*Stanley Paul*

1511 NORTH WELLS STREET CHICAGO, ILLINOIS 60610 312-751-2000

# Walter Payton, Inc.
### 1251 E. Golf Road • Schaumburg, Illinois 60173 • 312-605-0034

## SWEETNESS CHICKEN

12 choice chicken pieces (3-3 1/2 pounds)
1 1/2 cups orange juice
2 teaspoons oregano leaves
1/2 teaspoon garlic powder
1/2 teaspoon ground sage
1/2 teaspoon dried rosemary leaves, crushed
1/2 teaspoon dried thyme, crushed
salt and pepper to taste
paprika
1/4 cup orange marmalade
1 tablespoon cornstarch
3 cups hot cooked rice

*Place chicken in 13 x 9-inch baking dish, skin side down. Combine juice and seasonings. Pour over chicken. Sprinkle with paprika. Cover and bake at 350 degrees for 30 minutes. Turn chicken; sprinkle with paprika. Bake uncovered 30 to 40 minutes longer or until chicken is tender. Pour pan juices into sancepan; skim fat. Add marmalade and cornstarch dissolved in 2 tablespoons of water. Cook stirring until sauce is clear and thickened. Serve chicken and sauce over bed of rice. Garnish with orange slices.*

*Makes 6 servings*

# BENCHERS
## ·FISH HOUSE·

CAJUN BARBECUED PRAWNS

1 lb. Butter
1 tablespoon Pepper
1 teaspoon White pepper
1/2 teaspoon Cayenne red pepper
1 teaspoon Paprika
16 medium Raw Shrimp, peeled, deveined and butterflied
Lemon wheel and Parsley garnish

Melt butter in skillet and add spices and blend. Saute butterflied shrimp in seasoned butter for about one minute on each side. Place four cooked shrimp on individual plates and pour 1/4 of seasoned butter (or divide in two for entree portions) in center of each plate. Garnish with lemon wheel and parsley.

Serves: 4 appetizer servings or 2 entrees

BENCHERS FISH HOUSE
A signature of The Levy Restaurants
Sears Tower • 233 South Wacker Drive
Calder Level
Chicago, Illinois 60606
(312) 993-0096

*James Phillip*

Prepared by: Chef James Phillip

---

Sears Tower • 233 South Wacker Drive • Chicago, Illinois 60606 • (312) 993-0096

BENCHERS FISH HOUSE
*A Signature of The Levy Restaurants*

**WGN RADIO 720AM**
A Tribune Broadcasting Station
435 N. MICHIGAN AVE.
CHICAGO, IL 60611
312-222-4700

CHICAGO'S lakefront and CHICAGO'S people.....

one in the same. Unequalled anywhere.

Good luck with your efforts,

Wally Phillips

## STEAK BOURGUIGNONNE

For 4 persons:
- 3 lbs. Sirloin Steak
- 6 oz. bacon
- 7 1/2 oz white mushrooms
- 6 oz small onions
- 2 chopped shallots
- 2 glasses red burgundy wine
- 6 oz butter
- 1 teaspoon chopped parsley
- seasoning to taste

Chop the bacon in small bits and fry in pan until it reaches a blond color.
Cook small onions in butter then add the mushrooms cut in quarters, and mix together.

Fry the Sirloin Steak in butter according to your taste of cooking, then add the chopped shallots and the red wine, let it simmer to obtain the amount of sauce you require then add the balance of the butter.

Pour onto the meat, the onions, bacon and mushrooms.

Serve as a garnish some Dauphin Potatoes

## DAUPHIN POTATOES

Peel 1 1/2 lbs. potatoes to be finely shredded.
Put into a frying pan with oil and butter.
Fry deeply on one side, turn over and do other side.
The color of the potatoes should be light brown.

```
               Frederik Pohl
                 "Gateway"
           855 South Harvard Drive
              Palatine IL 60067
               (312) 991-6009
```

                                          29 September 1988

Dear Lakefront Partnership:

   It's not always possible to achieve perfection with
something that's not only simple and easy, but even guaranteed.
But here it is:  You start with a medium-sized pork butt, which
you cut into quarters lengthwise, then into quarter-inch slices;
put it in a large pot with about a quart of water and set it to
boil.

   While the pork butt is boiling, peel and quarter 6 medium-
sized potatoes; quarter two small onions; scrape and slice four
large carrots.  By the time you're finished doing that the pork
butt has cooked long enough to add all these vegetables to the
pot, along with pepper to taste.  (I prefer quite a lot, coarsely
ground.)

   After all this has boiled for 15-20 minutes, add one small
head of cabbage, cored and quartered.  Continue cooking until the
cabbage is as tender as you like it.  Serve.

   This is enough to feed at least eight people, but don't
worry about leftovers.  My personal opinion is that the soup gets
even better the next (or subsequent) days.  My personal opinion
is also that it freezes well, but then I happen to like the fact
that the freezing causes the cabbage and onions to disintegrate
and simply add body to the soup.

   I can't pretend to be the world's greatest chef.  In fact, I
have had many failures as a cook . . . but this ham and cabbage
soup has never been one of them.

                                          Hungrily yours,

                                          Pohl

# THE DUSABLE MUSEUM OF AFRICAN AMERICAN HISTORY, INC.

740 E. 56th Place • Chicago, IL 60637 • (312) 947-0600
In Washington Park

## A FAVORITE DESERT

When my brother, Harold Washington was in the Armed Forces, our Mom would regularly send him batches of cookies and other sweet goodies.

Apparently Harold shared them with some of his Army buddies because it was not uncommon for one of them to write "Mother Dear" requesting a goodie shipment of his own.

The below recipe is for one of those sweets sent to First Sargent Harold Washington. It has since become a family favorite which Harold and the rest of us, all came to look forward to at Holidays and special occasions.

8 oz. finely crushed walnuts
1 can of condensed sweetened milk
3/4 cup of margarine

8 oz. coconut (finely shredded)
3 cups of crushed graham crackers
Peanut butter morsels (approx. 12 oz.)

Melt margarine in a flat pyrex baking dish or cookie sheet (12"x15").
Spread a layer of crushed graham crackers (approx. 1/4' thick)
Cover entire bottom of baking dish. Press firmly into place.
Pour can of condensed milk over entire graham cracker layer.
Spread layer of peanut butter morsels
Add layer of crushed nuts and sprinkle with thin layer of shredded coconut.
Gently press into place.
Place in preheated oven at 300 for 15 minutes.
Remove from oven, cool and place in refrigerator until time to serve.
Cut into squares and go for it!

*Ramon B. Price*

Ramon B. Price, Chief Curator

EDWARD G. PROCTOR

REUBEN & PROCTOR
19 South LaSalle Street
Chicago, Illinois 60603

## **BUTTER TARTS**

FLOUR AND LINE MUFFIN TINS WITH REGULAR PIE PASTRY
ROLL THIN, ESPECIALLY FOR SMALL TARTS

Filling

1-1/2 Tablespoons butter (if hard, melt it a little to beat)

1 egg (large) - if small, use 2 eggs

3 Tablespoons of Half and Half

1 cup brown sugar

1 cup raisins (currants may be substituted if you prefer)

1/2 Teaspoon vanilla

Pinch of salt, if you wish

Mix all ingredients in order given and beat well until bubbles form on top of mixture. Fill muffin tins and bake at 400 degrees - 15 minutes or a little longer - check at 15 minutes to see if filling is brown and crust cooked.

NOTE: Sometimes it is good to beat egg a little before adding ingredients
Makes 36 small tarts or 12 regular size tarts

Edward G. Proctor

# CITY COUNCIL

## CITY OF CHICAGO

### COUNCIL CHAMBER
SECOND FLOOR, CITY HALL

**ROMAN PUCINSKI**
ALDERMAN, 41st WARD

6200 N. MILWAUKEE AVENUE 60646

TELEPHONE: 763-7300

**COMMITTEE MEMBERSHIPS**
INTERGOVERNMENTAL RELATIONS (CHAIRMAN)
AVIATION
CLAIMS AND LIABILITIES
FINANCE
HOUSING
MUNICIPAL CODE REVISION

---

My favorite dinner is fish..orange roughy and sole, preferably. Plus a green or yellow vegetable; lettuce and tomato salad; and fruit for dessert. For a more substantial meal, Betty serves pasta shells with tomato sauce. Our favorite fish recipe is very simple:

> One fish fillet per person
> Lemon 'n' Herb seasoning
> Paprika
> Margarine
>
> Rinse fish fillets in cold water. Pat dry. Place fillets on shallow baking sheet covered with metal foil. Spread margarine on fish--very lightly. Sprinkle with Lemon 'n' Herb seasoning and paprika. Bake at 400° for 15 minutes (if fish is thawed) or for 20 minutes (if fish is frozen. Turn oven to broil. Broil until lightly browned.

Another quick meal that we like is "Hamburger and Vegetable Packets", crusty bread, sherbet and beverage. For each "packet" proceed as follows:

> Place a ground beef patty on a square of metal foil. Sprinkle lightly with seasoned salt. Add one sliced, peeled, medium-sized potato, a sliced medium carrot, and a sliced small onion. Pull up the corners of the metal foil to seal in the meat and vegetables. Bake at 375° for one hour. When the package is opened, grated cheese may be added.

Super easy! And delicious!

I like to help Betty clean-up after a family meal. I am very fussy about how soiled dishes are placed in the dishwasher.

Roman Pucinski
Alderman, 41st Ward

## MUSSELS FOR SIX

George B. Rabb, President, Chicago Zoological Society, and Director, Chicago Zoological Park (Brookfield Zoo)

2 pounds mussels
sliced scallions
fresh garlic, 3-4 cloves chopped finely
butter
1 cup white wine  (Chenin Blanc complements well.)
1/4 teaspoon Thyme, freshly ground black pepper

Wash mussels under cold water, stripping beard of seaweed from them.  Mussels should be closed.

Saute garlic in butter over low heat.  Add the wine, increase the heat, and then add mussels, seasonings, scallions.  Shake pot a few times and steam until mussels open.  A glass lid on the pot is a help. Discard any unopened mussels.  Serve in broth, half-shelled or not.

Serve with french bread, slender french fried potatoes, and a salad.

*George B. Rabb*

**Carson Pirie Scott**
DEPARTMENT STORES

NEIL A. RAMO
PRESIDENT

## HOT CLAM DIP

\* \* \* \* \* \* \* \* \* \* \*

1-1/4 cups crushed Ritz Crackers (approximately 40 crackers)

1 can minced clams with juice

1 medium onion, minced

1/2 tsp. lemon juice

1 stick of melted margarine

Combine all ingredients. Place in a crock and bake at 350° for 30 minutes.

Serve with crackers and/or chips.

*Submitted by Neil A. Ramo*

ONE SOUTH STATE STREET • CHICAGO, ILLINOIS 60603 • (312) 641-4900

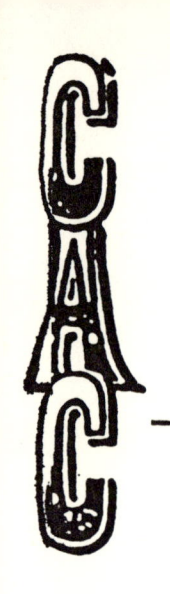

# CENTRAL ADVISORY COUNCIL
## FOR THE RESIDENTS OF THE CHICAGO HOUSING AUTHORITY

243 E. 32nd Street            Chicago, Illinois 60616

Telephone 312- 791-8731

SOUTHERN MIDNIGHT SNACK

The Southern Midnight Snack was a favorite of the 1930's depression era families of the deep south. Instead of desserts, children were served bowls of this nutritious mixture of cornbread and buttermilk.

Preheat oven to 350°

In a bowl: Mix together

- 2 cups corn meal (white or yellow)
- 2 teaspoons baking powder
- 1 pinch salt
- 1 pinch sugar
- 1 egg
- 3/4 cups buttermilk

Blend above ingredients well and pour into greased muffin pans or 8" pie pan.

Bake at 350° for 35 - 45 minutes until done

Cool bread, slice in sections and crumble in bowls filled with cold buttermilk.

Submitted By: *Artensa Randolph*
Commissioner Artensa Randolph
Chicago Housing Authority

**THE WHITE HOUSE**

WASHINGTON

## Gazpacho Soup

*Put into blender and liquify:*

2 14½ oz. cans of stewed tomatoes
1 cup peeled, chopped and diced cucumber
1 cup seeded and chopped green pepper
1 clove of garlic
2 tbsp. each of chives, parsley,
  basil and tarragon

1 cup clear beef stock or consommé
1 tbsp. worcestershire sauce
6 drops of tabasco sauce
6 twists of ground black pepper
  from pepper mill
Salt to taste

*For garnish:*

1 cup fresh tomato, peeled, seeded
  and finely diced
½ cup seeded and finely diced cucumber
½ cup seeded and finely diced green pepper
1 cup of croutons (white bread toasted with
  crust removed and then diced)

*Serve soup very cold. Pass garnish separately. Serves 6 people (makes about 1½ quarts).*

## Piccata of Veal

12 trimmed, thin slices of veal
½ cup flour
2 eggs, beaten in a small bowl
1 tbsp. chopped parsley
¼ cup grated romano cheese (optional)
¼ cup vegetable oil
½ cup vegetable oil
Salt and ground white pepper

Slowly heat the oil in a large teflon pan or iron skillet. Sprinkle veal on both sides with salt and pepper. Then dip each veal slice very lightly on both sides in the flour. Mix together the parsley and the beaten eggs. Put the veal into the egg mixture, turning each slice. Sauté egg coated veal in the hot oil to a golden brown on both sides. Remove to a serving platter. Serve Veal Piccata with pasta or rice and tomatoes.

Yield: 6 servings

With Best Wishes,

*Nancy Reagan*

## Café Provençal

1625 Hinman Avenue
Evanston, Illinois 60201
(312) 475-2233

*This recipe holds a lot of memories for me - it was the first "French" leg of lamb recipe I'd ever made - and the first time I liked lamb. The recipe was from my first cooking teacher - Denise Shorr in Fitchberg, Mass. I still make it - 20+ years later - and it gets raves —*

*Leslee Reis*
*Sept. 1988*

### GIGOT PERSILLE
(serves 6-8)

4 # leg of lamb trimmed of all outside fat
2 large cloves garlic, slivered
butter, softened
salt, freshly ground pepper
1/3 C. each: chopped onion, chopped parsley, breadcrumbs
1 clove garlic, crushed
1C. chicken stock or broth
2 T. dry white wine or dry vermouth
1 T. cognac or brandy

Preheat oven to 400°.
Using a small sharp knife make narrow deep slits randomly across leg. Insert garlic slivers into slits. Spread a thin coating of soft butter around the whole leg.
Roast for 20 minutes.
Remove from oven. Sprinkle with salt and pepper. Return and roast 35 min. more
<u>Sauce</u>: Combine onions, parsley, breadcrumbs and crushed garlic. Sprinkle over lamb. Cook 5-10 min. longer (until thermometer registers about 135-140° in thickest part of leg - med. rare). Transfer meat to platter and keep warm.

## Café Provençal
1625 Hinman Avenue
Evanston, Illinois 60201
(312) 475-2233

*Us — just for Georgia — You'll love this —*
*Leslee Reis*
*Café Provençal*

### Gingered Peaches — for Jean Louis

- 5 C. water
- 2½ C. sugar
- 1" of fresh ginger — julienned
- 3 sprigs fresh mint
- 8 ripe but firm peaches
- 1 ripe mango

Bring water, sugar, julienned ginger & mint to boil. Simmer 10 min. Add whole, unpeeled peaches; simmer 10 min. more. Remove peaches & cool til easy to handle.

Peel 2 peaches, halve and discard pits. Coarsely chop & process with mango (peeled & pitted), ½ C. sugar syrup from poachings, 1 T. of the julienned ginger and several fresh mint leaves. Process til smooth. Taste for fruit & spice balance. Adjust as desired.

Peel remaining peaches and slice into ½" thick wedges. Place wedges into individual dessert dishes or 1 large glass bowl. Pour puree over and chill several hours or overnight. Garnish with sprigs of fresh mint. Serve with your favorite cookie.

→ Serves 6

*\* This is a summer favorite, first made for Café Provençal's 5th Anniversary Party (in 1982) by Jean-Louis Bruneau — our Parisian Sous-Chef — and now by Leslee Reis — Chef-Owner —*

©1987
*Rolls Rice Enterprises – (312) 864-1577*

# Shake, Rattle, and Ronnie Rice

## Rock N' Roll Happiness

- 1 bunch watercress
- 1 cake of tofu
- 1/2 cup diced celery
- 2 average size carrots
- 4 oz. cucumber juice
- 1 cup scallions, sliced into small pieces
- 3 large turnips
- 1/3 yellow summer squash
- 2 oz. gefilte (male)

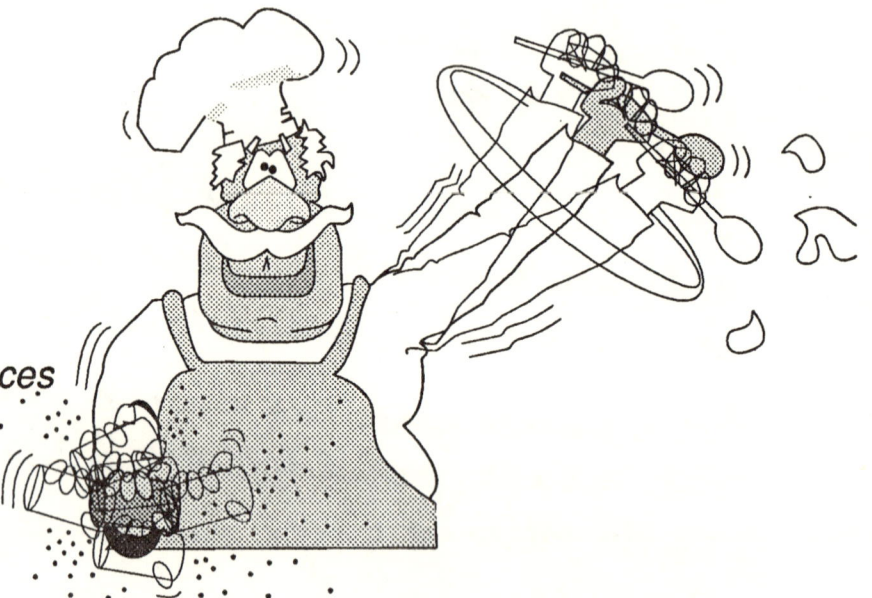

Blend all the above ingredients for 30 seconds in garbage disposal unit. Then grab your Lil' Darling, jump in your Little Deuce Coupe and cruise on over to Manny's on south Jefferson Street for some potatoe pancakes, kishke and gravy, brisket, hot pastrami, salami and beans, and other heavenly creations this side of Miami's Rascal House. See if you can go through the cafeteria line 3 times and spend $38 for lunch like me and my buddy (Merrill) did. And, make doubly sure you don't pass up the halavah at the candy counter. But remember to drive home with the windows open.

See ya later, alligator!

*Ronnie Rice*

**Chicago Tribune**

WILLIAM RICE
FOOD & WINE COLUMNIST

435 N. MICHIGAN AVENUE
CHICAGO, ILLINOIS 60611-4041
312/222-3141

WILLIAM E. RICE

## SHELLFISH AND MUSHROOM SALAD

1/2 pound shelled crabmeat or shrimp, cooked and chopped
1/2 pound squid or sea scallops, cooked and cut into rounds
1/2 pound raw mushrooms, sliced
2 cloves garlic, crushed
1/2 cup olive oil
1/3 cup lemon juice or white wine vinegar
1/2 teaspoon <u>each</u> oregano and thyme
freshly ground black pepper
2 tablespoons chopped parsley

Combine seafood in one bowl and mushrooms in another bowl. Add half the garlic, oil, lemon, oregano and thyme plus two grinds of pepper to each bowl. Mix ingredients together well with the dressing. Cover both bowls with plastic wrap. Let stand two hours at room temperature or up to eight hours in refrigerator. Stir each two or three times. Just before serving, mix the seafood and mushrooms together, adding salt to taste. Spoon onto serving plates and garnish with a sprinkle of chopped parsley.

Serves 4 to 6.

*This is a very nice make-ahead first course.*

*William Rice*

**Kraft** INC

John M. Richman
Chairman and
Chief Executive Officer

## CHOCOLATE CARAMEL PECAN CHEESECAKE

2 cups vanilla wafer crumbs
6 tablespoons PARKAY Margarine, melted
      *      *      *      *
1 14-oz. bag KRAFT Caramels
1 5-oz. can evaporated milk
1 cup chopped pecans, toasted
1 8-oz. pkgs. PHILADELPHIA BRAND Cream Cheese, softened
1/2 cup sugar
1 teaspoon vanilla
2 eggs
1/2 cup semi-sweet chocolate pieces, melted

Combine crumbs and margarine; press onto bottom and sides of 9-inch springform pan. Bake at 350 degrees, 10 minutes.

In 1-1/2 quart heavy saucepan, melt caramels with milk over low heat, stirring frequently, until smooth. Pour over crust. Top with pecans. Combine cream cheese, sugar and vanilla, mixing at medium speed on electric mixer until well blended. Add eggs, one at a time, mixing well after each addition. Blend in chocolate; pour over pecans. Bake at 350 degrees, 40 minutes. Loosen cake from rim of pan; cool before removing rim of pan. Chill. Garnish with whipped cream, additional chopped nuts and maraschino cherries, if desired.

10 to 12 servings

Sure to satisfy the most discriminating sweet tooth!

*John Richman*

Kraft Court, Glenview, Illinois 60025

# WJJD · WJMK

180 North Michigan Avenue • Suite 1200 • Chicago, IL • 60601 • (312) 977-1800

When one's all-time favorite restaurant closes, in this case because Fanny Lazzaro decided to retire and enjoy her 80s, it's like losing a member of the family. No more spaghetti at Fanny's of Evanston. No more finding a little oil painting you hadn't noticed before while dining on that extraordinary pasta. And above all, no more Fanny's salad dressing. So I set about trying to recreate Fanny's dressing. Is it as good? Not on your life. There's just one Fanny's; but it's not bad, and not very difficult to make.

## PHONY FANNY'S SALAD DRESSING

Place the ingredients in a blender or food processor and mix thoroughly.

| | |
|---|---|
| 1/2 cup olive (or salad) oil | 1/4 cup pecans |
| 1/4 cup red wine vinegar | 1 teaspoon Worcestershire |
| 3 teaspoons tomato paste | dash of bitters |
| 2 teaspoons sugar | pinch of sage |
| 1 teaspoon prepared mustard | 2 tablespoons orange juice |
| 1 small onion | 1 tablespoon molasses |
| 1 clove garlic | |

Makes a very tasty and thick dressing for a green salad. After eating, raise your glass of wine in a toast to our lakefront, and to Fanny who for all those years made the REAL Fanny's dressing.

*Reese Rickards*
Reese Rickards
WJJD NEWS

A DIVISION OF infinity BROADCASTING CORPORATION

HYATT REGENCY OAK BROOK
1909 SPRING ROAD
OAK BROOK, ILLINOIS 60521 USA

312 573 1234  TELEX 285373

*J.R. ROBERTSON*
*EXECUTIVE CHEF*

*MY FAVORITE TIME OF THE SEASON AT THIS TIME OF THE YEAR COMES ONE OF MY FAVORITE VEGETABLES, ASPARAGUS*

### WHITE AND GREEN ASPARAGUS RAVIOLI

| INGREDIANTS | UNIT | PREPARATION & SERVICE |
|---|---|---|
| Green Asparagus | 2 | Cut lower part of Asparagus in small pieces and mix with ground snails, chicken meat, garlic & shallots, season to taste. Fill in Ravioli Dough and cook. |
| White Asparagus | 2 | |
| Green Pasta Dough | | |
| Snails | 2 | |
| Chicken Meat | ½ oz. | |
| Peppered Ham | ½ oz. | |
| Garlic | to taste | Peel Red Peppers, Saute with shallots Deglaze with White Wine, Reduce, add cream reduce more, Puree the sauce and season to taste. Garnish with the Asparagus Spears and Julienne of Peppered Ham. |
| Red Pepper | | |
| Cream | for sauce | |
| White Wine | | |
| Shallots | | |

Asparagus is a member of the Lily Family which includes other vegetables and flowers such as onion, garlic, leek, lilies, tulips and gladiolas. There are two varieties of Asparagus, White and Green. Most of the Green Asparagus is domestic compared to the White Asparagus which is imported. The White Asparagus comes from Holland, France, Chile, Mexico, and South America. The best quality Asparagus is from France and Holland. They are less stringy and have a much sweeter flavor The White Asparagus is clipped while the stalk is still below ground. White Asparagus never sees sunlight. As soon as it shoots up it is quickly covered.

# FOREMOST SALES PROMOTIONS, INC.

**NATIONAL HEADQUARTERS**
5252 N. BROADWAY • CHICAGO, IL 60640
312/ 334-0077

## It's Delicious!
## FOREMOST TIPSY BRISKET
### Good Eating... 8 to 10 Servings

5 lbs Brisket
2 or 3 onions sliced
4 whole celery sticks
1 cup chili sauce
1 can dark beer
2 tsp. salt
¼ tsp pepper
Sprinkle liberally with garlic powder

Place onions in bottom of roaster. Season meat and place on top of onions, fat side up. Place celery stalks on top of meat and cover with chili sauce. Roast uncovered, basting periodically, for about 1 hour, 350° oven. Cover and cook 1 hour longer. Pour over the beer, recover and cook until tender, approximately 1 hour longer. Baste periodically.

If desired add small new potatoes and carrot chunks, seasoned with salt and pepper, about 45 minutes to 1 hour before meat is done. Test meat and vegetables for tenderness.

*Irving Robins*
*Chairman*

**FOREMOST** *Liquor Stores*
Each Store Independently Owned And Operated

# J. ALLEN HYNEK CENTER FOR UFO STUDIES

UFO Resource Facility
Library and Publication Sales

2457 W. Peterson Ave.
Chicago, IL 60659
(312) 271-3611

## CUFOS SUNFLOWER BREAD

1 package dry yeast
3 tablespoons sugar
1 teaspoon salt
3-1/2 cups white flour (and more for kneading)
2 tablespoons sunflower oil

1/2 cup milk
1/2 cup diluted lemonade concentrate
1 egg, at room temperature
1 tablespoon dried lemon peel
3/4 cup dry roasted sunflower seeds

Combine yeast with flour, salt and sugar. Heat milk and lemonade to 115° (yes, it will be curdled), and pour into dry ingredients. Mix egg, lemon peel, and sunflower oil. Add and beat for 3 minutes. Stir in the sunflower seeds. Scrape onto floured surface and knead 10 minutes, sprinkling with a little flour when sticky. Dough should be smooth and elastic. Return dough to oiled mixing bowl, cover with a clean towel, place in a warm spot out of drafts, and let rise until double. This will take about 2 hours. Punch down and let rest for 5 minutes. Shape, place in a loaf pan, cover, and allow to rise again till doubled. Preheat oven to 375°; bake bread for 40 minutes. Immediately remove from pan. Makes one loaf.

Jennifer Henderson
CUFOS Chef

Mark Rodeghier
Scientific Director

George Eberhart
Librarian/Archivist

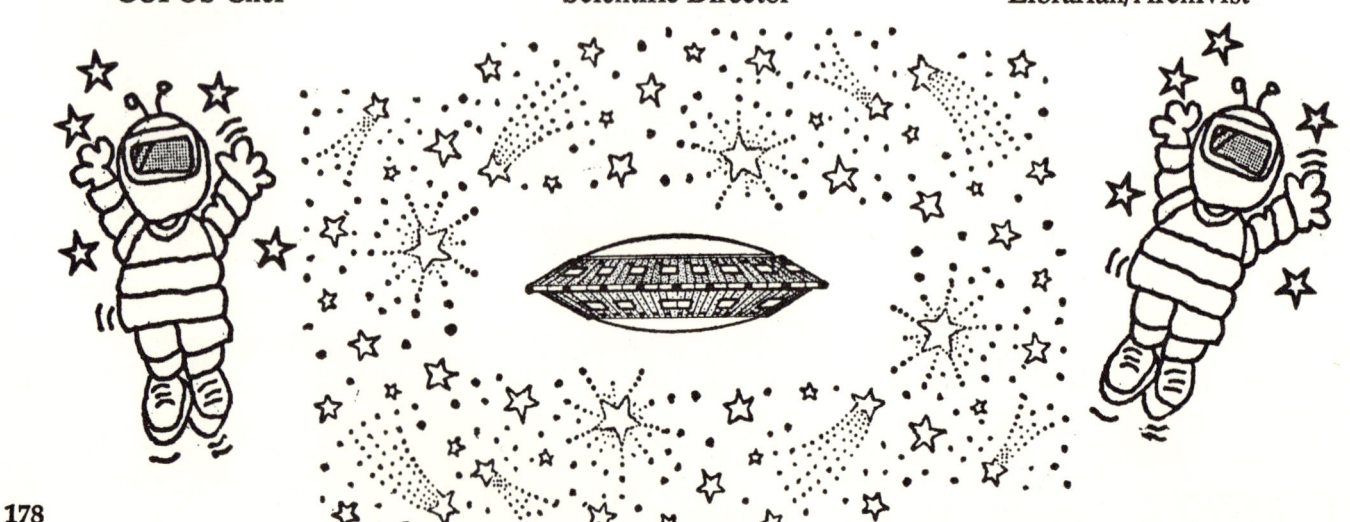

## TRUFFLE FILLED CHOCOLATE GLAZED PEARS

12 ripe but firm pears
Sprigs of mint for garnish

POACHING LIQUID:
- 2 c. sugar
- 8 cups water
- Zest of a large orange
- 2 cinnamon sticks

Bring to boil & cook for 20 min to develop flavor. Add

1 bottle white wine

Return to boil, add pears and poach gently for 10 - 30 min. Depends on size, type & ripeness of pears. Do not over cook.

FILLING & GLAZE:
- 1 1/2 Lbs Bittersweet chocolate
- 12 Oz Butter, unsalted

Melt together till smooth, for filling remove:

- 1 c Chocolate/butter mixture, add
- 2/3 to 1 c. whipping cream
- 1 1/2 to 2 oz liqueur (Grand Marnier, Pear William, Creme de Cocoa etc.)

Combine well & chill, whisking often till mixture holds its shape.

I prefer bosc pears. Pick only pears with stems. peel, level so they stand nicely. Core with melon baller. Hold in acidulated water.

I drain them on a rack with air space between them. Blot dry before filling and dipping.

I chill the pears after I fill them and before I dip them. Heat the Chocolate/butter mixture before dipping. Place dipped pears on wax paper, chill several hours. With the tip of a sharp knife make a slit for the stem of the mint sprig.

*Jimmy Rohr, owner*

**Jimmy's Place**
3420 N. ELSTON AV. CHICAGO IL 60618
RESERVATIONS : 539-2999

Wine & Spirits Marketing Consultant

**Mary Ross & Associates**
4278 N. Hazel 3f
Chicago, IL 60613

312/327-9748

My childhood memory is filled with wine and wines, of corks used as arithmetic counters, of corkscrews and glassware, the petunias in the backyard were planted in wine barrels, of labels picturing beautiful far-off lands for a little girl to dream on, of Dad's cerificates and awards for being one of the pioneers of the wine industry in Chicago and the U.S. Like M.F.K. Fischer, I feel, "Wine is Life. And I can no more think of my own life without wine... than I can remember living before I breathed."

I learned early that a splash of good wine will add natural fruit flavors to any recipe, but my Dad's signature dessert adds an extra sparkle to any occassion.

Take a tall parfait glass.
Fill 3/4 with good sherbet- lime or pineapple is best.
Poke a hole thru the sherbet. (This was my job. I used
    a chopstick.)
Chill in the freezer 'til the moment of service.
Fill almost full with green creme de menthe.
Top with Champagne or sparkling wine.


Good wine and good health,

Mary Ross

# PILOT KNOB
## A BED & BREAKFAST INN

CHOCOLATE CHIP SOUR CREAM COFFEE CAKE as served at our Bed and Breakfast Inn on the side of Pilot Mntn

*Norman Ross*

INGREDIENTS

1 egg
1/2 cup sugar
1 Tbs vanilla
1 cup sour cream
2 cups flour
1 tsp soda

STREUSEL

1/2 cup brown sugar
1/4 cup butter (chopped in pieces)
1/4 cup pecan pieces
1 cup chocolate chips

Preheat oven to 350 degrees
Cream first four ingredients
Add flour and soda

In separate bowl mix Streusel and set aside

Grease bundt pan
Pour in half of batter

Top with half of the Streusel
Add remaining batter and Struesel

Bake for 45-50 minutes at 350 degrees

If desire, dust with powdered sugar

Serve hot or cold

I wish you all the best in your efforts to protect and enhance our Lake Michigan shoreline.

Back in the 1920's my late father was one of the founders of the Polar Bear Club whose members chopped holes in the ice off Eastlake Terrace in Rogers Park, swam and then came to our apartment for breakfast prepared by my Mom.

Later, when competing in an annual Wrigley swim in Lake Ontario, Toronto, he either swam from the Evanston border to Navy Pier on his way to work each morning, or back home after work.   One day the lifeguard at Montrose Beach whistled him in as he was swimming north. "Where am I?" my Dad asked.   "Montrose Beach," said the guard. "Heck," my Dad said.   "I thought this was Milwaukee."   With that he dove back into the lake and swam north.

P.O. BOX 1280 • PILOT MOUNTAIN, N.C. 27041 • (919) 325-2502

# Shaw's
## CRAB HOUSE
### OYSTERS ALEXANDRA

Ingredients:

| | | | |
|---|---|---|---|
| 16 | Baked Oysters (Chesapeake Oysters) | | 1 cup Bechamel Sauce |
| 2 | lbs Spinach leaves steamed | | 1 T butter |
| 2 | Cups Romano cheese shredded | | 1 T flour |
| 1/2 | Cup mayonnaise | | 1 Qt milk |
| 2 | Oz Beer | | 2 to 4 T grated parmesan cheese |
| | | | 1 t ground cayenne pepper |

Juice of one lemon, 1 lemon, 1 lb rock salt, salt, white pepper

Directions:

a:  Bechamel Sauce- Melt butter over medium heat, add flour, stir, let cool in same pot. Bring milk to boil. Pour hot milk over cold roux (butter and flour). Bring to a boil stirring constantly, add salt and pepper, cook for 5 min.

1.  Creamed spinach -heat bechamel sauce (a) when hot add cooked spinach leaves, mix together. Verify seasoning.

2.  Cheese mixture-In a large bowl combine Romano cheese, beer and mayonnaise, add lemon juice and mix well. Add grated parmesan cheese til mixture is a dry consistency. Add cayenne pepper to taste.

-  Shuck oysters (remove oysters from shell) keep the bottom shells, reserve oysters in a cup.

-  Place 1 tsp of creamed spinach (1) on each half sheet.

-  Set one oyster on each spinach bed.

-  Top with cheese mixture (2) and bake in hot oven for 12 to 15 min.

-  Serve on a bed of rock salt with lemon wedge.

*This receipe was name after my Partner's Daughter*

21 East Hubbard Chicago, Illinois 60611
312-527-2722

# Mary Rubloff

## CAVIAR PIE

Line glass pie plate with finely chopped egg salad (slightly on dry side.)

Cover egg salad with finely diced onions

Spread caviar to cover.

Garnish with finely diced fresh parsley around rim.

After chilling to set, place dollop of sour cream in center and serve on toast points.

Delicious

305-832-7300 Two Breakers Row, Palm Beach, Florida 33480

**MARTY RUSSO**
3D DISTRICT, ILLINOIS

**COMMITTEE ON WAYS AND MEANS**

**COMMITTEE ON THE BUDGET**

**DEMOCRATIC STEERING AND POLICY COMMITTEE**

**DEPUTY WHIP**

# Congress of the United States
## House of Representatives
### Washington, DC 20515

OFFICES:
2233 RAYBURN BUILDING
WASHINGTON, DC 20515
202-225-5736

10634 SOUTH CICERO
OAK LAWN, IL 60453-5295
312-353-8093

April 1, 1988

### PEANUT BUTTER CAKE

1 pkg (1 lb, 3 1/2 oz) yellow cake mix
2 eggs
1/2 cup creamy peanut butter

### FROSTING

1 cup prepared chocolate syrup
1/4 cup light corn syrup
1 cup of creamy peanut butter
1/2 cup coarsely chopped peanuts

1. Preheat oven to 350F. Lightly grease & flour 2 (9-inch) layer cake pans.
2. Prepare cake mix as package label directs, using 2 eggs, amount of water specified on package, and 1/2 cup peanut butter.
3. Turn batter into prepared pans. Bake 25 to 30 minutes, or until surface springs back when gently pressed with fingertip.
4. Let cool in pans, 10 minutes. Turn out of pans; cool completely on wire rack.
5. Make Frosting: In medium bowl, combine chocolate syrup and 1 cup peanut butter. With portable electric mixer at medium speed, beat until combined.
6. Add corn syrup, and beat until frosting is creamy smooth and thick enough to spread.
7. On cake plate, put cake layers together with 3/4 cup frosting. Use rest to frost top and side of cake.
8. Sprinkle chopped peanuts over top of cake.

Makes 8 to 10 servings.

MR/kc

*Marty Russo*

# FRANCOIS, Inc.
## 156 Inverrary Lane
## Deerfield, IL 60015
## 312-541-4451

Wilted Lettuce with Bacon

1 head lettuce
Salt
2 thick slices bacon
1 medium onion, sliced

2 teaspoons sugar, about
¼ cup vinegar
½ cup water

First, wash and drain lettuce. Break into small pieces and place in mixing bowl. Sprinkle with salt and set aside.

Then, cut bacon into very small cubes and fry slowly with onions until brown. Add sugar and stir. Mix together vinegar and water. Add to skillet and bring to a boil.

Shake salty water from lettuce and place lettuce in salad bowl. Pour boiling vinegar-bacon mixture over lettuce. Toss gently.

Serves 6.

REMINISCING!

I ate Mom's Wilted Lettuce since I was knee high to a grasshopper. My late mother Mary made it often as I grew up, even in later years when I visited her in Miami Beach. Yet it was my sister Virginia Perlinski (Grayslake, IL) who reintroduced the treasured recipe to me (after Mom passed on) and to my daughter Christine Samaan. Both of them now have it perfected to a T --like Mom used to make. It took my Italian wife Gina about 8 preparations to get the knack of it -- the way I like it and now she too has it down pat.

After spending 13 years in Las Vegas broadcasting/telecasting, I never found a chef there who could make it like Mom -- and that adult Disneyland has the best chefs in the world -- NEXT TO CHICAGO.

STO LAT!!

*Sig Sakowicz*

# Abominable Snowman Delight

½ Gallon Vanilla Ice Cream
2½ Cups Shredded Coconut
1 Pint Sour Cream
1 Pkg Shredded Pecan Nuts
1 Can Sliced Pineapple
1 Can Naturally Sweetened Fruit Cocktail
1 Pkg Mini Marshmallows
1 Jar Maraschino Cherries
1 Pound Cake

Scoop ice cream into balls and roll them in shredded coconut. Place on a plate and refreeze while preparing sauce. Mix the fruit cocktail (drained), sour cream, pecans and marshmallows. Cut 1" slices of pound cake and place each on a plate. Add a slice of pineapple and put a coconut ball on top. Generously spoon sauce over balls, add a cherry and WOW!

**EXPRESS-WAYS CHILDREN'S MUSEUM**

Giraldo Rosales
Age 8 years
Beaubien Elementary, Third Grade

Express-Ways Children's Museum is a cultural institution dedicated to encouraging creative, participatory learning. Through interactive exhibits and programs, children are inspired to use the arts for discovery and self-expression.

For more information and public drop-in hours, call 527-1000.

Sincerely,

Dianne L. Sautter
Executive Director

## THE CHILDREN'S MUSEUM COOKS UP A LOT OF FUN

(312) 281-3222

## OFFICE OF THE MAYOR
### CITY OF CHICAGO

**EUGENE SAWYER**
ACTING MAYOR

HERE IS MY DAUGHTER SHERYL'S RECIPE FOR **SWEET POTATO PIE**.

**BLEND WELL**
SIX TABLESPOONS BROWN SUGAR
TWO TABLESPOONS WHITE SUGAR
HALF TEASPOON SALT
ONE TEASPOON CINNAMON
HALF TEASPOON GINGER
HALF TEASPOON CLOVE
HALF CUP DARK CORN SYRUP
THREE SLIGHTLY BEATEN EGGS

**MIX IN**
FOUR MEDIUM SIZED SWEET POTATOES, COOKED AND MASHED
ONE AND ONE HALF CUPS UNDILUTED EVAPORATED MILK
  (OR RICH CREAM)
ONE TEASPOON VANILLA (OR TWO TABLESPOONS BRANDY OR RUM)
3/4 CUP BLACK WALNUT MEATS (OPTIONAL)

- LINE 9 INCH PIE PAN WITH PIE CRUST
- BUILD UP A HIGH FLUTED EDGE
- POUR SWEET POTATO MIXTURE INTO THE PIESHELL
- BAKE THE PIE IN A HOT OVEN (425) FOR ABOUT ONE HOUR
OR UNTIL A KNIFE INSERTED IN THE FILLING COMES OUT CLEAN

BEST WISHES AND BON APPETIT!

*Eugene Sawyer*
MAYOR

**Schaefer's** A VINTAGE NAME IN SPIRITS
— SINCE 1936 —
9965 Gross Point Rd. • Skokie, IL 60076 • Phones: (312) 673-5711
673-5712
256-0700
256-0705

July 19, 1988

I'm a beef-lover. My favorite preparation is rare (is there any other kind?) tenderloin with a mushroom sauce that has been in our family for years. It's simple to prepare and absolutely delicious. Here's how:

### BEEF TENDERLOIN SAUCE

- 1 pound fresh mushrooms
- 2 cans (10.5 oz. each) beef broth
- 6 ounces sweet vermouth *
- 2-3 teaspoons cornstarch

Roast the tenderloin on a rack in a shallow roasting pan containing 15 ounces of beef broth. Slice mushrooms and sauté them in butter in a frying pan. Add to the sautéed mushrooms the remaining 6 ounces of beef broth that has been thickened with cornstarch (follow directions on box). Add 6 ounces of sweet vermouth and the drippings from the roasting pan. Continue to cook and stir until the sauce is thickened and clear. Season to taste. Warning: it can be addictive!

Enjoy with a nice bottle of California Cabernet Sauvignon or red Bordeaux.

To your health,

*George J. Schaefer*

\* I frequently substitute sweet vermouth for red wine in recipes. It adds an intriguing spice and "secret flavor".

CABLE ADDRESS: JUDOL

PHONE: (312) 477-6000

# JUDGE & DOLPH, Ltd.
*Division of Wirtz Corporation*

**Importing Distributors • Wholesale Liquor & Wine Dealers**

**2037-81 North Clybourn Avenue, Chicago, Illinois 60614**

November 8, 1988

When Ellie and I first got married, she was probably the worse cook I have ever known. I often would tell her after she prepared a meal that she couldn't even boil water without burning it.

Well, that was a longtime ago. Today, she is probably the best cook I know. One of our favorite recipes is a dish called Turkish Pilaf.

    6 T   butter
    Full ½ cup green peppers (cut into ½ inch pieces)
    1 cup canned or fresh tomatoes (we always use fresh)
    1 large clove garlic (put thru press)
    1 cup fresh mushrooms
    1 tablespoon salt, a little black pepper
    1 pound (2¼ cups) rice and about 2 cups water

Melt butter in heavy saucepan. Add green pepper, mushrooms and garlic, saute 5 minutes. Add tomatoes and seasonings, hot water, and rice. Stir only till mixed. Cover tightly; let come to quick boil, then let cook <u>slowly</u> over low heat about 25 to 30 minutes, until tender but not <u>soft</u>. Do not uncover during cooking and avoid stirring.

One might also find it delicious to add strips of cooked leftover chicken, meat or shrimp.

Enjoy! I certainly do everytime it's served.

Sincerely,

Norman H. Schatz
Executive Vice President

NHS/lct

**"The House That Cares"**

# Alan Schriesheim

**SALMON MOUSSE ARGONNE**

As a world center of research and development, Argonne National Laboratory plays host to hundreds of visitors from every continent each year. What they most often mention after they return to their homes are the extraordinary research facilities and staff, the hundreds of white deer that roam the Argonne site and the salmon mousse, my wife Beatrice's favorite recipe for our newcomers' welcoming dinners. The dish admirably combines the arts and sciences -- of convenient cuisine.

Alan Schriesheim, Director
Argonne National Laboratory

### Salmon Mousse

1 16 oz. can of salmon
2 envelopes Knox gelatin
2 T lemon juice
2 t dill weed
3/4 c chopped olives with pimientos
2 c Hellmann's mayonnaise
1/3 c chile sauce
1 T Worcestershire sauce
4 chopped hard boiled eggs
1/2 c chopped cucumber
1/4 c chopped onions

Drain the salmon and save the liquid. Add water to the liquid to equal 1/2 c and add gelatin. Bone and flake salmon. Place bowl containing gelatin plus juice in pan of hot water to dissolve gel.

Mix mayonnaise, chile sauce, Worcestershire sauce and lemon juice with mixer. Stir in salmon juice containing the dissolved gel. Add remaining ingredients. Turn into an oiled 1-1/2 quart mold (or two fish molds) and refrigerate.

* * * * * * * * *

*Chicagoland Association of Barbershop Chapters*

# THE BEST RECIPE IN THE WORLD

> MIX WELL AND STIR HEAVY DOSES OF HARMONY AND GOOD FELLOWSHIP AND YOU'VE GOT THE BEST RECIPE IN THE WORLD. AND, SIMPLY, THAT'S WHAT WE'RE ALL ABOUT.

Yours in harmony,

*Phil*

Philip Schwimmer

---

C.A.B.C. is an association of 15 member chapters, with 15 additional participating chapters (14 of which are female chapters) on our annual show calendar/chapter directory. Our international organization is the Society for the Preservation and Encouragement of Barbershop Quartet Singing in America. We are not-for profit and non-union.

# WJMK MAGIC 104 FM
## The Greatest Hits of All Time!

*"HOT MEXICAN DIP"*

1 lb. Ground Chuck (extra lean beef)
1 28 oz. can of diced tomatoes
1 pkg. French's Chili-O-Mix
1 bunch green onions - chopped
brick of Pinconing or Colby cheese, sliced
Taco chips

Brown ground beef. Remove from skillet & drain on paper towel - pat dry to remove grease.
Return beef to skillet. Add tomatoes, Chili-o-mix - bring to boil, then simmer 20 minutes.
In a baking dish, layer Chili - beef mix, sliced cheese (cover beef) & green onions. Repeat, using all ingredients, making approx. 3 layers, ending with cheese on top. (top layer of cheese melts best if it is *thinly* sliced)
Bake in oven at 425° for 20 minutes, then serve with Taco chips.

This is my "most requested" recipe - I can finally quit copying it over!

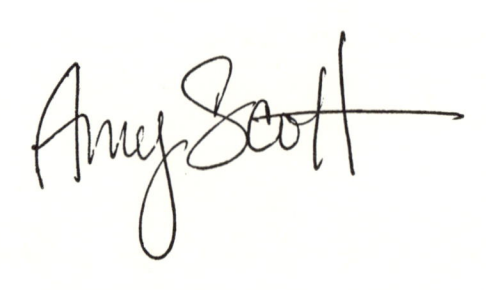

*Amy Scott*

180 North Michigan Avenue • Suite 1200 • Chicago, IL • 60601   (312) 977-1800

A DIVISION OF infinity BROADCASTING CORPORATION

**Jonathan Scott Enterprises, LTD.**

PRODUCERS OF THE AWARD WINNING TELEVISION SERIES

**Street beat**

JONATHAN SCOTT'S STREETBEAT HANGOVER RECIPE!

After a long, hard evening of videotaping mini-skirt contests, Jose' Cuervo look-alike contests, and Blues Brothers parties, I sometimes stumble home at 5 a.m., knowing full well that I have the same schedule the next day.

To meet the rigorous demands of the job, I follow this recipe:

- Three (3) regular aspirins (two is not good enough)

- Throw ten (10) drops of Wesson Oil on a skillet

- Wet and drop one (1) flour tortilla on the hot, oiled skillet. (corn is not as good)

- Carefully, cut, and drop cheddar cheese on the flour tortilla.

- Spoon out a teaspoon of La Prefirida or, LaVictoria Mild Salsa, or, Taco Sauce on the cheesed flour tortilla.

Repeat.

Bon Apetit!

*Jonathan Scott*

P.O. Box 14650 • Chicago, Illinois 60614    312-883-8810

The Crate and Barrel
Administrative Offices
725 Landwehr Road
Northbrook, Illinois 60062-2393
Telephone: (312) 272-2888
Telex: 724484
Fax: (312) 272-5276

## TENDERLOIN PIQUANT CHEZ CRATE

1 whole trimmed beef tenderloin - 5-7 lbs. (not larded)
Fresh cracked pepper
Garlic salt

¼ cup butter at room temperature
1 green pepper, seeded and sliced
1 red pepper, seeded and sliced
1 large Bermuda onion, sliced
2 Tblspns vegetable oil

1 cup tomato ketchup
3 garlic cloves, minced
3 Tblspns Worcestershire sauce
3 Tblspns chopped fresh parsley
1 Tblspn lemon juice
½ cup melted butter
¼ tspn salt

Remove beef tenderloin from refrigerator for ½ hour before rubbing with ¼ cup butter and seasoning with pepper and garlic salt. Broil meat for 6 minutes on each side to sear in juices. In the meantime, saute green and red peppers and onion in oil until slightly transparent, approximately 5 minutes. Do not brown vegetables. Set vegetables aside.

Mix the following ingredients together in a bowl for the sauce: ketchup, garlic, worcestershire sauce, parsley, lemon juice, ½ cup melted butter, and salt.

Remove meat from broiler. Put sauce over meat and then put vegetables on top of sauce. Let stand for ½-1 hour to marinate. Then bake uncovered in a 350° oven for 3/4 hour for rare. Remove meat from oven and let stand for 10 minutes before slicing into 1 inch pieces. Serves 6-8 people.

*Gordon and Carole Segal*

# Crate&Barrel

**CHARLES SHABICA & ASSOCIATES, INC.**
COASTAL CONSULTANTS
345 WALNUT STREET
NORTHFIELD, ILLINOIS 60093

(312) 446-4357

*I'M SORRY BUT THAT'S WHAT THEY'RE CALLED*

*SURE*

Edison

## SANDTARTS

MIX WELL TOGETHER
- 1/2 pound butter
- 1 pound sugar
- 3 egg yolks

Add enough flour to handle (cookie dough) about 4 1/2 cups

Roll VERY THIN and cut into diamond shapes
Brush with egg white
Sprinkle on sugar and/or cinnamon
Stick an unbleached almond on each (use egg white)
Put on greased cookie sheet & Bake in 375° oven for about 5 minutes
Remove from cookie sheet immediately to cool

This is Susie's Pennsylvania Dutch grandmother's recipe for which she is dearly loved.

Dr. Charles W. Shabica, President

# CITY COUNCIL
### CITY OF CHICAGO

## COUNCIL CHAMBER
CITY HALL, ROOM 209
121 N. LA SALLE STREET - 60602
744 6831

**HELEN SHILLER**
Alderman, 46th Ward

1138 West Montrose Avenue
Telephone: 878-4646

## BREAKFAST PIE

CRUST (You can use a prepared crust, graham cracker, or my favorite pastry crust). The pastry crust takes longer, but is worth the time.

Pastry Crust Ingredients:
- 1 and one-half cups flour
- Three-fourths cup of margarine or butter
- one-half cup sugar

Preparation:
1. Cut butter into flour and sugar with a fork or dinner knife. Mix with hands until completely mixed.
2. Refrigerate for 15 minutes to a half-hour.
3. Press into pie pan (a little extra may be left if it's a small 8" pan).
4. Prick the crust with a fork.
5. Line the crust completely with aluminum foil and add a little layer of dried beans.
6. Bake at 450 degrees for 10 minutes; lower to 350 degrees and bake for another 15 to 20 minutes or until golden brown (remove beans and foil for last five minutes if it is not browning well).
7. Cool

## FILLING

Filling Ingredients:
- 1 cup nonfat plain yogurt
- 1 cup lowfat cottage cheese (lowfat/no salt is preferable)
- 3 tablespoons honey
- 1 teaspoon vanilla

Preparation:
1. Press the ingredients through a colander or sieve or run through a food processor until smooth.
2. Pour into a cooled crust.
3. Cover the top with your favorite fruit. I prefer blueberries, strawberries cut in half or sliced peaches.

GRAHAM TOPPING (This is optional, but makes the pie much fancier.)

Topping Ingredients:
- 1 cup graham crumbs
- 6 tablespoons margarine or butter
- one-half cup of sugar

Preparation:
1. Melt butter then mix in the rest of the ingredients.
2. Sprinkle on top of the pie
3. Refrigerate the entire pie for at least an hour before serving.

# 7 INCH SALAD

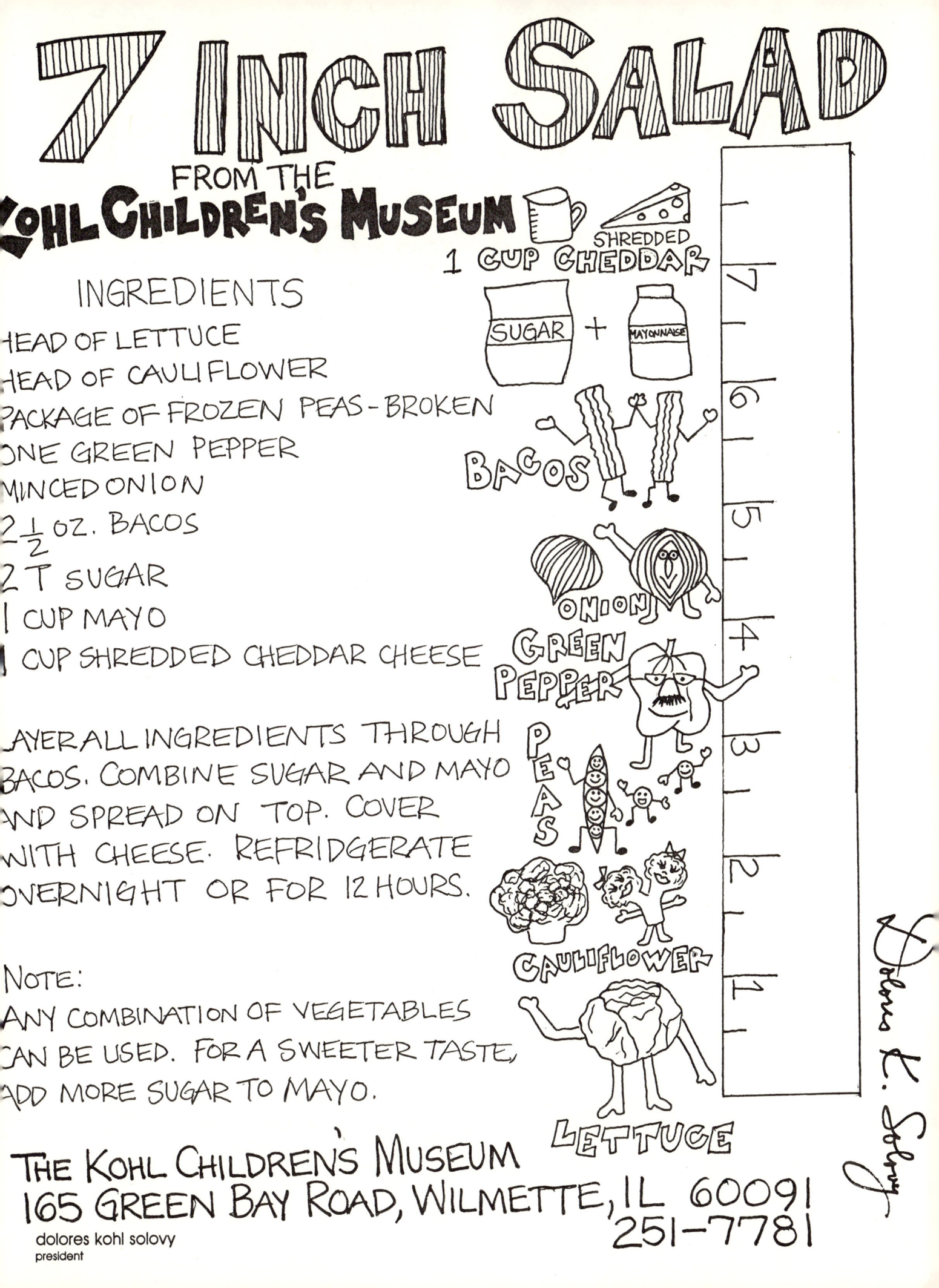

## FROM THE Kohl Children's Museum

### INGREDIENTS
- Head of lettuce
- Head of cauliflower
- Package of frozen peas - broken
- One green pepper
- Minced onion
- 2½ oz. Bacos
- 2 T sugar
- 1 cup mayo
- 1 cup shredded cheddar cheese

Layer all ingredients through Bacos. Combine sugar and mayo and spread on top. Cover with cheese. Refridgerate overnight or for 12 hours.

NOTE:
Any combination of vegetables can be used. For a sweeter taste, add more sugar to mayo.

The Kohl Children's Museum
165 Green Bay Road, Wilmette, IL 60091
251-7781

dolores kohl solovy
president

# THE ORCHESTRAL ASSOCIATION
# CHICAGO SYMPHONY ORCHESTRA
CIVIC ORCHESTRA OF CHICAGO • CHICAGO SYMPHONY CHORUS • ALLIED ARTS ASSOCIATION • ORCHESTRA HALL

220 SOUTH MICHIGAN AVENUE, CHICAGO, ILLINOIS • 60604

TELEPHONE: (312) 435-8122
TELEX: 25-3866
CABLE ADDRESS: CHICAGORCH

SIR GEORG SOLTI
MUSIC DIRECTOR

HENRY FOGEL
EXECUTIVE VICE PRESIDENT
AND EXECUTIVE DIRECTOR

## SIR GEORG SOLTI'S GOULASH

*Serves six*

| | | | |
|---|---|---|---|
| 1/2 pound onions | 250 g | Salt | |
| Two ounces lard | 50 mL | Four pints beef stock | 2 L |
| 2 1/2 pounds braising steak cut into 1/2 inch (1 cm) cubes | 1 Kg | Two tablespoons paprika use finest quality | 25 mL |
| 1/2 pound beef heart *(opt)* cut into 1/2 inch (1 cm) cubes | 250 g | 1/2 pound tomatoes | 250 g |
| Two garlic cloves | | Two green peppers | |
| One pinch caraway seeds | | One pound potatoes cut into 1/2 inch (1 cm) cubes | 500 g |

---

Peel and dice onions. Melt lard in heavy-bottom saucepan; saute onions but do not colour. Add beef (and heart if used) and saute for about ten minutes.

Chop and crush garlic, caraway seed and salt. Remove beef from heat and stir in paprika and garlic mixture. Add beef stock and return to heat with lid on and simmer for at least 1 to 1 1/2 hours.

Peel and dice tomatoes, core and cut peppers into rings and add to meat; simmer for a further 30 minutes adding more stock if required to keep to a soup-like consistency. Add potatoes and cook til all is tender.

Serve with little dumplings.

**Chicago Peregrine Release**

2001 N. Clark Street
Chicago, Illinois 60614
312/477/HAWK

The Chicago
Academy of Sciences

Lincoln Park Zoo

Illinois Department
of Conservation

Chicago Audubon
Society

### Squab Stuffed with Chestnuts

For six squabs take one pint chestnuts boiled and peeled of both shells. (An easy way to remove the inner shell is to take the outer shell off when about half boiled and set on the fire again for a few minutes.) Take a little more than a cup of bread crumbs. Brown all in a pan with lump of butter, size of an egg, with a little onion and salt and pepper to taste, then fill the squabs and place in oven until done.

Selected and submitted by Mark Spreyer (Director, Chicago Peregrine Release) from National Standard Squab Book by Elmer C. Rice (1901).

In 1988 for the first time since 1951, the cries of wild-hatched peregrine falcons could be heard in Illinois. Ironically, the cries of the federally endangered species were heard over the state's most densely populated city, and around the world's tallest building.

The parents were the products of two peregrine release projects. The female, was released in Minneapolis in 1985. The male was released in Chicago in 1986. Another Chicago male from that year, has taken up residence on the north side.

Of all the Chicago birds, "MacArthur" is most noteworthy. He is raising chicks with a Minnesota female in Milwaukee. This is the first record of two falcons, both only a year old, successfully breeding.

©The Chicago Academy of Sciences

# CHICAGO WILDFLOWER WORKS INCORPORATED

*HERE'S SOMETHING PRETTY ENOUGH TO EAT...*

## Wildflowers!

### EVENING YELLOW PRIMROSE

*Botanical Name*
*Onagraceae*

Uses: Vegetables and Salads

Roots taste like parsnips and are cooked like sweet potatoes.

### EVENING PRIMROSE FRITTERS

Clean and scrub one pound of roots and boil in a little water for about 30 minutes until they are tender.

Drain and mash.

Then mix in 1 oz. of warm butter, one tablespoon of flour, 2 eggs and a pinch of salt.

Mixture should be stiff.

Then shape into flat cake.
Coat with egg yolk and bread crumbs and
Fry until brown.

Serve with fish or meat.

Boiled roots when cold can be sliced and added to salads and stews.

### MANGE-TOUT WITH PRIMROSES SALAD*

Cook mange-tout one to two minutes until tender and still crunchy.
Drain and immediately plunge into iced water.
Drain again and dry.

Serve dressed with lemon juice and sunflower oil and scatter with freshly picked primroses for a delicate and refreshing spring salad.

* Mange-tout is similar to pea pods.

*Bernice B. Sproesser*
*Chicago Wildflower Works I, Inc.*

CHICAGO WILDFLOWER WORKS INCORPORATED, 1759 NORTH SEDGWICK, CHICAGO, ILLINOIS 60614   (312) 951-0789

# Stagman ETC

## Heavenly Glazed Party Nuts

Mix together 2 egg whites and 1 cup sugar — beat into peaks.
When beaten well, fold in 2½ lbs. of pecans and/or walnuts.
Spread sugar-nut mixture in cookie sheet with sides which has been sprayed with PAM.
Bake for 20 min. in a 325° oven. Then turn over nuts and continue baking for approximately another 20 min. or until lightly golden.
Let cool and then place in air tight container. They will stay fresh for 3 weeks.
P.S. For a change of taste add 2 tbls. of cinnamon to egg-sugar mixture.
They are the delights of any party.

Cookie & Barry Stagman

**COMMITTEES:**
TRANSPORTATION
HUMAN SERVICES
ENERGY AND NATURAL
 RESOURCES
LABOR AND COMMERCE
SMALL BUSINESS

## GENERAL ASSEMBLY
### STATE OF ILLINOIS

*James R. Stange*

STATE REPRESENTATIVE • 44TH DISTRICT

**CAPITOL OFFICE:**
ROOM 2137
WILLIAM G. STRATTON BUILDING
SPRINGFIELD, ILLINOIS 62706
217/782-6401

**DISTRICT OFFICE:**
2625 BUTTERFIELD ROAD
SUITE 221 WEST
OAK BROOK, ILLINOIS 60521
312/574-0171

### BEEF STROGANOFF

| | |
|---|---|
| 1½# | Sirloin, cut into ¼" strips |
| 2 | T. butter |
| 1 | cup celery, thinly sliced |
| 1 | Pinch garlic |
| 1 | T. parsley flakes (optional) |
| 5 | T. flour |
| ½ | cup butter |
| 2 | 10 oz. cans beef broth |
| ¼ | cup dry sherry |
| ¼ | cup tomato paste |
| 1 | cup sour cream |

In large skillet over medium high heat, brown sirloin in 2 tablespoons butter. Add celery, garlic powder and parsley. Cook 15 minutes, stirring frequently. In heavy 3-quart sauce pan, brown flour in ¼ cup butter, stirring constantly with wire whisk. Stir in beef broth. Cook until thickened. Stir gravy, sherry and tomato paste into sirloin mixture in skillet. Cook until sirloin is tender. Stir in sour cream and serve over hot cooked noodles or rice. Serves 6.

We find this dish is an excellent one to serve on election nights as we celebrate our Republican* victories!

\* No disclaimer intended ... it would be perfect for Democratic election parties also!!

state...uh..representative..illinois 58th

# grace mary stern
### 291 marshman street
### highland park, illinois 60035

New England fish chowder.. great for a cold night!

1 med. onion - chopped
oil to sauté it in
1 pkg frozen.. well, semi-frozen.. cod or haddock (or whatever)
1 large potato, peeled & in ½" cubes
water
milk
little bit of flour.. butter
salt & pepper

Sauté the chopped onion until soft. Add the potato & enough water to barely cover, & some salt. Simmer until nearly tender, add the fish & continue to simmer.

In another pan, melt -- oh, maybe 3 tbsp. butter. Add enough flour to thicken.. stir & then add milk, salt & pepper & bring it to a near-boil. (If it boils, the milk will curdle!) It should be slightly thickened.

Combine the two into a magnificent chowder & serve with a salad, crackers & cheese & whatever other good things you have in the fridge.

To piece it out the next day, add a can of creamed corn, reheat & serve (with gusto..)

Grace Mary

203

Mrs. Gardner H. Stern
1300 Lake Shore Drive, Chicago, Illinois 60610

## Tomato Pudding

Chop one 16 oz can of tomatoes and heat for five minutes.

Fill a casserole with loose bits of white bread, and stir in 1 1/2 sticks of melted butter.

Stir in 1 1/2 cups of brown sugar. Stir in the hot tomato mixture and salt to taste.

Bake covered in 325 oven for 20 or 30 minutes. Stir once or twice to thoroughly mix.

Hauchen S. Stern

# CHICAGO STING

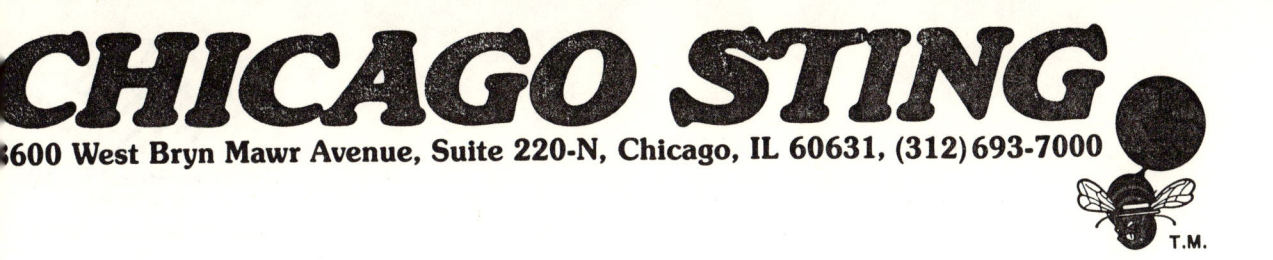

3600 West Bryn Mawr Avenue, Suite 220-N, Chicago, IL 60631, (312) 693-7000

RECIPE from LEE B. STERN

## VEAL

| 2 | Veal Chops, 10 ounces each |
| 1/2 tsp. | Lawry Salt |
| 1/2 tsp. | Mrs. Dash |
| 4 | Chopped Green Onions |

Sprinkle Lawry Salt and Mrs. Dash on both sides.

Broil 5 minutes each side.

Remove from oven, spread green onions on top, and broil 1 minute.

*Lee B. Stern*

Lee B. Stern
Owner and Chairman
CHICAGO STING

Michael T. Stirdivant

**SWEET POTATO SOUFFLE'**

6 Sweet potatoes, medium
1/2 teaspoon salt
2 tablespoons butter
1 egg beaten
1 teaspoon of Vanilla
1/2 cup raisins
3 tablespoons grated orange rind
1/4 cup whipping cream or half-and-half
Pinch of freshly grated nutmeg
1 cup miniature marshmallows

Boil the potatoes with the skins on until tender. Peel, and run the vegetables through a potato ricer into an electric mixing bowl. Add the remaining ingredients, except the optional marshmallows, and whip until light.

Place in a baking dish and top with the marshmallows. Bake at 375 degrees for 10-15 minutes or until the marshmallows brown and the dish is hot.

Serves 8

Michael T. Stirdivant
Executive Director

*The Club that beats the streets.*

**BOYS & GIRLS CLUBS** OF CHICAGO

**General Services Center**
625 West Jackson Boulevard
Suite 300
Chicago, IL 60606
(312) 648-1666

**Officers**
W. Clement Stone
*Honorary Chairman of the Board*
Robert B. Holzkamp
*President*
W. Mitchell LaMotte
*Past President*
John E. Swearingen
*Past Chairman*
Daniel A. Cotter
*Executive Vice President/
President's Council*
John J. Flieder
*Executive Vice President/
Development*
Mrs. Neele E. Stearns, Jr.
*Executive Vice President/
Woman's Board President*
Mural R. Josephson
*Treasurer*
Andre Rice
*Secretary*
Michael T. Stirdivant
*Executive Director*
Renae Ogletree
*Associate Executive Director/
Operations*

**Board of Directors**
John A. Breen
Keith J. Brown
Peter Bynoe
Denis H. Carroll
Theodore E. Cesarz
Richard H. Cooper
Mrs. Lester Crown
Hugh M. Dickinson
Thomas W. Fawell
Lee. F. Flaherty
Randall J. Gingiss
Bruce K. Goodman
Thomas Hill, Jr.
James L. Isham
Sheila King
William E. Lowry, Jr.
Adrian Lozano
Philip I. Mappa
Mrs. Graham J. Morgan
Mrs. Joseph G. Nellis
O. Robert Nottelmann
Norman Perlmutter
Jim Rose
Charles J. Ruder
Eugene E. Ruth
Patrick G. Ryan
Gordon Skeoch
Macey B. Smith
Mrs. William L. Smith
Robert A. Southern
Gary F. Spahn
Robert G. Streit
Mrs. John E. Swearingen
Albert G. Terrell
* Hon. Harold Washington
Mrs. Clayton E. Whiting, Jr.

**Trustees**
Jack Brickhouse
Isidore Brown
Wallace E. Carroll
Henry Crown
Thomas A. Dean
George M. Eisenberg
Hon. Saul A. Epton
Harold M. Finley
J. Burke Gelling
John D. Gray
J. Ira Harris
Robert S. Hartman
Addis E. Hull
Edward R. James
Joseph E. Luecke
Gordon M. Metcalf
David C. Meyers
Michael R. Notaro
Vernon J. Pellouchoud
Richard S. Pepper
Hon. Charles H. Percy
Sol Polk
Henry Regnery

* Deceased

### Crickettes
THE LADIES WHO LUNCH

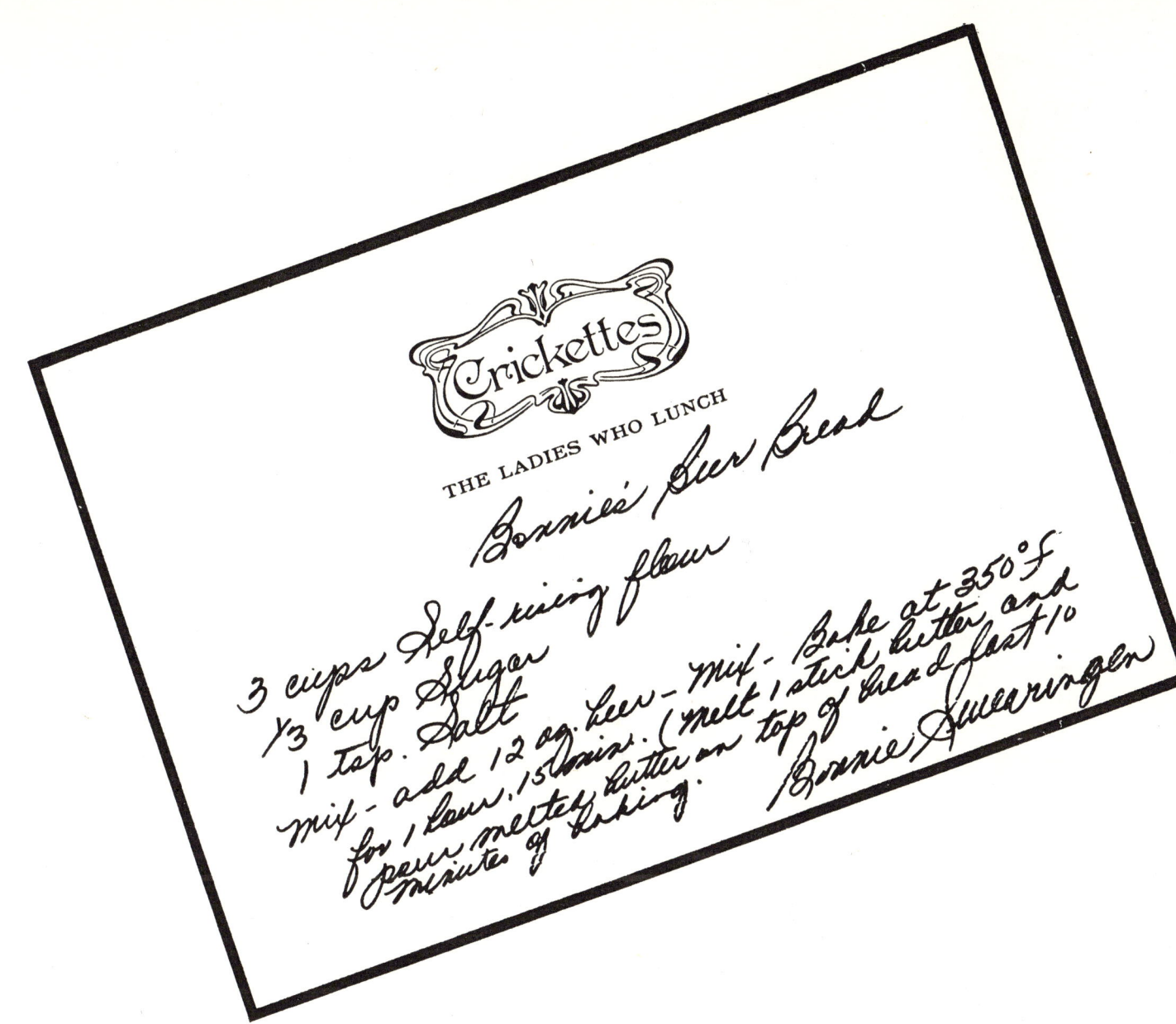

*Bonnie's Beer Bread*

3 cups self-rising flour
1/3 cup sugar
1 tsp. salt
mix - add 12 oz. beer - mix - Bake at 350°F
for 1 hour, 15 min. (melt 1 stick butter and
pour melted butter on top of bread last 10
minutes of baking.

*Bonnie Swearingen*

## Cheese and Chutney Canapes

| | |
|---|---|
| 1/4 lb | Grated sharp cheddar cheese |
| 3 oz | Cream cheese |
| 1/4 tsp | Dry mustard (small tsp) |
| 1/2 tsp | Worchestershire sauce (small tsp) |
| dash | Tobasco |
| 1 | Egg yolk |
| 1 | Egg white |

Beat egg white. Fold in above mixture into beaten egg white.

| | |
|---|---|
| 1/2 cup | Major Grey Chutney (chopped fine) |
| 6 slices | Crisp bacon, crumbled and mixed with chutney |

Butter toast rounds on one side and broil (do not burn)
(use regular sliced white bread). On unbuttered side pipe cheese
mixture with fork on border and fill center with chutney mixture.
Broil until cheese is melted.
Makes about 20 canapes.

## The "Bakery" RESTAURANT

2218 N. Lincoln Avenue  
Chicago, Illinois 60614

Reservations (312) 472-6942  
Open Tue.- Sat. 5 - 11 p.m.

### STOCK YARD INN MARINATED BEEF
*Serves 8*

1 pound boiled, broiled, or roasted beef, cut into julienne strips
1 large onion, cut the same as the beef
juice of 1 lemon
salt to taste
1½ tablespoons prepared mustard
2 tablespoons sugar
¼ teaspoon freshly ground black pepper
2 teaspoons (or more) curry powder
2 cups sour cream
½ cup white vinegar
salt to taste
lettuce leaves for decoration
sprinkling of paprika
sprinkling of chopped parsley for decoration

In a large bowl, mix together the beef and onion. Sprinkle with lemon juice and salt. Let stand at room temperature for 20 minutes.

In another bowl, mix the mustard, sugar, pepper, and curry powder until it forms a paste. Gently fold the sour cream and vinegar into the spice mixture. Fold this sauce into the beef and onions. Let it marinate in the refrigerator for at least 4 hours.

Taste for salt; add more if necessary. Serve on beds of lettuce, sprinkle with paprika and parsley.

CHEF'S SECRET   This recipe originated in Chicago at the famous Stock Yard Inn. Its secret is really in the quality of the meat used. Do not use any fat; use only the lean or marbled beef. If you feel the quality of the meat you have is not the best, cut the julienne strips very small—no bigger than matchsticks—and avoid cutting along the grain.

Marinating the beef and onions in the lemon juice and salt gives a very good taste to the beef, which will not be overpowered by the lemon. If you were to do the marinating with vinegar, the taste would be impaired.

*It is great picnic food at the beautifull beaches of dark studiey ous!*

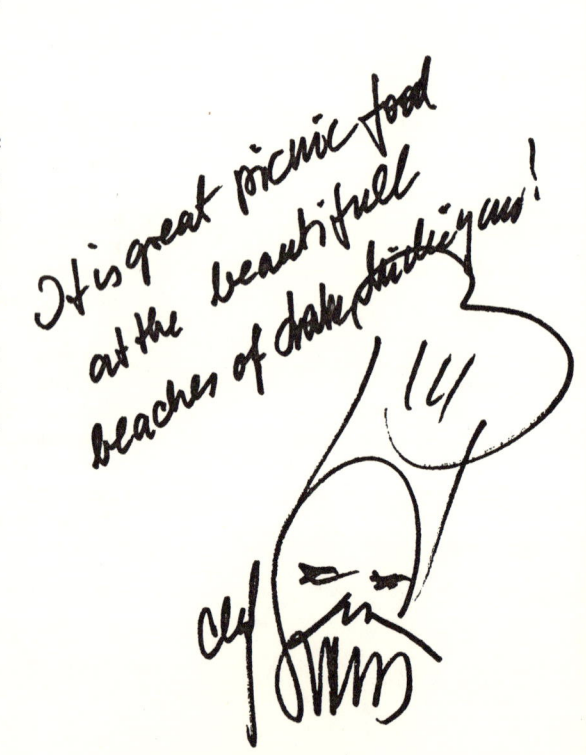

**CHICAGO WHITE SOX**
324 W. 35th STREET
CHICAGO, ILLINOIS 60616
(312) 924-1000

## CHICKEN BREASTS FLORENTINE

INGREDIENTS:
2 c. white sauce
1 c. cheddar cheese
1 T. butter
1/2 c. onion, chopped
1/2 lb. mushrooms
2- 10 oz. pkg. chopped spinach
1/4 tsp. dried basil leaf
1/8 tsp. nutmeg
1 1/2 tsp. salt
1/4 tsp. pepper
2 tsp. lemon juice
4 whole chicken breats, deboned and halved

DIRECTIONS: In large skillet, melt butter. Add onion and mushrooms and cook until tender. Add spinach. Cover and cook 5 minutes. Stir in spices and lemon juice. Turn into a shallow 3 qt. baking dish. Top with chicken breasts and pour cheese sauce over all. Bake, uncovered, in 375 degree oven for 45 minutes until chicken is tender.

Wonderful served with wild rice, fresh green beans and homemade rolls.

KERI THIGPEN

BOBBY THIGPEN

*Executive Mansion*
*Springfield, Illinois 62701*

LINCOLN LOGS

1½ cups diced, cooked chicken
1½ cups bread crumbs
1 cup walnuts, finely chopped
¼ cup celery, finely chopped
¼ cup onion, finely chopped
½ teaspoon salt
¼ teaspoon paprika

**THICK WHITE SAUCE MADE WITH:**

½ cup chicken stock
½ cup cream

Mix chicken, bread crumbs, walnuts, celery, onion, salt and paprika. Moisten with sauce. Form mixture into logs three inches long. Roll in bread crumbs and fry in oil. Drain and serve with white sauce.

Mrs. James R. Thompson

**DISTRICT OFFICE:**
8609 W. CERMAK ROAD
NORTH RIVERSIDE, IL 60546
312/442-0134

**CAPITOL OFFICE:**
ROOM 113 STATE HOUSE
SPRINGFIELD, IL 62706
217/782-8180

**COMMITTEES:**
APPROPRIATIONS I
PUBLIC HEALTH,
 WELFARE & CORRECTIONS
TRANSPORTATION

## ILLINOIS STATE SENATE
# JUDY BAAR TOPINKA
*State Senator - 22nd District*

These recipes were special to my mom who passed away recently, and I hope they become special to you-all.

My schedule as a State Senator doesn't leave me much time at home to bake, and I'd probably gain weight as well . . .so you can bake and have my calories!

Enjoy!

### APPLE YUM YUM CAKE

2 c. sugar
2 eggs
2 tsp. soda
1 tsp. cinnamon
4 c. apples, chopped fine
½ c. shortening
2 c. flour
1 tsp. nutmeg
1 c. chopped nuts
½ tsp. salt

Sauce:
1 c. white sugar
1 c. brown sugar
1 tsp. vanilla
1 c. whipping cream
½ c. butter

Cream sugar and shortening. Add eggs and dry ingredients. Add nuts and apples last. (Batter is very thick.) Bake in 9x13 inch pan at 350° for 1 hour. Serve warm with sauce and whipped cream.

Sauce: Mix all together and bring to boil. Use double boiler or it may curdle.

### GRANDMA'S BANANA CAKE

1½ c. sugar
½ c. butter
3 eggs
¾ c. buttermilk or soured milk
3 bananas, mashed
1 tsp. baking soda
1 tsp. baking powder
1 tsp. vanilla
½ tsp. salt
1 c. flour

Cream butter and sugar; add eggs one at a time and beat well. Add the milk with the soda. Add flour, baking powder and salt. Add vanilla and bananas last. Put in 9x13 inch pan. Bake at 350° until toothpick comes out clean about 40 minutes.

*Judy Baar Topinka*

COMMUNITIES SERVED: BERWYN, BROOKFIELD, CICERO, DOWNERS GROVE, ELMHURST, FOREST PARK, HILLSIDE, HINSDALE, LA GRANGE, LA GRANGE PARK, LISLE, NORTH RIVERSIDE, OAK BROOK, OAK BROOK TERRACE, RIVERSIDE, WESTCHESTER, WESTERN SPRINGS, WESTMONT

# Neiman-Marcus

## *Roasted Quail with Foie Gras*

*I have been lucky to have a friend who hunts quail and over the years has been kind enough to share them with me (Thanks Tim). Also working with foie gras has lead to trying new recipes. This is an easy, elegant, first course. Preparation and cooking time is about two hours which may be completed ahead. Serve with the remaining Sauterne, well chilled, and lightly buttered toast points.*

> *6 Cleaned Quail*
> *12 Tablespoons Foie Gras*
>   *(about 1/2 Pound)*
> *Truffle, 1 Large or 2 Small*
> *1 Cup Cognac*
> *Grape Leaves*
> *Salt Pork*
> *1/2 Cup Sauterne*
> *1/2 Pound Grapes*

*Remove wing tips from quail. Stuff each quail with 2 tablespoons foie gras and a thin slice of truffle. Place the stuffed birds in bowl. Sprinkle generously with fresh ground black pepper, pour over them 1 cup Cognac, and marinate for 1 hour.*

*Put wing tips in a sauce pan with 1 1/2 cups chicken stock and a bouquet garni of 4 sprigs parsley, 1 small stalk celery, 1 sprig thyme and half a bay leaf. Simmer 1 hour. Strain the broth, add the marinade from the quail and continue to cook until liquid is reduced by one-third. Reserve.*

*Wrap the quail in grape leaves, secure with toothpicks, cover the breasts with thin slice of salt pork. In roasting pan melt 6 tablespoons of butter. Arrange the quail in the pan and roast in very hot (450°) oven for 15 to 20 minutes. Discard the salt pork.*

*On an ovenproof platter arrange the quail and 1/2 pound seeded grapes. Heat together in a moderate (350°) oven. To the juices in the roasting pan add 1/2 cup Sauterne and bring to a boil. Continue cooking over high heat until reduced by one-half. Add the reduced broth and bring to a boil. Stir in 1 teaspoon flour mixed to a paste with 1 tablespoon butter, cook, stirring until slightly thickened. Stir in 1 tablespoon lemon juice and pour over quail.*

**CONNIE TOSHEFF**
*Lyons, Illinois*

737 N. Michigan Avenue
Chicago, Illinois 60611
312 642-5900

**Friends of the Parks**
53 West Jackson Boulevard • Chicago, Illinois 60604 • 312/922-3307

### Erma Tranter's Amaretto Torte

12 Italian Amaretti cookies (6 individually wrapped packages)

1 cup of butter

1 cup of sugar

5 eggs, separated

1/2 cup of flour

4 oz. semi-sweet chocolate, grated (or semi-sweet or milk chocolate chips, grated in blender)

1. Pulverize amaretti and set aside.
2. Pulverize chocolate and set aside.
3. Cream butter and sugar for 10 minutes.
4. Add egg yolks, beat for 10 minutes.
5. Gradually add flour and amaretti cookies.
6. Beat egg whites till stiff.
7. Fold egg whites into batter.
8. Bake in greased spring form pan at 350 for 40 minutes.
9. Sprinkle with confectioners sugar.

*Erma Tranter*

**Executive Committee**
Cindy Mitchell, *President*
James H. Ryan, *Vice President*
Jackie McKay, *Vice President*
Frank Diaz, *Secretary/Treasurer*
Steve Ballis
Kenneth Burkhart
Karen Davis
Leslie Douglass
John Drummond
David Sharpe
Guillermo Cannon Zuzunaga

**Board of Directors**
Jim Alter
John A. Bross Jr.
Baird Brown
Steve Christy
Diane Ciral
Kay Clement
Jane M. Curry
Oscar O. D'Angelo
William Drake
Leon D. Finney
Aaron Freeman
Judith Getzels
Mary Gray
Nancy Hays
Deone Griffith Jackman
Walter Kelly
Cristy Burnham Laier
Anthony F. Martin
John Massey
Gail Parrish
Stanley Paul
Alicia V. Pond
Howard Richards
Tom Ruben
Charles P. Schwartz, Jr.
Allen R. Smart
Donald Young
James W. Wagner

**Advisory Board**
George Cooley
Alyce DeCosta
Marvin Gordon
Henry Kahn
Victoria Post Ranney
Martin Reinhart
Lois Weisberg

**Executive Director**
Erma Tranter

serving as a catalyst for improving Chicago's parks

**Chicago**®

**Roger Tremblay**
Publisher

*KAHLUA VELVET FROSTY*

1 cup Kahlua or other coffee-flavored liqueur

1 pint vanilla ice cream

1 cup half-and-half

1/8 teaspoon almond extract

About 1 1/2 cups crushed ice

Combine all ingredients in container of electric blender. Blend until smooth. Yield: about 6 servings.

Roger Tremblay

# CHARLIE TROTTER'S

### Black Bass Tartare with Buckwheat Blini and Asian Vegetables

Sometimes one craves the exotic. Here is a dish that was inspired one afternoon on a stroll through San Francisco's China Town while contemplating all the wondrous produce and fish. Not only are the textures and tastes fabulous, but this dish is quite healthy as well! (Serves 4).

**Vegetables**
| | | |
|---|---|---|
| 8 | | Snow peas, blanched and finely julienned |
| 1/2 | C | Napa Cabbage, finely julienned |
| 1/2 | | Yellow bell pepper, finely julienned |
| 4 | | Shittakke Mushrooms, finely julienned |
| 1/2 | pkge | Enoki mushrooms |
| 25 | | Chives, cut to 2 inches long |
| 1/4 | C | Dried seaweed, reconstituted |
| 1/3 | C | Alfalfa Sprouts |

**Vinaigrette**
| | | | |
|---|---|---|---|
| 1/3 | C | Sesame oil | |
| 2 | T | Peanut oil | Whisk all vinaigrette |
| 1 | T | Miso | ingredients together. |
| 1 | T | Soy sauce | |
| 3 | T | Rice wine vinegar | |
| | | Black pepper to taste | |

**Buckwheat Blini**
| | | | |
|---|---|---|---|
| 1/2 | T | Dried yeast | Proof yeast with |
| 3/4 | C | Water | water, 15-20 minutes. |
| 3/4 | C | Flour | Add flour. Let rise 1 hour. |
| 3/4 | C | Buckwheat flour | Combine buckwheat flour, |
| 2 | T | Melted butter | butter, milk, egg yolk. |
| 3/4 | C | Milk | Let rise 1 hour. |
| 1 | | Egg yolk | |
| 2 | | Egg whites | Whip egg whites, fold in. |

**Bass Tartare**
| | | | |
|---|---|---|---|
| 8 | oz | Black sea bass, chopped up | |
| 1 | | Garlic clove, finely chopped | |
| 2 | t | Ginger, finely chopped | |
| 1 | T | Cilantro, finely chopped | |
| 1 | T | Rice wine vinegar | |
| 1 | T | Soy sauce | Combine all tartare |
| 1 | T | Hoisin sauce | ingredients. |

**Instructions:** Toss the vegetables in a large bowl with the vinaigrette. Cook the blini to the size of 1-inch discs, about 24. Arrange the vegetables on 4 plates. Divide the tartare into 4 servings and mound on vegetables in center of plates. Serve approximately 6 blini with each tartare.

*Chas. H. Trotter*

*816 W. Armitage Chicago, Illinois 60614 312/248-6228*

**McDonald's**

Fred L. Turner
Chairman

Direct Dial Number
312/575-3333

Twoallbeefpattiesspecialsaucelettucecheesepicklesoniononasesameseedbun.

Translated -- that's a Big Mac!

*[signature: Fred L. Turner]*

McDonald's Corporation • McDonald's Plaza • Oak Brook, Illinois 60521

**L'ESCARGOT**
on Michigan
701 north michigan avenue
chicago, illinois 60611

MOUSSE AU CITRON VERT ET KIWI

Yield---1 large terrine (8 servings)

5 egg yolks
65g sugar
Juice of 2 limes
Zest of 1 lime (grated)
65g milk
4 gelatin leaves (available at specialty stores)
5 egg whites
50g sugar

8-9 ripe kiwis (sliced)
Fresh genoise or 2 pkgs. ladyfingers
Simple syrup (2 parts sugar to one part water, boiled until sugar dissolves, and cooled)

½ pint heavy cream whipped with ½c sugar

To make mousse:

Soak gelatin leaves in cold water for at least 10 minutes. Blanch the finely grated lime zest in boiling water at least 2 times. In a seperate bowl, mix egg yolks and milk. In the small bowl of an electric mixer, put egg whites, and reserve until later. In a small pot, mix lime juice, blanched lime zest and 65 grams of sugar. Add egg yolk & milk mixture to this. Thin the mixture stirring constantly with a wire whip until it comes to a boil. Drain water from gelatin leaves and add leaves to the hot mixture, stirring until dissolved. Whip egg whites to a froth on the medium speed of an electric mixer, add 50 grams of sugar to the egg whites little by little, and continue mixing until they hold stable peaks. Gently fold whites into the hot lime/gelatin mixture.

Assembling the dessert

Fill terrine mold one third of the way up with lime mousse. Sprinkle with halved kiwi slices. Fill the mold another 1/3 with mousse. Sprinkle with kiwi. Place a very thin layer of genoise or sliced lady fingers on top of the kiwis. Sprinkle the cake well with simple syrup to moisten it. Repeat a kiwi layer, then repeat another genoise layer, moistened with syrup. Cover with plastic wrap and put in the refrigerator at least 6 hours or overnight.

Unmolding & Decorating

Simply place terrine in hot water for a few seconds until it can be unmolded easily. Unmold on to serving platter. Run a line of sliced kiwis down the middle of the terrine, then pipe sweetened whipped cream alongside the kiwis. Use an electric knife ( or extremely sharp knife) to slice. Pass kiwi sauce. This dessert is best when eaten the same day it is made.

Kiwi Sauce

Grind peeled kiwis in a food processor only a few seconds. (too long will discolor them) Add a bit of water to lighten the puree. Add sugar until desired sweetness. Stir & serve with dessert.

• Petit Déjeuner • Déjeuner • Dîner • Joie de vivre •

tel. 337-1717

# PopsPopsPopsPopsPopsPopsPopsPopsPopsPopsPopsPops
### For Champagne

Here's an appetizer that helped get Pops started and had many, many of our customers wondering: "What is a whoopie?".

## Whoopies

1½ long loaves French bread
4½ 8 oz. packages Philly cream cheese
1 doz. medium eggs - hard boiled & chopped fine
1 bunch scallions - chopped fine
4 stalks celery - chopped fine
1½ T. brown mustard
½ T. yellow mustard
2 t. dry mustard
1½ t. salt

Cut ends off bread & discard. Slice loaf lengthwise leaving one side in tact. Remove center of bread and chop in food processor. In mixer blend cream cheese, mustards & salt. In large bowl combine cheese mixture, chopped bread & remaining ingredients.

Fill center of loaves with mixture and put loaf back together. Slice ¾" circular "finger sandwiches" & serve slightly chilled.
    Enjoy!
                    Lin Lellerkey

2934 N. Sheffield • Chicago, Illinois 60657 • (312) 472-1000

# The Chicago Academy of Sciences

## RUBBABOO

Rubbaboo is a favorite dish with the northern voyageurs, when they can get it. It consists simply of pemmican (deermeat) made into a kind of soup by boiling water. Flour is added when it can be obtained, and it is generally considered more palatable with a little sugar. Pemmican is supposed by the benighted world outside to consist only of pounded meat and grease; an egregious error; for, from some experience on the subject, I am authorized to state that hair, sticks, bark, spruce leaves, stones, sand, etc., enter into its composition, often quite largely, especially if the meat has been pounded by the Indians. Rubbaboo is made in open kettles, of snow water. It is decidely the best way to cook pemmican at night, and I have occasionally found a gallon or so make a very good supper when on a voyage. I was a little shy of it for a while after learning how two packet men were once made into pemmican near Fort Good Hope, a few years since, by starving Indians.    Contributed by Robert Kennicott (1861).


Robert Kennicott (1835-1866) was the founder of the Chicago Academy of Sciences. He described a rubbaboo as "any queer mixture". Kennicott died at the age of 30 while exploring Alaska in search of a telegraph route linking the United States and Europe. The reports he sent back were instrumental in convincing the United States to purchase Alaska.


Submitted by Ronald Vasile, Archivist, Chicago Academy of Sciences.

*Ron Vasile*

Mrs. (Mary-Frances) Bill NECK

## My Mother's Wonderful Sandwich Filling — one of Bill's favorites!

1 lg. whipped cream cheese
2 hard-boiled eggs
1 med. white onion
2 med. green bell peppers
3 small jars whole pimentos
1 cup walnuts
2 Tbsp. Heinz chili sauce (cause it's not sweet)
salt, pepper, paprika

Chop all ingredients coarsely. (except cheese & chili sauce). Mix all together with chili sauce — AND then blend with cream cheese. Salt, pepper, paprika to taste. Chill! Serve!! — Accept Applause!!!

## Judy Vessely
### MUSIC FOR ALL OCCASIONS
1633 East Avenue
Berwyn, Illinois 60402

(312) 484-4720

PINEAPPLE NUT COOKIES

1 cup butter
1 cup granulated sugar
1 cup brown sugar
2 eggs
1 cup of crushed pineapple, well drained
1 cup chopped nuts
4 1/2 cups sifted flour
1 teaspoon baking soda
1/4 teaspoon salt
1 teaspoon vanilla

Cream butter and sugars until light and fluffy. Add eggs and beat well. Add pineapple and nuts. Mix in flour which has been sifted with soda and salt. Add vanilla. Drop by teaspoonsful on greased cookie sheet. Bake 15 minutes in 350 degree oven.

These cookies will add to any sweet table at private parties or when one desires a good cookie for their own use.

*Judy Vessely*

Music for all occasions: CONVENTIONS, BANQUETS, WEDDINGS, RECEPTIONS, DANCES, PROMOTIONS, PARTIES, FASHION SHOWS, SHOW BANDS, STROLLING VIOLINISTS, DINNER MUSIC
One musician to a twenty piece band or orchestra - any combination desired - strolling or stationary
Elegance in Sound from Old Favorites, Contemporary, Dixieland, Rock, Jazz, Disco, Ethnic, Semi-Classic, Classic, the Big Band Era, and Country Western Music. Music for special theme parties available.

# The Drake

LAKE SHORE DRIVE
CHICAGO, ILLINOIS 60611 (312) 787-2200
A VISTA INTERNATIONAL HOTEL

The following recipe, developed by The Drake Hotel's Executive Chef Leo Waldmeier, has become one of the signature dishes for the Cape Cod Room. During a special Cajun Festival at The Drake Hotel, Chef Waldmeier personally consulted with and visited the restaurant of the chef that made Cajun food popular - the famous Paul Prophomme. The crab cakes have a slight tang, but still allow the flavor of the crabmeat to come through.

## MARYLAND CRAB CAKES WITH MUSTARD SAUCE
### (Serves 4)

MUSTARD SAUCE:

- 2 tsp. chopped shallots
- 1 tsp. butter
- 1 c. heavy cream
- 2 2/3 c. fish stock
- 1/2 tsp. dry vermouth
- 1 tsp. prepared mustard
- 1/2 tsp. dry mustard
- 1/3 c. dry white wine
- Salt and pepper

CRAB CAKES:

- 1 lb. (2 c.) fresh Maryland crabmeat
- 1/3 c. finely diced pimento
- 1/3 c. finely sliced spring onions (green part only)
- 1 c. mashed potatoes
- 1 egg
- 1 tsp. (generous) Tabasco
- 1/2 tsp. Worcestershire sauce (or to taste)
- 2 c. fresh bread crumbs
- 4 Tbls. butter
- Salt and pepper

Prepare Mustard Sauce: Saute shallots in butter in a medium-size saucepan. Stir in remaining sauce ingredients. Cook over medium heat, stirring constantly, for 7 minutes. Strain through cheesecloth. Keep warm over simmering water.

Prepare Crab Cakes: Mix crabmeat gently with other ingredients, except bread crumbs and butter. Divide into 8 equal portions and shape into patties (3 oz. each). Coat each patty with crumbs on all sides.

Heat half the butter in a 10-inch skillet over medium heat. Saute 4 crab cakes until brown on undersides; turn and brown second side. Remove from skillet and keep warm. Repeat with remaining butter and 4 crab cakes.

Spoon mustard sauce onto service plates. Arrange crab cakes over sauce.

Garnish with snow peas, toasted pine nuts, glazed baby carrots with sprout attached, and glazed turnips.

Susan Wayman
Project Coordinator

City of Chicago
Department of Cultural Affairs
Navy Pier

600 East Grand Avenue
Chicago, Illinois 60611

744-4219

## Susan's WAKE-UP COFFEE CAKE

1 BEATEN EGG
1/2 CUP SUGAR
1/2 CUP MILK
2 TABLESPOONS MELTED CRISCO
1 CUP FLOUR
1/2 TEASPOON SALT
2 TEASPOONS BAKING POWDER

COMBINE EGG, SUGAR, MILK AND SHORTENING.
ADD FLOUR SIFTED WITH SALT AND BAKING POWDER.
MIX WELL AND POUR INTO 8-INCH SQUARE GREASED PAN.

### WAKE-UP COFFEE CAKE TOPPING

1/4 CUP BROWN SUGAR
1 TEASPOON CINNAMON
1 TABLESPOON FLOUR
1 TABLESPOON MELTED BUTTER
1/2 CUP BROKEN NUT MEATS

COMBINE AND SPREAD EVENLY OVER DOUGH.
BAKE IN 375° OVEN 20-25 MINUTES.

Note: This is a never-fail recipe of my Dutch grandmother who lived up the lake in Holland, Michigan. One of its great advantages is that the ingredients are usually on hand in your kitchen. The other is that you can make it with your eyes closed, while the coffee is brewing.

*Susan Wayman*

# NAVY PIER

# Friends of the Chicago River

53 WEST JACKSON BLVD • SUITE 1135 • CHICAGO, ILLINOIS 60604 • (312) 939-0490

*President*
Jerome E. Sterling
Procter & Gamble Mfg. Co.

*Vice President*
*Programs*
Susan Namest
WFMT Radio

*Vice President*
*Development*
Emma Kowalenko
Historian/Consultant

*Vice President*
*Administration*
Susan K. B. Urbas
Chicago River Aquatic Center

*Secretary/Treasurer*
Ed Zotti
Writer

*Executive Director*
Beth White

*Directors*

William E. Espinosa
Design Plus Architecture

J. William Fredrickson
North Park College

Jeffrey Green
Devco Commercial Real Estate

Timothy J. Griffin
Trkla, Pettigrew, Allen & Payne

David W. Jones
State of Illinois
Dept. of Energy
& Natural Resources

Paul F. McCarthy
Chicago From The Lake

Rose Morreale
CMC Real Estate Corp.

*Advisors*

Commissioner Joanne Alter
Metropolitan Sanitary District

Sharon L. Burge
Tishman Speyer Properties

Robert Cassidy
Editor/Publishe

John Hogan
Commonwealth Edison

Sheila Leahy

RECIPE FOR A RIVER RENAISSANCE

Combine and mix well...

1 dirty Chicago River (this can easily be obtained by pouring the raw sewage of a booming city and the wastes from steel, lumber and packing industries into a nearly flat river bed; making sure that the water barely flows).

1 100-year effort by the Metropolitan Sanitary District to protect the city's drinking water supply (again, easy to do, just follow the recipe below:

1. build 3 canals higher than the river into which they flow, forcing the river waters southward;
2. add locks to keep the river and lake waters separate;
3. season with pumping stations to remove harmful wastes from the now reversed river waters;
4. fold in deep tunnels to further improve the river water quality)

Sprinkle on top...

1979 Friends of the Chicago River (recruit members from those interested in urban development and planning, history, ecology, cartography, canoing, rowing, and the improvement of their city environment) - organized to promote and protect the Chicago River.

Bake for 10 years...

When done the Renaissance will offer Chicago a cleaner river, suitable for boating, rowing, canoeing, etc; a river whose stench has been largely eliminated allowing for pleasant parks and outdoor cafes to be built on its banks, a river that will attract activity and development...a river that will be seen by all as a valuable resource.

*Beth White*
*Executive Director*

# The Chicago Temple

First United Methodist Church, Clark and Washington Streets, Chicago, IL 60602, 312/236-4548

**Ministers - William D. White,  Carol L. Cory,  George E. David**

Norma Lee Barnhart
**Diaconal Minister - Music**

Nicolette Owen-Pfaff
**Director Christian Education**

## RECIPE FOR SELF-EXAMINATION

1. Am I consciously or unconsciously creating the impression that I am a better person than I really am? In other words, am I a hypocrite?
2. Am I honest in all my acts or words, or do I exaggerate?
3. Do I confidentially pass on to another what was told to me in confidence?
4. Can I be trusted?
5. Am I a slave to dress, friends, work or habits?
6. Am I self-conscious, self-pitying or self-justifying?
7. Did the Bible live in me today?
8. Do I give it time to speak to me everyday?
9. When did I last speak to somebody else with the object of trying to win that person for Christ?
10. Am I enjoying prayer?
11. Am I making contacts with other people and using them for the Master's glory?
12. Do I pray about the money I spend?
13. Do I get to bed on time and get up on time?
14. Do I disobey God in anything?
15. Do I insist upon doing something about which my conscience is uneasy?
16. Am I defeated in any part of my life? Am I jealous, impure, critical, irritable, touchy or distraught?
17. How do I spend my spare time?
18. Am I proud?
19. Do I thank God that I am not as other people, especially as the Pharisee who despised the publican?
20. Is there anybody whom I fear, dislike, disown, criticize, hold a resentment toward or disregard? If so, what am I doing about it?
21. Do I grumble or complain constantly?
22. Is Christ real to me?

*William D. White*

William D. White
Senior Minister

*This recipe for self-examination from John Wesley is over 250 years old.*

# THE LAKESIDE GROUP

600 North McClurg Court  Chicago, Illinois 60611
312-787-6858

I can't imagine a greater feeling than sitting out at Navy Pier in the evening and enjoying this Cajun dish, looking back at one of the most beautiful cities in the world.

## GRILLED CAJUN SHRIMP ON JAMBALAYA RICE

4 servings     Cajun Pepper Sauce

2# 10-15 shrimp, 24 jumbo shrimp

1 cup small diced spanish onion

1/2 cup small diced red pepper

1/2 cup small diced green pepper

1/2 cup small diced carrots

1/2 tablespoon cayenne pepper

1 fresh jalapeno seeds removed or canned 1 1/2

1 tablespoon pickapepper sauce

salt to taste

tomato sauce

1 cup rice

3/4 cup chicken stock

1/2 cup cajun sauce

3 scallions diced in circles for garnish

Peel clean and devein shrimp, leave tail intact. Keep on ice. Sautee all the above ingredients except tomato sauce until tender. Onion will be translucent, add tomato sauce simmer for 15 min. Season with salt to taste. Sauce should be hot and spicy. Cool. May be made 48 hours ahead. Mix rice, stock, cajun pepper sauce, bring to a boil, cover and simmer for 15 minutes till tender. Marinate shrimp in cajun sauce for 1/2 hour. Grill over hot fire approximately 2 minutes on each side. Cook shrimp just till done. Serve on cajun rice, garnish with diced scallion rounds. Hea rest of sauce on side for those who enjoy it hot.

THE CHICAGO CATERERS            Gregory Wenger, Chef

Sincerely,

John D. Wilson
President
THE LAKESIDE GROUP, INC.

**WRIGLEY BUILDING RESTAURANT**
410 North Michigan Avenue
Chicago, Illinois 60611
Telephone 312 - 944-7600

### Wrigley Building Restaurant
# COBB SALAD

| | | | |
|---|---|---|---|
| 1/2 | head iceberg lettuce | 1 | chicken breast, cooked, boned and skinned |
| 1/2 | bunch watercress | | |
| 1/2 | head romaine | 6 | strips bacon, cooked |
| 1 | small bunch chicory endive | 1 | avocado, peeled |
| 2 | tbsp. minced chives | 3 | hard-cooked eggs |
| 2 | med. tomatoes | 1/2 | cup Roquefort cheese, crumbled |

Chop lettuce, watercress, endive and romaine in very fine pieces using knife or food processor.
Mix together in a large wide bowl, or individual wide shallow bowls. Add chives. Peel, seed and dice tomatoes. Dice chicken breast, bacon, avocado and eggs. Arrange chopped ingredients in narrow strips or wedges across top of greens.
Sprinkle with cheese and chill. Just before serving, toss with 1/2 cup of dressing of your choice.
Makes 6 or more luncheon entree servings.

*Julie A Wrigley*

# LANDMARKS PRESERVATION COUNCIL OF ILLINOIS

The Landmarks Preservation Council of Illinois was founded in 1971 during the battle to save Adler & Sullivan's Chicago Stock Exchange on LaSalle Street. Since that time, LPCI has become a statewide voice for preserving the best of our history and architectural heritage. LPCI was instrumental in saving the Marquette Building, Chicago Public Library Cultural Center, Chicago Theatre and many other prominent landmarks. Our mission is to preserve the character and vitality provided to Illinois communities by historic architecture.

## NEIGHBORHOOD TREASURE

This tasty dish provides long-term enjoyment and nourishment for the mind, body and pocketbook.

Take one old building with architectural merit
    (Scrape off aluminum, asphalt or fake brick
     siding before preparation.)

Add one developer with vision
    (Not available in all locales.)

Add one financial institution

Add one preservation architect

Mix gently to avoid bruising egos. Sprinkle in generous amounts of community input, sage preservation advice, and seasoned salt-of-the-earth builders.

Cook at medium heat until building returns to original colors and beauty.

Serves any number, for years to come.

Sincerely,

Carol S. Wyant
Executive Director

---

**LANDMARKS PRESERVATION COUNCIL·OF ILLINOIS**

EXECUTIVE COMMITTEE
Susan Baldwin, President
Seymour H. Persky, Executive Vice President
Victoria Granacki, Vice President, Chicago Programs
William Hood, Vice President, Development
Bradford J. White, Vice President, Legislation
Toni Sons Kibort, Vice President, Personnel
Susan Glover Godlewski, Vice President, Membership
Paul L. Wertheimer, Vice President, Public Relations
Leslie H. Kenyon, Vice President, Statewide Programs
Devereux Bowly, Chairman, Preservation Fund
John E. McFadden, Secretary
William E. Ellis, Treasurer
J. Bradley Shafer, Member-At-Large

BOARD OF DIRECTORS
Susan Jantorni Allen
Salvatore A. Barbatano
John W. Barriger
Susan S. Benjamin
Robert Berkoff
Marianne Guerrini Boe
Ben A. Borenstein
Michael S. Bozich
Janet Gates Conover
Beth Ingram Davis
Howard S. Decker
Royal R. Faubion
Neil Gaston
Janet A. Gilboy
Patrick J. Glithero
Cynthia M. Haviland
Susan Kaufmann-Horwitz
Harry J. Hunderman
Walker C. Johnson
Robert C. King
Larry D. Kuster
Michael J. McNerney
Grayson Mitchell
Langdon Neal
Roger R. Nelson
Gail A. Niemann
Gordon Lee Pollock
John Power
Tobin M. Richter
Letticia Robinson
Edward K. Uhlir
Rolf A. Weil
Emese Wood
John C. York

ADVISORY BOARD
Gerald Adelmann
Lachlan Blair
Kathleen Roy Cummings
Wim de Wit
Barbara Donnelley
Harriet Gulis
Maureen Gustafson
W. R. Hasbrouck
Frank Heitzman
Nancy L. Kaszak
Harold Lichterman
Nellie Longsworth
Robert Meers
William E. O'Neil
Ellen Kettler Paseltiner
David C. Roston
William D. Staley
Jacqueline Vaughn
John Vinci
Judith Carmack York

HONORARY BOARD
Carl W. Condit
Stanley Freehling
Charles C. Haffner III
Irving J. Markin
Hope McCormick
Nancy Stevenson
Harry Weese

EXECUTIVE DIRECTOR
Carol S. Wyant

The Monadnock Building
53 West Jackson Boulevard
Chicago, Il. 60604
312-922-1742

# MUSSELS MAYFAIR

## MUSSELS:

3 lbs. greenlip mussels (or domestic)

3 shallots (chopped)

2/3 cup white wine

1 bay leaf

\* Scrub and debeard the mussels. Place wine, shallots, and bay leaf in large pot. Bring to a boil and simmer 1-2 minutes. Add mussels and cook covered until mussels just begin to open (approx. 4 mins.) Remove from heat. When mussels are cool enough to handle, remove from shells and place back in cleaned shell half. Place on baking sheet and set aside.

## BUTTER COMPOSE:

1 shallot (minced)

2 cloves garlic (minced)

2 teaspoons parsley (chopped)

3/4 lb. sofften butter (unsalted)

2 tablespoons pernod liqueur

3 tablespoons bread crumbs

1 teaspoon herbs de provence

2 tablespoons sun-dried tomatoes (minced)

salt & pepper to taste

\* Combine shallot, garlic, parsley and butter in the bowl of a food processor. Using pulsing motion, mix until smooth. Add pernod, breadcrumbs, herbs, and sun-dried tomatoes. Mix to incorporate. Season with salt and pepper to taste.

Cover each mussel with butter mixture and refrigerate until firm. Brown under preheated broiler (3-5 minutes). Splash additional Pernod on sizzling mussels and serve immediately. (Serves 4)

GREGORY NFCHAK - EXECUTIVE CHEF

# CHICAGO

## DON ZIMMER'S ECLAIR CAKE

**Dough**
1 cup water
1/2 cup butter (1 stick)
1 cup flour (not sifted)
4 eggs

**Topping**
2 squares semi-sweet chocolate
2 tbs. butter
1 cup powdered sugar
2 tbs. milk
1 tsp. vanilla

**Filling**
2 packages (3 1/2 oz. each) instant French vanilla pudding
2 1/2 cups milk
1 (8 oz.) LeCreme whipped topping
1 tsp. vanilla

**Dough**-- Heat butter and water to rolling boil. Stir in flour all at once over low heat (with wooden spoon). Beat with spoon until a ball is formed. Beat in eggs one at a time with electric beater. Spoon on cool pizza pan to form a circle (with hole in the middle). Bake at 400 degrees for 45-50 minutes (until brown). Cool away from drafts. When cool split horizontally and fill with pudding filling.

**Filling**-- Mix pudding and milk (with mixer). Beat in whipped topping and vanilla.

**Topping**-- Melt chocolate, then add rest of ingredients. Spread over top. Refrigerate.

Chicago Cubs, Wrigley Field
1060 West Addison Street
Chicago, Illinois 60613
312/281-5050

# Zimmerman's

ALL PHONES (312) 332-0012

213 WEST GRAND AVENUE • CHICAGO, ILLINOIS 60610

July 14th, 1988

## Max Zimmerman's Lox Omelette

### Ingredients

1 large onion minced
1 green pepper chopped
1 red pepper chopped
1/4 lb fresh lox - shredded
6 eggs
black pepper to taste

Yield: 4 servings

### Directions

In large frying pan, saute first three ingredients adding about 2 oz. of water to prevent drying.

Beat eggs lightly in a bowl then add to mixture and follow this with the lox and pepper. Cook slowly on a low flame until lightly fluffed. Serve at once.

### Serving Suggestion

Excellent with bagels and cream cheese

At our house this is a Sunday favorite with everyone -- especially good with champagne.

Culinarily yours,

*Max Zimmerman*

Max Zimmerman

OPEN FROM 8:30 A.M. TO 8 P.M. — SUNDAYS NOON TO 5 P.M.

# RECIPE INDEX

## APPETIZERS AND SNACKS

* Aunt Barb of Bloomingdale's Crab Puff Appetizer, *Ed Curran*, 43
* Carols's Pita Suprise, *Carol R. Nolan*, 152
* Caviar Mousse, *Marion Meyerson*, 140,141
* Caviar Pie, *Mary Rubloff*, 183
* Cheese and Chutney Canapes, *Bonnie Swearingen*, 207
* Escargots with Herbed Brie in Phyllo Dough w/Lemon Caper Butter Sauce, *Michael Folz*, 69
* Frank's Dip, *Cary Gott*, 88
* Heavenly Glazed Party Nuts, *Cookie & Barry Stagman*, 201
* Hot Clam Dip, *Neil A. Ramo*, 167
* Hot Mexican Dip, *Amy Scott*, 192
* Oysters Alexandra, *Yves Rouband*, 182
* Salmon Spread, *Karen McKay*, 136
* Shrimp Binyon, *Hal Binyon III*, 12
* Southern Midnight Snack, *Artensa Randolph*, 168
* Whoopies, *Linda Verhey*, 218

## SOUPS, CHOWDERS & LOVE POTIONS

* Avocado Soup, *Elizabeth L. Hollander*, 102
* Blackeyed Peas Jumbalayi, *Marva Collins*, 38
* Ever Changing Voyageurs Soup, *Larry Hill*, 100
* Fish Soup, *Bernard F. Brennan*, 18
* Gazpacho Soup, *Nancy Reagan*, 169
* Ham & Cabbage Soup, *Frederick Pohl*, 162
* Hearty Hodgepodge, *Jim Keane*, 112
* Dorothy's Special Beef Stew, *Lauri A. Neal*, 149
* Lazy Pierogi, *Fred Hudy*, 103
* Lobster Newburg, *Carol J. Callahan*, 25
* New England Fish Chowder, *Grace Mary Stern*, 203
* Plantain Soup, *Leon M. Lederman*, 121
* Potato-Onion Soup, *Sheli A. Lulkin*, 126
* Pumpkin Bisque Soup, *Dr. Duncan*, 62
* Real Boston to Chicago Fish Chowder, *Phil Elmes*, 66
* Rubbaboo, *Ron Vasile*, 219
* Traditional Polish Bigas, *Lucyna Migala*, 142
* Wild Rice Soup, *Paul Harvey*, 94
* Zuppa di Scarolaor La Pozione d'Amore, *Nicholas Patricca*, 157

## BREADS

* Blueberry Scones, *Mary Ann Childers*, 31
* Bonnie's Beer Bread, *Bonnie Swearingen*, 207
* Cinnamon Nut Biscuit Rolls, *Rene Arend*, 3
* CUFOS Sun Flower Bread, *M. Rodeghier*, 178
* Evening Primroses Fritters, *Bernice Sproesser*, 200
* Hush Puppies, *Bill Cullerton*, 42
* Irish Soda Bread, *Raymond Chadwick*, 29
* Pecan Pullapart, *Donald N Hensel*, 97
* Pizza Dough, *Anthony Mantuano*, 132
* Popover Power, *Samuel B. Casey, Jr.*, 28
* Southern Midnight Snack, *Artensa Randolph*, 168
* Tofu Loaf, *Jeff Gresko*, 90
* Whoopies, *Linda Verhey*, 218

## PASTA

* Baked Fettuccini with Perch Florentine, *Patrick Hammer*, 93
* Broccoli-Stuffed Shells, *Barbara Dore*, 58
* Fettuccini Robert, *Robert Billings*, 11
* Great Wall Canned Lamb Spagetti, *McGuire Gibson*, 84
* Jocko's No Cook Tomatoe Sauce for Pasta, *Christine Goldshmidt*, 85
* Paglia E Fieno, *Chef Mike Ditka*, 55
* Pasta Allegra, *Joe Cappo*, 27
* Pasta Con Broccoli, *Michael J. Madigan*, 131
* Pasta with Clam Sauce Eduardo, *Ed Berger*, 7
* Pizza al Quattro Formaggi, *Anthony Mantuano*, 133
* Quick Baked Mostaccioli Casserol, *Phil Georgeff*, 82
* Tagliatelle with Zucchini and Walnut Sauce, *Lauren Bannon*, 5
* White and Green Aspararus Ravioli, *J.R. Robertson*, 176

## Rice

* Turkish Pilaf, *Norman Schatz*, 189
* TV Dinner Fried Rice, *Peter Hawley*, 95
* Wild Rice Casserole, *Jane Edwards*, 64
* Wild Rice Soup, *Paul Harvey*, 94

## VEGGIES & DRESSINGS

* Artichokes in Honor of Courtenay, *Sara Paretsky*, 156
* Blackeyed Peas Jumbalayi, *Marva N. Collins*, 38
* Broccoli-Stuffed Shells, *Barbara Dore*, 58
* Cabbage Tamales, *Timothy C. Evans*, 67

* Dauphin Potatoes, *Wally Phillips*, 161
* Dill Carrots, *Gerald W. Adelmann*, 1
* Evening Yellow Primrose, *Bernice Sproesser*, 200
* Fresh Tuna Salad with Avacado and Pesto, *Michael Foley*, 73
* John Garrison's South Jersey Baked Limas, *John Garrison*, 81
* Joko's No Cook Tomato Sauce, *Christine Goldschmidt*, 85
* Kugelis, Lithuainian Potato Pudding, *Stanley Balzekas, Jr.*, 4
* Lil' Tommy's Mushroom Salad, *Tommy Edwards*, 65
* Mama's Chicago Beach Salad, *Lillian K. Chorvat*, 32
* Mange-Tout with Primrose Salad, *Bernice Sproesser*, 200
* My Daughter Sheryl's Sweet Potatoe Pie, *Mayor Eugene Sawyer*, 187
* My Mother's Wonderful Sandwich Filling, *Mrs. (Mary-Frances) Bill Veeck*, 220
* Ona's Potatoes, *Ona/ William Dietrick*, 54
* Phony Fanny's Salad Dressing, *Reese Rickards*, 175
* 7-Inch Salad, *Beth D. Fisher*, 197
* Shellfish and Mushroom Salad, *William E. Rice*, 173
* Spinach Jade Souffle, *Diana Nicholas*, 150
* Sweet Potato Frites, *Michael Foley*, 72
* Sweet Potato Souffle, *Michael T. Stirdivant*, 206
* Tangy Salad Dressing, *Josephine Minow*, 144
* Tagliatelle with Zucchini and Walnut Sauce, *Lauren Bannon*, 5
* Tofu Loaf, *Jeff Gresko*, 90
* Tomato Pudding, *Mrs. Gardner H. Stern*, 204
* White and Green Aaparagus Ravioli, *J. Robertson*, 176
* Wilted Lettuce with Bacon, *Sig Sakowicz*, 185
* Wrigley Building Restaurant Cobb Salad, *Julie A. Wrigley*, 227

## MEATS
### BEEF

* Al's Favorite Chili, *Alan Dixon*, 56
* Bare Meat, *Johnny Morris*, 145
* Beef Strogonoff, *James R. Stange*, 202
* Beef, Tenderloin Sauce, *George Schaefer*, 188
* Big Mac, *Fred L. Turner*, 216
* Bobby Christian's Hot Dog Scaloppine, *Bobby Christian*, 33
* Bruce Dumont's Burger Boats, *Bruce Dumont*, 61
* Chipped Beef in Wine-Mushroom Sauce, *Dorothy Fuller*, 79
* Corey Deitz's "Crock-A-Smile Donewell Chili" *Corey Deitz*, 51
* Dorothy's Special Beef Stew, *Lauri A. Neal*, 149
* Five-Way Chili, *Jery Buster*, 21
* Green Pepper Ginger Beef with Oyster Sauce, *Stanley Paul*, 158
* Hamburger and Vegetable Pockets, *Roman Pucinski*, 165
* Hot Mexican Dip, *Amy Scott*, 192
* Meat Loaf, *Ardis Krainik*, 117
* Pepperloin, Mustard Sauce, *Warren Buttler*, 23
* Rich's Favorite Stew, *Richard and Margaret Daley*, 46
* Rugby (Meat) Balls, *Ray Dempsey*, 52
* Sir Georg Solti's Goulash, *Sir Georg Solti*, 198
* Steak Bourguignonne, *Wally Phillips*, 161
* Steak Tartare, *Martin J. Oberman*, 153
* Steve Dahl's Tacos, *Steve Dahl*, 45
* Stock Yard Inn Marinated Beef, *Louis Szathmary*, 208
* Szechuan Steak Shish Kebabs, *Maryclaire Collins*, 39
* Tenderloin Piquant Chez Crate, *Gordon and Carole Segal*, 194
* Tipsy Brisket, *Irving Robins*, 177
* Tyranno Burgers, *Willard L. Boyd*, 13

### LAMB

* Gigot Persille, *Leslee Reis*, 170
* Great Wall Canned Chinese Lamb Spagetti, *McGuire Gibson*, 84
* Helena's BBQ Sauce and Lamb, *William F. Dietrick*, 54

## FOWL
### CHICKEN

* Chef Johann Lustenberger's Chicken Breast Baked in Phyllo Dough, *Johann Lustenberger*,127
* Chicken Breasts Florentine, *Kari & Bobby Thigpen*, 209
* Grandma Bilandic's Fried Chicken, *Michael and Heather Bilandic*, 10
* Individual Chicken Pot Pies, *Essee & Irv Kupcinet*, 118
* Jerry Coleman's Paella, *Jerry Coleman*, 34
* Lemon Chicken, *Barbara L. Kipper*, 114
* Lincoln Logs, *Mrs. James R. Thompson*, 210

* Marinated Grilled Chicken, *Sam & Melanie Bronfman*, 19
* Sesame Chicken with Cumberland Sauce, *Barbara Flynn Currie*, 44
* Sweetness Chicken, *Walter Payton*, 159

## DUCK, LARK, PHEASANT, QUAIL and SQUAB

* Breast of Duck Grilled with Sesame Seed Oil, *Michael Foley*, 72
* Larks, *Hope McCormick*, 135
* Quail, *Hope McCormick*, 135
* Quail in Wine, *Robert P. Gwinn*, 92
* Roasted Quail with Foie Gras, *Connie Tosheff*, 212
* Squab Stuffed with Chestnuts, *Mark Spreyer*, 199
* Stuffed Wild Quail with Cognac Sauce on Crouton with Pheasent Liver Pate, *Leo M. Henikoff*, 98, 99

## TURKEY

* Cholestrol Free Quiche, *Misty and John Davis*, 48
* Turkey Meatloaf, *William C. Bartholomay*, 6

## PORK

* Bloomie's Baked Apples with Sherry Pork Chops, *Brian H. McMahon*, 137
* Dr. Bratwurst's The-Way-It-Should-Be-Done-Brats, *Henry Kisor*, 115
* Ham & Cabbage Soup, *Frederick Pohl*, 162
* Heliocentric Pork Chops, *Zofia Sadlinska-Kasper*, 110
* My Mom Hanky's Spam Balls, *Jonathon Brandmeier*, 17
* Pork Carnitas, *Jeff Koligian*, 116

## VEAL

* Dr. Bratwurst's The Way-It-Should-Be-Done-Brats, *Henry Kisor*, 115
* Piccata of Veal, *Nancy Reagan*, 169
* Veal, *Lee B. Stern*, 205

## SEAFOOD AND FISH

* Barry's Secret Recipe, Lake Michigan Smelt, *Barry Bernsen*, 9
* Baked Fettuccini with Perch Florentine, *Patrick Hammer*, 43
* Black Bass Tartare with Buckwheat Blini and Asian Vegetables, *Charlie Trotter*, 215
* Braised Turbot on a Bed of Daikon with Whole Grain Mustard Sauce, *Yoshi Katsumura*, 111
* Cajun Barbequed Prawns, *James Phillip*, 160
* Calamari Risotto, *Michael Foley*, 73
* Caper Casserole, *Alan R. Johnston*, 106
* Captain Gorstayn's Lake Trout, *Capt. Gorstayn*, 87
* Commander's 5-Star Plate (Crab Alfranco), *Jess Franco*, 74
* Crabmeat Remoulade, *Loleta A. Didrickson*, 53
* Crevettes Armoricaine, *Lou Conte*, 40
* Deep Fried Carpaccio of Salmon Chinois, *Arnald J Morton and Alexander S. Dering*, 146, 147
* Escargots with Herbed Brie in Phyllo Dough with a Lemon Caper Butter Sauce, *Michael Folz*, 69
* Fish Soup, *Bernard F. Brennan*, 18
* Fresh Tuna Salad and Pesto, *Michael Foley*, 73
* Grilled Cajun Shrimp on Jambalaya Rice, *John D. Wilson*, 226
* Hot Clam Dip, *Neil A. Ramo*, 167
* Italian Style Salmon Steaks on a Grill, *Louis T. Galante*, 80
* Jerry Coleman's Paella, *Jerry Coleman*, 34
* Lake Trout Braised with Reisling and Savory Cabbage, *Chef John Draz*, 59
* Lobster Newburgh, *Carol J. Callahan*, 25
* Maryland Crab Cakes with Mustard Sauce, *Leo Waldmeier*, 222
* Max Zimmerman's Lox Omelette, *Max Zimmerman*, 231
* Musical Casserole, *Bozo*, 14
* Mussels Mayfair, *Gregory Zifchak*, 229
* Mussels for Six, *George B. Rabb*, 166
* New England Fish Chowder, *Grace Mary Stern*, 203
* Orange Roughy and Sole, *Roman Pucinski*, 165
* Oysters Alexandra, *Yves G. Rouband*, 182
* Pasta with Clam Sauce, *Ed Berger*, 7
* Real Boston to Chicago Fish Chowder, *Phil Elmes*, 66
* Red Snapper with Coconut Sauce, (Pescado Con Salsa de Coco), *Leon M. Lederman*, 121
* Salmon a la Shedd, *William P. Braker*, 16
* Salmon Mousse Argonne, *Alen Schriesheim*, 190
* Salmon Spread, *Karen McKay*, 136
* Sauteed Sea Scallops with Capers and Roasted Red Peppers, *Ray Capitanini*, 26
* Seafood Gumbo, *Paul Freeman*, 76

* Shellfish and Mushroom Salad, *William E. Rice*, 173
* Shrimp Binyon, *Hal Binyon III*, 12
* Spiced Shrimp with Sweet Onions, *Walter Jacobsen*, 104, 105
* Turbot and Cabbage Terrine with Beure Blanc, *J. Joho*, 107

## CASSEROLES, QUICHES and SOUFFLES

* Aunt Irma's Mexican Quiche, *James S. Kahn*, 108
* B.O. Plenty's Chuck Wagon Casserole, *Steve Locher*, 123
* Caper Casserole, *Alan R. Johnston*, 106
* Cholesterol-Free Quiche, *John and Misty Davis*, 48
* Corn Souffle, *Renee S. Crown*, 41
* Musical Casserole, *Bozo*, 14
* Quick Bake Mostaccioli Casserole, *Phillip Georgeff*, 82
* Spinach Jade Souffle, *Diana Nicholas*, 150
* Sweet Potato Souffle, *Michael T. Stirdivant*, 206
* Wild Rice Casserole, *Jane Edwards*, 64

## BREAKFAST FOODS
### PANCAKES, OMLETTES, AND SUCH

* Breakfast Pie, *Helen Schiller*, 196
* Chocolate Chip Sour Cream Coffee Cake, *Norman Ross*, 181
* Cookie's Berry Butter and French Toast, *Cookie*,
* Max Zimmerman's Lox Omelette, *Max Zimmerman*, 231
* Ona's Potatoes, *Ona/ William Deitrick*, 54
* Palmer House Griddle Cakes with Stewed Red Cherries, *John Lunney*, 128, 129
* Strawberry/Banana Wheat Pancakes, *Richard Dayhoff*, 49
* The Lowly Bowl of Oatmeal Comes of Age, *Johnny Frigo*, 77
* Trencherman's Breakfast, *Earl Nightingale*, 151
* Wake-Up Coffee Cake, *Susan Wayman*, 223

## DESSERTS
### CAKES, COOKIES and BROWNIES

* A Favorite Dessert, *Harold Washington's Mother (Submitted by Ramon B. Price)*, 163
* Apple Yum Yum Cake, *Judy Baar Topinka*, 211
* Art Berman's Favorite Chocolate Chip Cookies, *Art Berman*, 8
* Aunt Lana's Curran(t) Cookies, *Ed Curran*, 43
* Bill's Favorite Apple Crisp, *Bill Paar, Jr.*, 155

* Chocolate Caramel Pecan Cheese Cake, *John M. Richman*, 174
* Chocolate Chip Sour Cream Coffee Cake, *Norman Ross*, 181
* Chocolate Mousse Cake, *Ellis B. Levin*, 122
* Don Zimmer's Eclair Cake, *Don Zimmer*, 230
* Erma Tranter's Amaretto Tarte, *Erma Tranter*, 213
* Fairmont Hotel's Baked Alaska, *John Coletta*, 36, 37
* Frango Raspberry Chocolate Pecan Torte, *Phillip B. Miller*, 143
* Frank Lloyd Wright's Chocolate Indulgence, *Mary McLeod* 138, 139
* Grandma's Banana Cake, *Judy Baar Topinka*, 211
* Heavenly Brownies, *Dr. Joseph M. Chamberlain*, 30
* Loukoumathes, *Skip Griparis*, 91
* Lustful Cheesecake, *Maggie & William D. Long*, 125
* Meringue Cake With Fresh Exotic Fruits And Flowers, *Zaranda Gowenlock*, 89
* Mrs. Emmett Dedmon's Fabulous Cookies, *Mrs. Claire Dedmon*, 50
* My Mother's Hazelnut Cake, *Dirk Lohan*, 124
* Nusskuchen (Nut Cake), *Virginia B. Macdonald*, 130
* Peanut Butter Cake, *Marty Russo*, 184
* Pecan Pullapart, *Donald N. Hensel*, 97
* Pineapple Nut Cookies, *Judy Vessely*, 221
* Poppy Seed Cake, *Sensei John Nanay*, 148
* Poppy Seed Cake, *Pat Langenberger*, 120
* Rum Cake, *Danny Davis*, 47
* Sky High, *Audrey and Greg Fischer*, 68
* Sour Cream Chocolate Chip Cake, *Doug Collins*, 35
* The Honeymoon Cake, *Jaki Mari*, 134
* Tootsie Roll Cheese Cake, *Melvin J. Gordon*, 86
* Wake-up Coffee Cake, *Susan Wayman*, 223

## CHOCOLATE

* Arthur Berman's Favorite Chocolate Chip Cookies, *A.L. Berman*, 8
* Chicago Fudge Pie, *Ann Gerber*, 83
* Chocolate Carmel Pecan Cheesecake, *John M. Richman*, 174
* Chocolate Chip Sour Cream Coffee Cake, *Norman Ross*, 181
* Don Zimmer's Eclair Cake, *Don Zimmer*, 230
* Frank Lloyd Wright's Chocolate Indulgence, *Mary McLeod* 138, 139

* Heavenly Brownies,
  *Dr. Joseph M. Chamberlain*, 30
* Mrs. Emmett Dedmon's Fabulous Cookies,
  *Mrs. Dedmon*, 50
* Semifreddo al Cioccolato, *Mark Hilan*, 101
* Sour Cream Chocolate Chip Cake,
  *Doug Collins*, 35
* Tootsie Roll Cheesecake, *Melvin J. Gordon*, 86
* Truffle Filled Chocolate Glazed Pears,
  *Jimmy Rohn*, 179

## MOUSSES, PUDDINGS, AND SOUFFLES

* Black Cherry Pudding, *Michael Butler*, 22
* Hasty Pudding, *Lauren Kaminsky*, 109
* Mousse Au Citron Vert Et Kiwi, *Alan Tutzer*, 217
* Pineapple Flan,
  *Leon M. Lederman, Tita Jensen*, 121
* Steve and Jayne Allen's Chocolate Mousse,
  *Steve & Jayne Allen*, 2
* Tomato Pudding, *Mrs. Gardner H. Stern*, 204

## PIES and TARTS

* Best-Ever Lemon Pie/Never-Fail Meringue,
  *Ann Landers*, 119
* Breakfast Pie, *Helen Shiller*, 196
* Butter Tarts, *Edward G. Proctor*, 164
* Chicago Fudge Pie, *Ann Gerber*, 83
* Mile-High Strawberry Pie, *Renee S. Crown*, 41
* My Daughter Sheryl's Sweet Potatoe Pie,
  *Mayor Eugene Sawyer*, 187
* Pear Tart, *John B. Duff*, 60
* Plum Pie, *Ed Burke*, 20
* Sand Tarts, *Charles Shabica*, 195
* Shoo Fly Pie, *Chapman Kelley*, 113

## OTHER GOODIES

* Abdominable Snow Man Delight,
  *Dianne L. Sautter*, 186
* Gingered Peaches, *Leslee Reis*, 171
* My Dad's Signature Dessert, *Mary Ross*, 180
* Snow Birds, *Jane Byrne*, 24
* Southern Midnight Snack, *Artensa Randolph*, 168

## DRINKS

* Glogg, *William F. Dietrick*, 54
* Kahlua Velvet Frosty, *Rodger Tremblay*, 214
* Mother Tucker's Punch, *Dave Helland*, 96
* My Dad's Signature Dessert, *Mary Ross*, 180

## AND MORE

* The Best Recipe in the World,
  *Philip Schwimmer*, 191
* Captain Gorstayn's Lake Trout,
  *Captain Gorstayn*, 87
* FROYD (For Reality Of Your Dreams), *Froyd*, 78
* Jonathon Scott's Street Beat Hangover Recipe,
  *Jonathon Scott*, 193
* Making a Dive Site, *Patrick Hammer*, 93
* Neighborhood Treasure, *Carol S. Wyant*, 228
* Party Stew a la Limelight, *Tom Doody*, 57
* Recipe for a River Renaissance, *Beth White*, 224
* Recipe for Self-Examination,
  *William D. White*, 225
* Roast Impala, *Earl Nightingale*, 151
* Rock N' Roll Happiness, *Ronnie Rice*, 172
* Rubbaboo, *Ron Vasile*, 219
* Scuba Diver, *Patrick Hammer*, 93
* Sediment Soup, *Mary Durkin*, 63

## FOR YOUR PET

* Armadillo's Surprise, *Lester Fisher*, 70
* Bobcat's Burgers, *Lester Fisher*, 71
* Crow's Cuisine, *Lester Fisher*, 71
* Ferret's Fare, *Lester Fisher*, 70
* Guinea Pig's Salad Supreme, *Lester Fisher*, 70
* Junior Possum's Plate, *Lester Fisher*, 71
* Olga's Delight, *Olga*, 154
* Porcupine's Pleasure, *Lester Fisher*, 70
* Prairie Dog's Pie, *Lester Fisher*, 71
* Rabbit's Salad Bar, *Lester Fisher*, 70
* Raccoon's Delight, *Lester Fisher*, 70
* Tarantula's Treats, *Lester Fisher*, 71
* Turtle's Hash, *Lester Fisher*, 71

# THE MONTEREY VINEYARD®
## is proud to support

*Quantity*

*The SAN FRANCISCO CELEBRITY CHEFS COOKBOOK with proceeds to benefit the San Francisco Ballet. Foreword by Pierre Salinger.   $9.95          _____

*The SOUTH FLORIDA (MIAMI) CELEBRITY CHEFS COOKBOOK with proceeds to benefit the Museum of Art Fort Lauderdale. Foreword by Don Schula. $9.95   _____

**CHICAGO Celebrity C·H·E·F·S**

If you would like to order additional copies of the CHICAGO CELEBRITY CHEFS COOKBOOK which will help support the Lakefront Partnership's effort to preserve and enhance Chicago's lakefront, send $9.95

*(Quantity)*   _____

Please add $2.00 for postage and handling (two or more books, $3.00)
Make checks payable to CELEBRITY CHEFS COOKBOOKS

If you would like to order CELEBRITY CHEFS COOKBOOKS for MIAMI, SAN FRANCISCO, or CHICAGO please send order and payment to:

PEANUT BUTTER PUBLISHING
200 Second Avenue West
Seattle, Washington 98119
(206) 281-5965

BILL TO:                                              SHIP TO:

NAME _____        _____

ADDRESS _____        _____

CITY _____ ST___ ZIP_____   _____

[ ] Payment Enclosed $ _____   [ ] Charge
Visa or Master Card # _____  exp date ____
*(Circle One)*
Signature _____

THANK YOU